TEENAGE PREGNANCY

TEENAGE PREGNANCY

Developing Strategies for Change
in the
Twenty-First Century

Edited by
Dionne J. Jones
and
Stanley F. Battle

Transaction Publishers
New Brunswick (U.S.A.) and London (U.K.)

New material this edition copyright (c) 1990 by Transaction Publishers, New Brunswick, New Jersey 08903.
Originally published as Vol. 12, Nos. 1 & 2 of *The Urban League Review*.

Library of Congress Catalog Number: 89-20420
ISBN: 0-88738-818-3
Printed in the United States of America

\ 1

Library of Congress Cataloging-in-Publication Data

Teenage pregnancy: developing strategies for change in the twenty-first century / edited by Dionne J. Jones and Stanley F. Battle.
    p.   cm.
    ISBN 0-88738-818-3
    1. Afro-American teenage mothers.   2. Afro-American teenagers--Family relationships. 3. Teenage pregnancy--United States.
I. Jones, Dionne J. II. Battle,Stanley F.
HQ759.4.T4319   1990
306.85'6--dc20

                                                    89-20420
                                                    CIP

CONTENTS

RESEARCH REPORTS

1
Editor's Overview
Strategies for Alleviating Teenage Pregnancy in the Twenty-First Century

Dionne J. Jones

This special issue of the *Review* was developed as a result of a continuing concern over the issue of teenage pregnancy. The prevalence of premarital sexual activity, pregnancy, and childbearing among teenagers in the United States is well documented. In 1985, there were nine million fifteen-to-nineteen-year-old teenage girls in the United States, approximately 93 percent of whom had never been married. Of these teenagers, 3.6 million (40 percent) were sexually active and only about half of these used some method of contraception. Further, 850,000 (9 percent) became pregnant and 270,000 (3 percent) gave birth. For 110,000 of those fifteen-to-nineteen-year-olds who gave birth in 1985, there was at least one previous birth.[1]

Disaggregating the numbers by race and ethnicity, it is seen that although minority teenagers do not account for the majority of births to teenagers, they are disproportionately likely to give birth. African-American teenagers are also disproportionately more likely to be unmarried.[2] However, these racial/ethnic differences may be a reflection of the decisions made by these groups regarding marriage, sexual activity, contraceptive use, and abortion. Moreover, these decisions may be related to higher poverty rates and lower academic skills among African-American and Hispanic young females, as well as unemployment and low wages among young African-American males.[3]

Little information is presently available on adolescent male reproductive behaviors and the response of these young men to parenthood. In 1985, there were 9.4 million fifteen-to-nineteen-year-old males, 98.5 percent of whom had never been married. The data suggest that on average, adolescent males are more sexually active than adolescent females of the same ages. Results of a 1983 survey of young adults (twenty years and older) revealed that 64 percent of the males had become sexually active by the time they were eighteen, compared with 44 percent of the females. By age twenty the proportions were increased to 83 percent for young men and 74 percent for young women.[4]

Contrary to popular belief, teenage pregnancy and childbearing are stressful events not only for teenage mothers, but also for the teenage males who become fathers. Of concern is the fact that the socioeconomic, health, emotional and psychological well-being of many of these youth tend to be below standard. Their knowledge of, and access to health care facilities and resources appear to be limited, if and when these exist at all.

Teenage pregnancy is a major reason cited by many African-American females for dropping out of school.[5] The related literature suggests that many students who drop out of school do not return. Thus, these teenagers often find themselves in a cycle of poverty out of which it is hard to break. Generally, the noncompletion of a high school education limits the life earning potential among the teenage population. The outlook is even gloomier for the African-American teenage population, whose unemployment rate in 1987 was 34.7 percent, compared with 14.4 percent for White teenagers.[6]

Viewing teenage pregnancy from a health perspective, there are numerous attendant problems. For example, due to the lack of early prenatal care, teenage mothers are more likely than most women in other age groups to experience problems during pregnancy. Further, they are more likely to give birth to low birthweight or premature babies. The chances of survival beyond the first year for these infants are very slim. Of those infants who do survive, many experience problems with school learning and are classified as educable mentally retarded or learning disabled. Moreover, because of the immaturity of many teenage parents, they lack adequate parenting skills to provide a nurturing and supportive environment for these children. Added to this, they lack the financial wherewithal to provide for their children. Thus, many experience emotional and mental problems trying to cope with parenting.

Although some teenage pregnancies are the outcome of casual sexual encounters, many are the result of close long-standing relationships. As such, many teenage fathers desire to continue their relationship with the mothers of their children and to provide various kinds of support.[7] However, because large numbers of these young fathers are unable to find employment, they often cannot meet their financial obligations to their children.

Given the adverse effects of teenage pregnancy, with all of its implications, a multidisciplinary approach must be taken by professionals to attack this problem head on. Just as the problem has multiple dimensions and causations, so too, the strategies used for remediation and amelioration must be multifaceted, multidimensional and multiobjective. There are no instantaneous solutions and this must first be acknowledged by all professionals concerned. Long range goals must be established, with measurable objectives outlined to meet the goals. Both macro- and micro-level planning must be undertaken simultaneously; that is, at the federal government, as well as at the local community level. Further, the outcomes of programs must be shared with all concerned either through the mass media or through related professional vehicles. Equally important, successful programs must be duplicated nationally.

In addition to massive efforts by the multidisciplinary professional communities, there must be commitment at the federal, state and local government levels to make teenage pregnancy a top priority. More funds must be made available to support programs as well as research and demonstration projects. In addition, there must be support for the evaluation and analyses (impact, implementation, or ethnographic) of these programs.

One dimension of the multifaceted programmatic strategies should include education and the development of strong basic skills. Another dimension should focus on jobs and skills building to prepare these youth for the labor force. There should also be extracurricular and social support to help build and enhance self-esteem and to develop a strong sense of family values among these youth. Sexuality and parenting skills should be another component of comprehensive health care.

The National Urban League (NUL) and its local affiliates have been involved in a variety of program and policy initiatives to address teenage pregnancy. For example, in 1984, through its Affiliate Development of Adolescent Pregnancy/Parenting Project (ADAPP), the League became a part of the Charles Stewart Mott Foundation's Network of Too-Early Childbearing programs. This impact evaluation model has facilitated documentation by the League of the effectiveness of strategies and interventions designed to reduce pregnancy among teenagers.

Another nationally administered demonstration project conducted by the League was "Reducing the Incidence of Pregnancy Among Minority Adolescents." This project developed a curriculum, "Saying No and Meaning It: A Guide for Parents." The curriculum was used as a training manual in a series of workshops designed specifically for minority parents. The workshops addressed both adolescent sexuality issues and skills necessary to enhance the quality of parent-child communications.

In 1985, NUL launched the Adolescent Male Responsibility Program to provide services and programs to adolescents who are fathers as well as to those who are not. As part of this program, a successful public awareness campaign was launched via the media: radio, newspapers and posters. Nearly half of the 113 Urban League affiliates have participated in these three projects. In addition, all affiliates are involved in local youth-directed activities.

In the policy arena, NUL has worked vigorously with a variety of groups to impact on legislation pertaining to the health and welfare of adolescents and children, particularly with regard to teenage pregnancy. Thus, the League has worked closely with congressional members, staffers, and committees, legislative think tanks, and other community-based organizations to give input in the redrafting of teenage pregnancy legislation.

Consistent with the multifaceted nature of the problem and its multiple solutions, the articles included in this issue of the *Review* address various aspects of the problem of teenage pregnancy and suggest various remedial approaches. Special emphasis is given to African-American male involvement. In the Guest Editor's comments, Stanley Battle addresses a number of factors related to teenage pregnancy and out-of-wedlock births.

The first three articles set the stage by providing the underlying perspective of the environment in which African-American youth are reared today. In particular, they delineate the role of the social system in determining the hierarchical arrangement of the people within it.

In the first article of this volume, "African-American Inner City Youth and the Subculture of Disengagement," Ronald Taylor presents two opposing viewpoints regarding the social disengagement of African-American youth from traditional institutional life. Through little fault of their own, Taylor observes, many of these youth become adapted to their environments and engage in antisocial behaviors. Taylor notes that in order for programs that address teenage pregnancy to be effective with these youth, more information is needed about their attitudes, perceptions, and behavior relative to sexuality and fatherhood.

The second article in this trilogy, "African-American Youth at Risk," by Bruce Hare, proposes that the American social system should be viewed from a structural deterministic perspective in order to understand the disproportionate allocation of African-Americans to the lowest slots of the social system. Hare argues that racism, classism and sexism negatively impact on African-American families, and particularly on the socialization of African-American youth. He calls for the African-American community to become organized, form coalitions, provide organized collective activities for youth, and demand enforcement and protection of our rights from the federal and local governments to save our youth.

In the third article, "A Strategy of Responsible Militancy: A Template for Today's African-American Youth," Robert Washington points out that the "twin evils" of poverty and racism in America are the culprits responsible for producing a system of social stratification that prevents African-Americans from sharing equitably in the benefits and products of society. Thus, he proposes a strategy of responsible militancy as both a mind set and a tactic which should be used by African-American youth to bring about desired change.

In "Reading and Writing as Risk-Reduction: The School's Role in Preventing Teenage Pregnancies," Karen Pittman observes that the school has a role to play in providing access to information on sexuality, counseling, and services. However, Pittman notes, in addition to the provision of such information and services, the school must provide quality education for all students beginning at the preschool and elementary school levels.

Stanley Battle's article, "African-American Male Responsibility in Teenage Pregnancy: The Role of Education" also addresses the importance of education in the prevention of teenage pregnancy. Battle highlights effective programs that have been developed specifically for males in several cities. He concludes that male responsibility can be perpetuated if African-American adolescents are provided with positive experiences in school and encounter positive African-American male role models.

In "The Responsibility of the African-American Church as a Source of Support for Adolescent Fathers," Althea Smith compares the traditional role of the African-American church on issues of concern to the African-American community with its current stance on teenage pregnancy. Noting that the African-American church has taken a conservative position on this issue of pressing concern to the African-American community, Smith urges that it should take a more progressive stance.

John Taborn's article, "Adolescent Pregnancy: A Medical Concern," discusses some health conditions associated with teenage pregnancy and shows that they are partially correlated with race, age and socioeconomic status. Various complications that lead to maternal mortality, infant mortality, and low birthweight babies are presented and reasons cited for the inappropriate use of medical care by adolescents.

In a similar vein, Alva Barnett describes some of the health consequences associated with adolescent pregnancy and motherhood among African-Americans. Within a cultural context, her article, "Factors that Adversely Affect the Health and Well-Being of African-American Adolescent Mothers and Their Infants," presents several strategies for effective and relevant service interventions.

In "The African-American Adolescent Male and School-Based Health Clinics: A Prevention Point of View," Robert and Helen Evans assert that problems related to adolescent health and childbearing are most often researched and discussed from the female's perspective. Urging that services and programs be expanded to include adolescent males, the Evans' describe the services utilized by both male and female adolescents at two school-based health clinics.

In "Dispelling Myths About Teenage Pregnancy and Male Responsibility: A Research Agenda," Betty Watson, Cyprian Rowe, and Dionne Jones present evidence to challenge many commonly held misconceptions about the nature and magnitude of teenage pregnancy. They reject the notion of a linear relationship between poverty and the value system of adolescent males and females. Further, they assert that the perpetuation of a system of incorrect and partially incorrect beliefs has taken programmatic and policy emphases away from necessary systemic socioeconomic solutions to the problem.

Judith Rozie-Battle presents an analysis of pertinent legislation and court decisions as they affect adolescent fathers in "Adolescent Fathers: The Question of Paternity." Specifically, she addresses paternity issues, child support concerns, and the legal rights and responsibilities of unwed and/or adolescent fathers. Special concerns of African-American adolescent fathers are addressed.

The final three articles in this volume present the findings of research studies conducted with African-American adolescent males. Together, they shed light on some key areas of functioning of minority adolescent males, particularly African-Americans.

In the first research report, Neela Joshi's article, "An Epidemiological Perspective of Minority Teenage Males: A Preliminary Report," the preliminary results of a quasi-experimental study are presented. The study focuses on the sexual behavior, use of contraceptives and fatherhood status of 150 minority males under the age of nineteen.

In "Reaching African-American Male Adolescent Parents Through Nontraditional Techniques," Leo Hendricks and Annette Solomon utilize data from studies conducted in four cities to provide suggestions for reaching out to African-American male adolescent parents through nontraditional means. Specifically, strategies are given for reaching this population, planning the initial assessment meeting, and helping them stay in treatment or a counseling relationship. Finally, suggestions are made for the fathers to be helpful not only to themselves, but also to the mothers and their children.

Finally, Leanor Boulin Johnson and Robert Staples' article "Family Planning and the Young Minority Male: A Pilot Project" seeks to promote sexual responsibility and ultimately the reduction of unwanted, out of wedlock births among minority adolescents. They propose goal-directed support and assistance to unwed fathers and potential unwed fathers age 14 to 24.

In conclusion, the studies and analyses presented in this edition are all agreed with respect to the nature of the problem of teenage pregnancy. A key component to its solution is deemed to be a broadening of focus to include adolescent fathers in existing programs and services. Most important, perhaps, is that there must be ongoing information and education for both male and female adolescents.

Of special note is the fact that the National Urban League has adopted a policy to use the term "African-American" instead of "Black-American" or "Black" in all of its publications and other public communications. The change is reflected in this and all future editions of the *Urban League Review*. This change represents a maturing of our community in terms of how we view ourselves and our collective interests, as well as in terms of the wider regard we seek to command, both domestically and internationally. As editor of the *Review*, I believe that the new policy is particularly appropos of the current edition. Indeed, teenage pregnancy and other social problems involving our young people are, in some measure, consequences of negative or confused self-imagery which is not adequately informed by the extensive, positive history of our people. Thus, the self-concept of our youth in today's society must be reinforced if they are to realize their full productive potential. Adopting the term African-American is one of the ways in which we are serving this need.

NOTES

1. Karen Pittman and Gina Adams, *Teenage Pregnancy: An Advocate's Guide to the Numbers*, A Publication of the Adolescent Pregnancy Prevention Clearinghouse (Washington, DC: Children's Defense Fund, 1988), p. 4.

2. Ibid., p. 18.

3. Ibid.

4. Ibid., pp. 31-32.

5. Antoine M. Garibaldi and Melinda Bartley, "Black School Pushouts and Dropouts: Strategies for Reduction," *Urban League Review* 11 (1 & 2) (Summer 1987, Winter 1987-88): 227-235.

6. U.S. Department of Commerce, Bureau of the Census, *Current Population Reports* Series (P-25, No. 1022), "United States Population Estimates By Age, Sex, and Race: 1980-1987."

7. Jacqueline Smollar and Theodora Ooms, *Young Unwed Fathers: Research Review, Policy Dilemmas and Options.* Summary Report, Dept. of Health and Human Services (Washington, DC: GPO, 1987).

2

Teenage Pregnancy and Out-of-Wedlock Births

There has probably never been a time for African-American people in the United States to begin to define the circumstances, needs and imperatives of African-American family life and the development of African-American children, as there is now. We are quite aware of the negative perceptions of the African-American family. One important aspect of this situation is the occurrence of pregnancy and out-of-wedlock births among African-American adolescents. Indeed, the number of single parent families represents a major concern in the African-American community and unplanned births are at the heart of the issue.

The phenomenon of unprecedented rates of adolescent pregnancy and childbearing in the 1970s, often referred to in crisis terms as an "epidemic," appears to be receding in the 1980s. By 1986, fertility rates for teenagers had declined. Yet these birth rates, especially for younger teenagers are still disturbingly high. They are not only among the highest levels ever observed for the United States, but they are among the highest in the Western industrialized world.[1]

While the number of births to teenagers (656,000 in 1970, 562,000 in 1980, and 472,081 in 1986) gives us the dimensions of the problem, these aggregate numbers mask the distinct differences among age groups within the adolescent population.[2] Childbearing rates of teenage women declined from their peak levels in 1973 through 1986 (the most recent year for which data are available). While the birth rate for younger mothers (ages 14 and 15) declined least from its peak level in 1973, the birth rate for older mothers (ages 18 and 19) sharply decreased over the past few decades. The decline for very young adolescent mothers has been an average of approximately 28 percent from peak year to present, whereas birth rates for older mothers have declined by more than 47 percent. A combination of factors may have contributed to the sharper decline in rates for older teenage mothers, namely, increased use of contraception, changing patterns of sexual activity, attitudes of control, self-esteem, and autonomy. These appear to manifest themselves with growing maturity.

While the uneven decline in birth rates within the adolescent cohort is noteworthy, the dramatic story of recent decades has been the sharp decrease in teenage births

TABLE 1
Percentage of Births to Unmarried Women Younger Than 20, by
Age and Race, 1985

Age	All Races	White	Black	Hispanic
Total under 20 years	58.7	45.1	90.0	51.9
Under 15 years	91.8	82.4	98.7	79.0
15-17 years	70.9	57.8	95.4	60.6
18-19 years	50.7	38.0	85.5	53.8

Source: K. Pittman and G. Adams, *Teenage Pregnancy: An Advocate's Guide to the Numbers*. A Publication of the Adolescent Pregnancy Prevention Clearinghouse (Washington, D.C.: Children's Defense Fund, 1988), p. 19.

legitimated by marriage. In 1980, this figure dropped to 52 percent. The number of out-of-wedlock births to women under twenty years of age tripled between 1960 and 1981. Almost 50 percent of all births to women under age nineteen are out-of-wedlock.[4] The phenomenon of out-of-wedlock births is highlighted due to the fact that the number of births to married women has declined. Thus, a higher proportion of children are now "illegitimate," and the number of children living with an unmarried mother has increased by a factor of more than four. The disproportionate share of out-of-wedlock births to young African-American women is illustrated in Table 1.

The disproportionate incidence of births to unwed young African-American women is cause for intense concern. However, the aggregate figures mask a significant trend. There was a decrease of 10 percent in one decade (1971-1981) in the out-of-wedlock rate for African-American women (15-19), while the rate for White women in that age group increased by almost 57 percent. A decline in out-of-wedlock birth rates occurred in every age group for African-American women, while the rates for White women increased substantially for all ages between 15 and 24. Yet, the problems associated with teenage sexual activity and pregnancy are felt more profoundly in the African-American population since it is, essentially, a young population. In 1987, the median age for African-Americans was 27.2 years compared to 33.0 for Whites. Nationally, 18.8 percent of the African-American population was in the 15-24 age group compared to 15.3 percent of Whites.

It is difficult to account with specificity for the rise and fall in out-of-wedlock rates by age and race. However, it is reasonable to assume that for young African-American teenage women, the concerted efforts through various social programs have produced a downward trend. The upward trend for White females is accounted for, perhaps, by an increase in sexual activity.

Although the rate of out-of-wedlock births is extremely high in this country, significant variations by age and race should be emphasized. Younger age groups within the cohort show the least decline. Along racial lines, it is observed that the rate is increasing for young White women and decreasing slightly for young African-American women. However, this should not obscure the fact that very high rates of out-of-wedlock births exist for African-Americans, especially in large urban areas. In this regard, a recent study disclosed that in Chicago, Illinois, forty-five out of one hundred children were born out-of-wedlock.[6]

Whether or not the high proportion of out-of-wedlock births signals the beginning of a family formation that will be accepted without societal stigma remains to be seen. Certainly, societal attitudes toward "illegitimacy" have changed substantially. Especially interesting are the studies that corroborate a marked change among adolescents; more teenagers feel they will never get married or do not intend to get married. They also believe that having a child out-of-wedlock will not hurt their chances for marriage.

In the final analysis, as we move toward the year 2000 and this country attempts to strengthen its competitive position in the world, we must begin to better understand the needs of African-American adolescents. If not, we will experience a continuation of the problems associated with teenage pregnancy and childbearing.

NOTES

1. Melvin Zelnick and John Kantner, "Sexual Activity, Contraception Use and Pregnancy Among Metropolitan-Area Teenagers: 1971-1979," *Family Planning Perspectives*, 12(5) (1980).
2. Allen Guttmacher Institute, *Teenage Pregnancy: The Problem That Hasn't Gone Away* (New York: Guttmacher Institute, 1981).
3. Unpublished data from the National Center for Health Statistics, Washington, D.C. Also Zelnik and Kantner, "Sexual Activity . . ."
4. Allen Guttmacher Institute, *Teenage Pregnancy*.
5. U.S. Bureau of the Census, Current Population Reports Series (P-25, No. 1022), "United States Population Estimates by Age, Sex and Race: 1980-1987."
6. Zelnik and Kantner, "Sexual Activity . . ."

3

African-American Inner City Youth and the Subculture of Disengagement

Ronald L. Taylor

This article gives a psychosocial perspective of African-American youth. It assesses two opposing viewpoints that have been advanced as being responsible for the social disengagement of African-American youth from traditional institutional life. Further, it points to conflicting institutional expectations that produce conflicts in the orientation of youth who often become confused about the relationship between school and employment/ unemployment. Thus, many of these youth make adaptations to their environments and become involved in antisocial behaviors. Finally, the article stresses the need for gaining a better understanding of the attitudes, perceptions and behavior of African-American youth, as well as the impact of society on their psyches. It is only with such an understanding that programmatic efforts can be effective in bringing about responsible male behavior with regard to sexuality and fatherhood.

In addressing the issue of African-American male responsibility in teenage pregnancy, it is essential to take into account the relative impact of recent social, economic, and ecological changes on the attitudes and behaviors of African-American youth. This framework is important in order to understand how such changes have shaped the evolving sense of African-American males and their life chances. The following analysis examines competing explanations for the deteriorating conditions among African-American youth in central cities across the country. It also proposes alternative interpretations of their current predicament. Further, it identifies some gaps in our knowledge concerning the attitudes and behavior of African-American youth, particularly as they are related to responsibility in unwed teenage pregnancy.

ASSESSING THE LOCUS OF AFRICAN-AMERICAN YOUTH'S SOCIAL PROBLEMS

In scrutinizing the problems of African-American youth in this country, especially the problems of African-American males, we can find numerous explanations for their increasingly desperate predicament, as well as proposed solutions to eradicate their problems. One point of view suggests that the locus of the social problems of African-

American youth is associated with perverse demographic trends, deteriorating local economies, and functional transformations in the structures of urban areas during the past two decades.[1] It is argued that attention to the structural problems of these youth (i.e., improving their access to quality education, employment opportunities, and prospects for decent incomes) will substantially reduce, if not entirely eliminate, high rates of unemployment, early parenthood, school failure, crime and substance abuse among them.

An alternative perspective, while acknowledging the role of structural changes in the economy and the society at large in diminishing the life chances of African-American youth in the inner cities, emphasizes the spread of self-destructive values and behaviors among these youth as both cause and effect of their multiple social problems.[2] In the view of Eleanor Holmes Norton, former chairman of the Equal Employment Opportunity Commission, the "self-perpetuating culture of the ghetto" is at the core of the crisis among African-American youth.[3] The spread of this predatory subculture, characterized by crime, violence, drug addiction, illegitimacy, and welfare dependency, has grown powerful and "ruthless in its demands for conformity."[4] Mired in a malignant way of life, without adequate education or marketable skills, a growing number of African-American youth seem unable or unwilling to escape.

Recently, there has been renewed emphasis on the subcultural values and norms of inner-city youth as impediments to material improvements in their condition. Various writers are calling for more attention to the attitudes and values of the African-American underclass, in concert with the exercise of greater moral leadership in addressing their problems. Glenn Loury, the African-American Harvard economist, contends that the breakdown of values, norms, and moral behavior of a segment of the inner city population is part cause and part effect of economic deprivation, and as such requires the sort of attention and moral leadership that only African-Americans are in a position to provide. He writes:

> When faced with the ravages of black crime against blacks, the depressing nature of social life in many low-income black communities, the alarming incidence of pregnancy and unwed black teenagers, or the growing dependency of blacks on transfer from an increasingly hostile polity, it is simply insufficient to respond by saying 'This is the fault of racist America. These problems will be solved when America finally does right by its black folk'. Such a response dodges the issue of responsibility, both at the level of individual behavior (i.e., the criminal perpetrator being responsible for his act), and at the level of the group (the black community being responsible for the values embraced by its people) (p. 11).[5]

A recent essay authored by thirty prominent African-American scholars and civil rights activists, entitled *Black Initiative and Governmental Responsibility,* acknowledges the crisis of norms, values, and behavior among impoverished segments of the African-American community. These scholars note that this crisis imposes a moral imperative on African-American leadership to more forcefully articulate, reaffirm, and reinforce the African-American value heritage.[6] The African-American value heritage refers to the system of values which has sustained the African-American community in difficult times. This system, however, has been subjected to enormous and diverse social changes in recent decades.

Regardless of which perspective writers employ in explicating the problems of African-American youth in this country, all agree that the predicament of these youth is both qualitatively and quantitatively different from the conditions experienced by African-American youth two decades ago. Disagreements occur over the sources of these differences and appropriate strategies for their resolution. To be sure, disagreements among scholars, policymakers, and leaders of the African-American community over the causes of and solutions to African-American youth problems are a function of differences in political perspectives, angle of vision, and/or levels of analysis. Those accustomed to viewing the whole of contemporary society as a network of interdependent parts, are likely to stress the consequences for individual and group behavior of changes in the nature of these interdependencies.

Similarly, those confronting the realities of life on the local or community level, often find it difficult to sort out the role of adverse structural conditions to which the behavior and attitudes of African-American youth are a response. The inclination at this level is to point to the self-destructive behaviors and norms of African-American youth as sustaining, if not causing, the problems they confront. In short, the issue is not that one or the other perspective is in error in its analysis of the problem, but that each perspective tends to pay insufficient attention to the other.

It is undoubtedly the case, as some social scientists have shown, that the dramatic increase in the youth component of central city African-American populations during the past two decades has been a major contributing factor to the worsening conditions among African-American youth in this country. As William Wilson has observed: "On the basis of these demographic changes alone, one would expect Blacks . . . to account disproportionately for the increasing social problems of the central city" (p. 83).[7]

A similar conclusion is advanced by James Wilson who hypothesizes that the dramatic increase in the size of the African-American youth component of central city African-American populations has had an "exponential effect on the rate of certain social problems" (p. 17).[8] He suggests that there may be "a 'critical mass' of young people such that, when that number is reached, or when an increase in that mass is sudden and large, a self-sustaining chain reaction is set off that creates an explosive increase in the amount of crime, addiction, and welfare dependency" (p. 18).[9] Yet, as James Wilson explains, changes in the age structure of the African-American population cannot alone account for the magnitude of African-American youth problems in recent years: "Detroit . . . had about one hundred murders in 1960 but over five hundred in 1971, yet the number of young persons did not quintuple" (p. 17).[10]

Several major factors must be added to changes in the age structure of central city African-American populations. For example, there was a precipitous decline in the number of jobs available to African-American youth in primary and secondary labor markets. This was a result of industrial relocations from the urban core to other areas of the city and suburbs, as well as of the shift in economic activity from manufacturing to more technical-service oriented industries. These developments have had a severe impact on this population, and in conjunction with the continual outflow of middle-income families and resources from the city to the suburbs, have contributed to a number of social and economic problems of inner city residents. Kasarda noted that some of these problems included:

> a widening gap between urban job opportunity-structures and the skill levels of disadvantaged residents (with correspondingly high rates of structural unemployment), spatial isolation of low-income families, and intractably high levels of urban poverty (p. 41).[11]

Thus, demographic trends, deteriorating local economies, changes in the structures of urban areas, and the resulting social isolation of growing segments of low-income families, may be seen as principal causes of the desperate plight of African-American youth and the underclass in central cities. Such major developments may also be observed to have produced powerful secondary consequences for the experiences and behavior of African-American youth in inner cities which can hardly be ignored.

AFRICAN-AMERICAN YOUTH AND SOCIAL DISENGAGEMENT

It is generally acknowledged that the institutional contexts of family, school, media, workplace, peer group, and the criminal justice system interact to produce a code of rules internalized by youth as a guide to behavior and as a frame of reference for interpreting experience. To the extent that such institutional contexts are in relative harmony with one another, they are experienced by youth as a relatively coherent structure which helps to facilitate the transition to adulthood. However, where such institutional contexts are in conflict or disarray, youth are likely to internalize this conflict and experience a lack of coherent structure in their psychosocial organization.[12] In this context, as Ianni observes, "youth are left to chart their own course or, much worse, to pick a route from among the often confusing signals put out by the family, the peer group, the school, and the workplace" (p. 36).[13] The results are often a growing sense of futility, alienation, and resistance to any formal structure among youth.

Thus it may be argued that one of the major consequences of recent structural changes in the economy and the society at large for African-American inner city youth has been the creation of considerable conflict and confusion in the institutional contexts experienced by these youth. The result has been that the "facilitating environments" which had heretofore sustained these youth in their transition to adulthood have all but disappeared.[14] Indeed, in many inner city neighborhoods, the church is all that remains of formal organization,[15] although youth gangs have emerged in some communities to fill the void created by the collapse of coherent social institutions.[16] However, it is important to stress that while the progressive disappearance of these facilitating institutions did not create the array of social problems among African-American inner city youth, their rapid demise has undoubtedly exacerbated such problems.

Conflict in the network of social institutions that structure the lives and experiences of African-American youth can be easily illustrated and documented by focusing on the contradictory expectations of families, schools, and employers with regard to the respective role of each in providing the necessary preparation and resources for youth employment. In addressing the locus of institutional responsibility for high rates of unemployment among African-American youth, school officials point to the lack of parental guidance and involvement as the principle problem, while employers and job training professionals cite the failure of schools to provide basic education and attitudes necessary for employment. For their part, parents tend to be critical of all three for failing to discharge their responsibilities.

Such finger pointing, as Ianni observes, is not merely a case of passing the buck, "but represents an agency focus on particular institutional prerogatives and expectations for youth."[17] Nevertheless, such conflicts in institutional expectations are likely to produce conflicts in the orientations of youth, many of whom may understandably become confused about the relationship between schooling, work, and unemployment. Even more confusing is the recognition that completing high school is no guarantee of gainful employment or improved life chances.

Largely in recognition of the growing inability of institutional mechanisms at the community level to respond effectively to the needs and problems of central city youth, a variety of social programs were created at the federal and state levels during the past two decades to address their problems. But the proliferation of such programs at the community levels has often added, rather than diminished, confusion among youth, as some social agencies compete with and displace, traditional institutions of socialization such as home, school, and church.

This observation is not intended as an argument against the value and need for such programs or agencies—the need has been well established. It does, however, alert us to their potential as sources of conflict and confusion in the normative orientations of African-American youth. Flagrant and open lawlessness in many inner city neighborhoods is another source of normative confusion among African-American youth. In the presence of widespread noncompliance with—and nonenforcement of—the law, many youngsters are forced to develop their own detrimental principles of conduct and morality, in association with other youth.[18]

Since poor African-American youth are far more dependent on the limited resources of their communities than are the youth of more affluent communities, even slight changes in the quality and quantity of resources available to them can have immediate and adverse consequences. There is little question that the quality of life for a significant number of inner city African-American youth has seriously deteriorated during the past two decades. For instance, youth unemployment has soared, access to quality education has diminished, and the "concentration effects" of impoverished segments of inner city residents have taken hold.

Propelled by a disappearing local economy, disintegrating community institutions, social isolation, and spatial concentration, a *subculture of disengagement* has apparently surfaced among some segments of the African-American youth populations in central cities across the country. This is evidenced by the rise of African-American teenage gangs and violent behavior, the spread of drugs and alcohol abuse, increases in teenage homicide and suicide rates, and the growing tendency among inner city youth to shun schooling and work for less productive, but more lucrative, criminal pursuits. Recent research indicates that poverty and unemployment are not sufficient to explain these developments. Similarly, continuing discrimination and racial segregation are inadequate to explicate these trends, although all are implicated in the process.[19]

What is here being referred to as the "subculture of disengagement" is by no means new. Elements of it can be found in the work of a number of writers.[20] For instance, in his study of the aspirations, motivations, and experiences of African-American youth in Watts, Los Angeles during the late 1960s, Douglas Glasgow outlined the responses of these youth to limited access to mainstream opportunities:

> Where the avenues to mainstream achievement are closed to them, underclass youth so often seek success within other available systems, sometimes in the illegitimate sector of the mainstream and other times in both the legitimate and deviant spheres of the Black community. Still others, with increasing frequency, withdraw from participation in either of these directions, choosing instead to gain livelihoods through hustling, welfare-connected programs, or other low-income or poverty programs (p. 155).[21]

To be sure, the "subculture of disengagement" has little in common with the so-called "culture of poverty" outlined by some writers. It does, however, have its origin in the limited opportunities and growing disarray in the socialization matrix experienced by African-American youth.

As recent ethnographic research conducted by Williams and Kornblum,[22] and Mac-Leod[23] make clear, the tendency toward progressive disengagement from the norms and values of the larger society is not a phenomenon limited to poor African-American youth marooned in the inner cities. This tendency can be found among poor White youth in urban areas as well. African-American and White youth most at risk of becoming involved in the "subculture of disengagement" are those who do not have social support systems or are not involved in institutions in their communities or neighborhoods. Others include those frustrated and increasingly alienated by years of underprivilege or material deprivation, as well as those who perceive few alternatives beyond the street gangs and the underground economy for survival.

When one takes the trouble to converse with these youth, it is clear that they "do not easily relinquish the American Dream and do not fool themselves when they take routes to maturity that are self-destructive or confirm them in their status as second-class citizens."[24] Yet their material deprivation and day-to-day experiences dictate that they have little choice but to succumb to the perverse influences of the street.

Clearly, these developments in the attitudes and behavior of a growing segment of African-American youth in our cities are every bit as important to address as are the structural or economic problems that created them. For as the number of African-American youth who come to embrace the self-destructive features associated with social disengagement from the larger society increases, the more difficult it will be to retrieve them as social and economic conditions improve. After all, these are not super-beings possessed of some extraordinary capacity to deflect or neutralize the incessant assaults on their physical and psychological well-being. Moreover, when new opportunities present themselves it is difficult for these youth to lay aside coping strategies devised to survive a hostile and dangerous environment.

This much is clear, or ought to be, from the results of the Manpower Demonstration Research Corporation's *Youth Incentive Entitlement Pilot Project*. This project was conducted during the late 1970s and early 1980s. It was the first national experiment of its kind designed to discover what worked and what did not with respect to improving the employment prospects of African-American and other disadvantaged youth.[25] The *Youth Incentive Entitlement Pilot Project* guaranteed jobs to youth between the ages of 16 and 19 if they stayed in school or returned to school. Some 80,000 youth nationwide participated in the project.

The results of this experiment were encouraging: the prospect of real employment did decrease the school dropout rate, and had a significant effect on the overall youth employment rate. But the project encountered serious difficulties in achieving more positive results in the attitudes and behavior of its participants. Their expectation of failure, low self-esteem, and "exaggerated sense of victimization" diminished their efforts and undermined their progress toward self-improvement. Such debilitating attitudes and insecurities were difficult to overcome in an environment that fed and sustained them.

It would be an egregious mistake to blame African-American youth for the adaptations they are forced to make to circumstances that are beyond their control. But it would be equally serious to ignore or minimize the long-term consequences of these adaptations for the youth themselves and the society at large. The argument that African-American teenage crime and delinquency, school failure and unwed pregnancy, drug abuse and violent behavior are largely responses to the morass of social and economic problems, while undeniably the case, nonetheless has the effect of absolving youth of the responsibility for their actions and the choices they make. As such, it feeds the public perception of disadvantaged African-American youth as lacking in capacity for responsible decisions and conduct.

PREGNANCY, PATERNITY, AND RESPONSIBILITY

Until we get a better understanding of the dynamic interplay between recent structural changes in society and the attitudes, perceptions and behavior of African-American youth, our best efforts to design programs to address the problems of teenage pregnancy and early parenthood, crime and substance abuse, employment and school failure, will continue to yield moderate results among these youth. Our knowledge about adolescent African-American male attitudes toward fatherhood and family responsibility is especially deficient, since empirical research in this areas lags far behind that available on African-American adolescent females, as does our service delivery to these young men. In fact, until quite recently, little attention was given to their inclusion in counseling and other support mechanisms available to females. Much of what we know about the attitudes of African-American male youth toward fatherhood and family responsibility is founded on myths and stereotypes of these young men.

What little empirical evidence exists on the subject, however, contradicts many commonly held views.[26] Apart from anecdotal cases, there is little evidence to support the popular view that the typical African-American teenage father has a "fleeting, casual relationship with the young mother, and few emotions about the pregnancy"; that teen fathers "are rarely involved in the support and rearing of their children"; that they have some psychological need to prove their masculinity; or that they are especially wise and knowledgeable about sex and sexuality.[27] On the contrary, studies show that the majority of teenage fathers continue to date the mother during pregnancy and after childbirth, help to support her by providing money, transportation, and gifts, and continue to be involved in the lives of the mother and child for an average of 18 months after the baby is born.[28]

In addition, research indicates no significant psychological differences (e.g., self-image, intellectual functioning, and coping style) between teenage fathers and male youth in general. They do, however, experience considerable psychological stress and conflict over the simultaneous roles of teenager and father.[29] Teenage fathers also differ from nonfathers in their views about out-of-wedlock births and attitudes toward abortion. They are more likely than nonfathers "to believe that pregnant teenagers should be allowed to get an abortion, to accompany them in going for abortions, and to give emotional support after abortions."[30] In addition, such fathers are more likely to have been born to teenage parents themselves and to accept teenage pregnancy as a common occurrence.[31]

Although teenage fathers are generally uninformed about sex, pregnancy, and the effectiveness of contraception, they are no more deficient in this regard than are their nonfather peers. In short, as Robinson's review of related literature indicates, teenage fathers do not normally abandon their female partners, but demonstrate a desire to participate in childbirth and childrearing, and attempt to maintain contact with the mother long after the baby is born. They also report a desire or intention to provide financial support during and after pregnancy.

There is evidence that suggests teenage fathers are willing to provide financial support to the mother of their children where circumstances make it possible for them to do so. Attempts to formalize their financial obligation, however, have met with considerable resistance at the national and state levels, led by social welfare professionals and, in some cases, members of the judiciary, who fear African-American and other minority males would be subjected to harassment, discriminatory treatment, and abridgements of their civil rights.[32] While such fears are not unfounded, strong public resistance to extralegal remedies may have the unintended effect of conveying to young men the message that little is expected of them by way of support for children they father. Fortunately, for African-American families and communities, the majority of African-American teenage males desire to support, both financially and emotionally, their sexual partners and the children they bear, but often find it difficult or impossible to do so given their meager resources and lack of marketable skills.

CONCLUSION

In conclusion, it must be acknowledged that the social problems of African-American youth, in general, and male youth in particular, are far more complex today than they were two decades ago. These problems will not yield to remedial solutions predicated on the assumption that they are a direct consequence of dysfunctional values and behavioral norms on the one hand, or of structural forces on the other. What seems required is a far more complex model of interaction of the sort proposed by Giroux among others, if we are to move beyond the "structure-agency dualism" dilemma. Giroux argues persuasively for the need "to understand more thoroughly the complex ways in which people mediate and respond to the interface between their own lived experiences and structures of domination and constraint."[33]

Indeed, the growing body of field research in this area indicates a "synergistic" relationship between structural or socioeconomic changes in the broader society and the subcultural norms and behavior of youth, each reinforcing the effects of the other. It is, therefore, unlikely that a focus solely on the maladaptive attitudes and behavior of African-American youth will significantly diminish the magnitude of their difficulties. Similarly, the provision of training and employment opportunities alone will not eliminate the debilitating aspects of the daily lives of these youth. This view was forcefully argued nearly twenty-five years ago by Kenneth Clark.[34] What is required is concerted action at both levels if the life chances of African-American inner city youth are to improve. Given the complexity of these problems, solutions must be long-term ones, sustained over generations, not abandoned with changes in the national administration.

One is inclined to agree with a recent editorial on race relations in this country which observed that the moral responsibility and leadership required for addressing the situation of African-American youth and the underclass must come first from our national political leaders in Washington, who can make White Americans understand their stake in solving these problems, and the national commitment required.[35] With such a commitment, African-American leadership will then be able to redirect more of its energy and resources toward addressing these problems on the community level as they manifest themselves in the self-destructive behaviors of African-American youth.

What is more, they can do so without fear of White apathy or the tendency to blame these youth for their adversities. To cite the editors of *The New Republic*: "It is too late now for Ronald Reagan to credibly provide such leadership. A president who thinks that segregation has ended in South Africa should not be expected to grasp the more subtle racial problems of our society . . . his administration has taught largely complacency, and a premature feeling of triumphalism, which makes it all the more urgent for other leaders to begin".[36] No better prescription for the ills of African-American youth would be more effective.

NOTES

1. John D. Kasarda, "Caught in the Web of Change," *Society* 21 (1983): 4-7.
2. Nicholas Lemann, "The Origins of the Underclass," *The Atlantic Monthly* 257 (1986): 31-55.
3. Eleanor Holmes Norton, "Restoring the Traditional Black Family," New York Times Magazine (June 2, 1985): 43.
4. Ibid.
5. Glenn C. Loury, "The Moral Quandary of the Black Community," *Public Interest* 79 (1985): 9-22.
6. Committee on Policy for Racial Justice, *Black Initiative and Government Responsibility* (Washington, DC,: Joint Center for Political Studies,1987).
7. William Wilson, "Inner-City Dislocations," Society 21 (1983): 81-87; and William Wilson, *The Truly Disadvantaged* (Chicago: University of Chicago Press, 1987).
8. James Q. Wilson, *Thinking About Crime,* (New York: Basic Books, 1975).
9. Ibid., p. 18.
10. Ibid., p. 17.
11. Kasarda, "Caught in the Web of Change."
12. Francis Ianni, *Home, School, and Community in Adolescent Education* (New York: Columbia University, Institute for Urban and Minority Education, 1983).
13. Ibid., p. 36.
14. D.W. Winnicott, The Maturational Processes and the Facilitating Environment (New York: International Universities Press, 1965).
15. William Wilson, "Inner-City Dislocations."
16. Wall Street Journal, "Lords of the Slums: Chicago Street Gangs Treat Public Housing As Private Fortresses," September 30, 1988, pp. 1 & 13.
17. Ianni, *Home, School, and Community,* p. 30.
18. Terry Williams and William Kornblum, *Growing Up Poor* (Lexington, MA: Lexington Books 1985); and Ianni, *Home, School, and Community.*
19. Richard Freeman and Hary Holzer, eds. *The Black Youth Employment Crisis* (Chicago: University of Chicago Press, 1986).
20. Claude Brown, *Manchild in the Promised Land* (New York: New American Library, 1965); Kenneth Clark, *Dark Ghetto,* (New York: Harper Press 1965.); and Ulf Hannerz, *Soulside* (New York: Columbia University Press, 1969).
21. Douglas G. Glasgow, *The Black Underclass,* (New York: Vintage Books, 1981).
22. Williams and Kornblum, *Growing Up Poor.*
23. Jay MacLeod, *Ain't No Makin' It* (Boulder, CO: Westview Press, 1987).
24. Williams and Kornblum, *Growing Up Poor.*
25. Manpower Demonstration Research Corporation, *Findings on Youth Employment: Lessons for MDRC Research* (New York: Manpower Demonstration Research Corp., 1983).
26. Bryan Robinson, "Teenage Pregnancy from the Father's Perspective," *American Journal of Orthopsychiatry* 58 (1988): 46-51.
27. Bryan Robinson, *Teenage Fathers,* (Lexington, MA: Lexington Books 1987).
28. F.P. Rivera, P.J. Sweeney, and B.F. Henderson, "A Study of Low Socioeconomic Status, Black Teenage Fathers, and Their Nonfather Peers," *Pediatrics* 75 (1985): 648-656; and R. Vaz, P. Smolen and C. Miller, "Adolescent Pregnancy: Involvement of the Male Partner," *Journal of Adolescent Health Care* 4 (1983): 246-250.
29. J.E. McCoy and F.B. Tyler, "Selected Psychosocial Characteristics of Black Unwed Adolescent Fathers," *Journal of Adolescent Health Care* 6 (1985): 12-16; I. Nakashima and B.W. Camp, "Fathers of Infants Born to Adolescent Mothers," *American Journal of Diseases of Children* 138 (1984): 452-454; and Bryan Robinson and R.L. Barret, "Self-Concept and Anxiety of Adolescent and Adult Fathers," *Adolescence* (1987).
30. Robinson, "Teenage Pregnancy from the Father's Perspective," p. 47.
31. Rivera et al, "A Study of Low Socioeconomic Status."
32. Blanche Bernstein, "Shouldn't Low Income Fathers Suppot Their Children?" *The Public Interest* 66 (1982): 51-71.
33. Henry Giroux, *Theory and Resistance in Education* (South Hadley, MA: Bergin & Garvey, 1983), p. 108.
34. Clark, *Dark Ghetto.*
35. *The New Republic,* "Rethinking Race," February 9, 1987, pp. 7-10.
36. Ibid., p. 10.

4

African-American Youth at Risk

Bruce R. Hare

This article begins with the premise that it is largely environment, rather than biological or cultural disorder that is responsible for the overrepresentation of African-Americans in the lower echelons of society. After briefly reviewing biological and cultural deterministic explanations that have been advanced to justify the disproportionate location of African-Americans in the lower slots of the social system, the article develops a third ideological perspective. It shows how through structural determinism, the social system determines the hierarchical arrangement of people within it, over either their biological or cultural dispositions. Biological and cultural explanations are shown to be steeped in racism, classism and sexism. Several policy recommendations are offered to save our youth.

There comes a period in every person's life when the tasks of moving from childhood dependency to adult independence are to be accomplished. It is ideally at this time that a fusion of mental readiness and structural opportunity makes this passage possible. The continuous and smooth movement of youth from childhood to adulthood, from school to work, from parents' abode to their own abode, is essential both to the future well-being of the individual and society. Thus, it is in the interest of a society to provide its young people *both* the training (aptitude) and the opportunities (structures) necessary to accomplish these tasks.

Were such conditions being optimally accomplished for African-American youth, they would be demonstrating a pattern of self-development, at the very least commensurate with that of their white and more likely middle class counterparts. They would be raised in psychologically and economically stable homes, sucessful in school, optimistic about their program and their futures, and successfully transitioning from school to work. They would furthermore as African-American youth demonstrate patterns of self-discipline, and commitments to self, family, and community, reflecting the legacy of

Originally published in *The State of Black America 1988*. Reprinted with permission of the National Urban League, Inc.

struggle for equity and justice of which they are a part. Such does not, however, appear to be the case. Not only do our youth remain "disadvantaged" as regards other youth, but they are at greater risk than at any other time in recent history. Not only are they being denied their structural opportunity, as reflected in their highest high school drop-out and eviction rates, their lowest college attendance, and their well-beyond fifty percent unemployment rates, but they are also reflecting alarming attitudinal forma-tions as well.

These youth reflect a lower sense of control over their destinies and an absence of political and collective consciousness, as would be unfortunately expected of children of the post "civil rights," "black nationalism" eras. They are subsequently short on mentors, and long on rugged individualism. The soaring rates of out-of-wedlock births, "babies having babies" among increasingly younger African-American girls with irre-sponsible and abandoning African-American boys, the rising crime and drug abuse rates, and the increasing violence committed by our youth against each other and our elders also speak to a rising despair and declining discipline among our African-Amer-ican youth.

While we recognize the role of dramatic change in the American economy and psychological climate in general that are causal to this shift, we cannot afford to be content with system blame and allow an entire generation of our youth to go down the drain. It is within this context that this detailed analysis of the state of African-Amer-ican youth will be undertaken. Such an analysis, however, could not be undertaken in a theoretical vacuum and thus will be accompanied by an analysis of the workings of the American social system and the state of African-Americans. Policy recommendations for increasing the life-chances of our youth will be suggested in the conclusion of this article.

OVERVIEW: ON BEING AN AFRICAN-AMERICAN

It should be stated from the outset that this overview of the condition of African-Americans begins from the premise that it is largely environment, rather than any mystical, within-group, biological, or cultural disorder which is responsible for the overrepresentation of African-Americans among the losers in the society. Much as a slave may have been defined as ill or maladaptive for failing to adjust to slavery, we have failed to adjust to poverty, racism, and discrimination.

For as long as recognition of the "disadvantaged" status of African-Americans has existed, an assortment of explanations has been advanced to justify their disproportio-nate location in the lower slots of the social system. The notion of biological (genetic) inferiority is an example of the "bad genes" explanation for the inferior social position of African-Americans. A revised and more liberal, although equally devastating, argu-ment appeared with the emergence of cultural inferiority explanations. This justifica-tion of discrimination shifts the blame from the genes of the group to the culture of the group, while subtly retaining a victim-blame focus. While the second explanation does represent a kind of progress, under the assumption that culture can be improved, both perspectives serve to maintain the locus of blame within the group itself, while leaving the system unchallenged. In neither mode has it been posited as a tenable hypothesis that differential attainment is a requirement of the American social order and that processes are operative within the system that increase the probability that African-Americans will be disproportionately allocated to the lower slots.

While acknowledging the relative underattainment of African-Americans, this writer adopts a third ideological perspective in search of an explanation—that being that the relative academic and economic failure of African-Americans in the American social order is functional, if not intended, given racism and the differential distribution of wealth, power, and privilege in the social structure. It is posited that both the biological and cultural explanations serve largely to justify current race, class, and gender inequalities. Furthermore, it is argued that the myth of equal opportunity serves as a smoke screen through which the losers will be led to blame themselves, and be seen by others as getting what they deserve. One might simply ask, for example, how can both inheritance of wealth for some and equal opportunity for all exist in the same social system?

Bowles and Gintis posit that the unequal distribution of wealth, power, and privilege is, and historically has been, the reality of American capitalism and that such a system must produce educational and occupational losers.[1] This writer further argues in what he terms "class-plus" analysis, with classism as the engine and racism as the caboose, that African-Americans have simply been chosen to absorb an unfair share of an unfair burden in a structurally unfair system.

As indicated in Figure 1, our structural determinism approach assumes that the character of the social system is preponderant as the determiner of the hierarchical arrangement of people within it, over either their biological or cultural dispositions. It is further argued that, in addition to the inherent intergenerational inequality caused by inheritance, the educational system, through its unequal skill-giving, grading, routing, and credentialing procedures, plays a critical role in legitimating structural inequality in the American social system. The triangles in Figure 1 represent the following: triangle 1, the assumed hierarchical distribution of intelligence—many low, few high; triangle 2, the assumed similar distribution of cultural readiness; triangle 3, the actual sratifying function of schools—many enter, few make it to the top; and triangle 4, the actual distribution of occupation prestige and power—many low, few high.

The biological and cultural deterministic traditions have argued that schools merely respond to innate genetic or cultural differences in ability when they receive and stratify youngsters. The occupational structure is further assumed simply to respond to the schools when it slots people into hierarchical positions on the bases of credentials and skills given in schools. The structural argument goes from right to left instead of left to right, and charges that the social system needs people to replenish its ranks at all levels of skill and credentials, and that in producing such differences the schools respond to structural needs rather than innate differences. It is further assumed that such ascribed characteristics as one's race, sex, and social-class background deliver differential treatment, consequently increasing the probability of lower educational attainment and

FIGURE 1

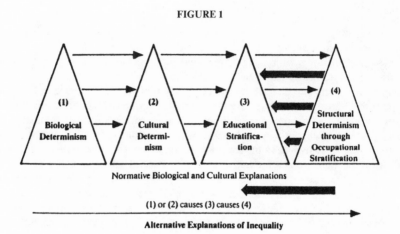

Normative Biological and Cultural Explanations

(1) or (2) causes (3) causes (4)

Alternative Explanations of Inequality

---

lower occupational placement among people of color, women, and people of lower-class origin. The amount of inequality explained by biology or culture becomes notably minor in such an analysis, since such a system would theoretically be compelled to stratify a population of identical culture and biological characteristics.

The March 1986 issue of *Crisis* presents a series of dire statistics on African-American youth. For example, it was reported that "86% of Black youth live in poverty . . ., 1 out of every 22 Black males will be killed by violent crime . . ., 51% of violent crime in the U.S. is committed by Black youth . . ., 1 out of every six Black males will be arrested by the time they reach 19 . . ., 40% of Black children are being raised in fatherless homes."[2] The magazine also puts the current high school dropout rate at 72 percent. Given the structural issues presented, and the already known precarious state of the adults, one might wonder specifically how a people of equal innate childhood potential arrive at such a disadvantaged youth status. To be sure, early indicators do exist in the over 45 percent unemployment rate of African-American youth, but the process of structuring differential perceptions, access, and attainment among African-American youngsters is begun early on.

The cornerstone of the health of an adult is the capacity to take care of one's own, and one's own self. The mechanism through which this task is made possible is employment. As we enter 1988, not only do African-Americans remain twice as likely to be unemployed as whites, but when they are employed they can expect to hold lower-status positions and to be paid less even if holding the same occupational positions as their white counterparts. The social and psychological consequences of job discrimination remain enormous both for the individuals and the relationships within the community and its families.

ENVIRONMENTAL INFLUENCES

The Role of Home

Ideally, the homes in which African-American children would blossom would consist of stable and successful parents who were capable of meeting their material and spiritual needs, providing discipline, and interceding on their behalf in the outside worlds of school, work, and community. They would be parents who would confidently challenge the school to teach their children. They would do the kinds of things that would facilitate their children's learning, such as reading to them, helping them with their homework, rewarding their successes, and exposing them to experiences and the world of knowledge. In short, such parents would provide their children with a safe, secure, and protected environment in which they would flourish with positive role models and develop both the skills and optimism necessary for a successful future.

While there are many African-American youth who, in fact, are blessed with such conditions, a significantly larger number find themselves in quite the opposite situation. It is important to emphasize that the existence of some privileged African-American individuals, be they children or adults, does not contradict or deny the endangered status of the African-American community as a whole. African-American youth are four times more likely than their white counterparts to grow up in a poor household and are as likely to grow up in a one-parent household as not. They are, therefore, at high risk of exposure to the kinds of family instability and turmoil associated with deprivation. In such circumstances, they are also more likely to fall victim to child abuse, inadequate nutrition, poor health care, drugs, crime, and material deprivation. They are more likely to live in below-par crowded quarters, with relatives other than their biological parents, and in foster care. Given such possibilities as these, it is a wonder that they survive and thrive as well as they do. Fortunately, indicators are that they are loved and feel loved, but there is no denying that many African-American youth must also suffer the consequences of the pressure under which they and their parents live.

The significant absence of fathers both as successful role models and partners in the socialization of the youth is likely to have profound, although different, effects on both boys and girls. For example, there is evidence that this absence of fathers may be partially causal to reported differences in academic achievement, favoring African-American girls over African-American boys. Allen[3] suggests that since African-American parents are role models for their chidlren and are harder on their same-sex children, the boys lose both the model and disciplinarian. Lewis reports that African-American mothers are in fact harder disciplinarians on their daughters.[4] Thus to the extent that adolescent development requires boys to break from their mother's control the absence of fathers is posited to contribute significantly to a loss of control as well as the increased probability that such boys will also reject school and be recruitable to, and controlled by, explotive males of the peer and street cultures.

To the extent that poor, young girls see their mothers coping "successfully" as single parents, they may be led to believe that they can do the same. In fact, Mayfield[5] suggests "motherhood" as a road to recognized adult status. The rapid rise in the "illegitimacy" rate among young African-American girls, which is as high as 50 percent in some cities, who are literally abandoned by their children's young fathers and left to rear their children in poverty, speaks to the seriousness of this issue. It is worth emphasizing that acknowledging these negative possibilities neither denies existing strengths of African-American families nor removes the system from its responsibility for creating the conditions that are causal to these patterns. The fact, however, remains that socialization and control problems do exist among African-American youth, and particularly poor African-American youth.

The Role of School

It has been said that schools are places that people attend most and know the least about. Education to Americans remains the symbolic key to advancement. The historic 1954 Supreme Court decision[6] declaring segregated schools inherently unequal represented what many hoped would be the turning point. Many believed it would bring an end to inferior education. However, over thirty years later the dream of the *Brown* decision remains to be realized, particularly in our cities. The underlying desegregation notions, that sprinkling a few African-American children in a predominantly white school would not depreciate the assumed higher quality of education and that sprinkling a few white children in a predominantly African-American school would appreciate the quality, are both racist and questionable. However, the fact that the wait for desegregation has allowed for significant "in the meantime" declines in predominantly African-American urban school systems is unquestionable. The education of our youth in urban systems has largely become an exercise in social control and babysitting by outsiders.

While much has been written about the achievement gaps between African-American and other ethnic groups on standardized tests, as through suggestions concerning the innate ability and motivational problems of the youngsters, less has been offered about the possible role of the school and teachers in the creation and forwarding of such differences. Nevertheless, there exists a body of literature on teacher expectations and differential treatment of children of different characteristics that might shed alternative light on the causes of these achievement differences.[7]

While conventional wisdom would have us believe that every child begins the greater quest for status at the same starting line, with the same track shoes, with only aptitude determining placement at the starting line, there is ample evidence to suggest that such egalitarian theories are myths and distortions of facts. For example, Cicourel and Kitsuse, examining the egalitarian assumption in a study of educational decision makers, concluded that quite the opposite is true. They reported that their research "supports the view that the student's progress in this sequence of transitions is contingent upon the student's biography, social and personal adjustment, appearance and

demeanor, social class, and 'social type' as well as his demonstrated ability and performance," and they concluded that "the professed ideal of equal access to educational
opportunities for those of equal ability is not necessarily served by such procedures"[8].
Lavin, in a study on predicting academic performance, concluded, "some evidence
suggests that implicit subjective criteria are involved in teacher grading practices. We
refer here to the possibility that certain characteristics of the student, such as his sex and
social class background, affect the quality of the relationship between the student and
the teacher."[9]

Katz concludes, in an analytic study of teacher attitude, that "the meaning of these
teacher differences is that on the average, children from low income homes, most of
whom are Negro, get more than their fair share of classroom exposure to teachers who
really are unqualified for their role, who basically resent teaching them, and who
therefore behave in ways that foster, in the more dependent students, tendencies toward
debilitating, self-criticism."[10]

While older research has attempted to attribute the lower attainment of African-
American youth to low self-esteem, more recent studies, when controlling for economic
background, have found no significant race differences in general or area-specific
(school, peer, and home) self-esteem. Nevertheless, consistent with the hypothesis of
differential treatment, achievement differences remain even when economic background is controlled.[11]

As previously noted, the school plays a unique role in allocating people to different
positions in the division of labor through routing and grading practices. Relative success in school is, in fact, the major avenue through which discrimination in the job
market is justified. Given racism as well as sexism and classism in a stratified America,
it has been posited that the disproportional allocation of African-Americans, women,
and people of lower-class origin to the lowest labor slots is functional, and that their
relative academic failure is essential to getting the job done. For example, such procedures as differentially allocating girls to home economics and sewing courses, lower-
class youngsters to slower tracks, and African-American children to compensatory
programs are common school practices with long-term educational and occupational
implications. Thus, it is argued that structured educational failure legitimizes job discrimination while eliminating legal recourse—one cannot successfully sue an employer
for failing to give a desired job if one arrives relatively unqualified.

It should be noted that such a process does not require a conscious conspiracy to
operate, rather it is posited that Newton's law of inertia regarding material objects is also
applicable to notions. Begging the issue of origins, continuing educational discriminatory practices merely require that school personnel, like other people, act on socialized unconscious beliefs in established stereotypes, which then have the capacity to
become self-fulfilling prophecies. Such a process requires a conspiracy to stop, not to
continue.[12] There is little reason to assume that if such processes and attitudes exist in
the general culture, they would not be operative in the schools. The fact that the schools
simultaneously homogenize attitudes while differentiating skills increases the proba-

bility that the youngsters themselves will accept their outcomes as the consequence of their own attributes or deficiencies.

This discussion, while not denying the existence of achievement gaps, has attempted to offer a structural alternative to conventional victim-blame type explanations. Such a notion appears not at all inconsistent with reported findings of gross race differences in academic achievement.

The Role of Peers

As early as pre-adolescence, African-American children show a trend toward higher peer self-esteem than white children, and higher ratings of the importance of such social abilities as being popular and good at sports and games. The fact that they do not differ from white children in general self-esteem or home self-esteem, but tend toward lower school self-esteem, as well as significantly lower standardized reading and mathematics performance, suggests that a shift from school to peers may already be beginning to take place.[13]

It may be theorized that as African-American children age and progressive lose in school evaluations, they may shift toward peer evaluations in search of higher possibilities of success and ego enhancement. As stated by Castenell in a study of area-specific achievement motivation, if an adolescent is "discouraged by significant others, or through repeated failure, to perceive achievement (as possible) within the school environment, then that adolescent may choose to achieve in another arena."[14] Cummings and others have reported evidence that as African-American children grow older, their values are more influenced by peers than by other groups, and that the maintenance of ego and self-respect increasingly requires peer solidarity.[15] These authors further support the possible existence of a progressive shift in motivation and attachment from the school to the peers among African-American youth, and particularly poor African-American youth. What is more important, they suggest that such a shift is a logical pursuit of "achievement" and positive strokes, and a flight from failure and ego-damaging experiences. Since the benefits are short-term, in that they are unlikely to pay off in the adult occupational structure, the African-American adolescent peer culture may also be viewed as a long-term "wash-out" arena although a short-term achivement arena.

Consistent with Castenell's area-specific achievement motivation notion, Maehr and Lysy question traditional restricted cultural and academic notions of achievement motivation.[16] They posit that contextual conditions are important in expressions of achievement motivations, and that the particular form in which achievement is expressed is determined by the definition that culture gives to it. They further indicate that their definition suggests that motivation is manifest in a broad range of activities, and that motivational questions are ultimately about the ways in which, rather than whether, people are motivated. In some communities, such abilities as mastering street-wiseness, playground sports, sexually, domestic and childrearing chores, supplementing family income, and taking on other aspects of adult roles at an early age provide youth opportunities to demonstrate competence. It should be noted that although the larger culture views these patterns as maladaptive and strange, they are, within the cultural milieu, perfectly realistic, adaptive, and respected responses to reality.

The African-American youth peer culture may be regarded as a long-term failure arena because even though it succeeds in providing alternative outlets for achievement through the demonstration of competence, as through street, athletic, and social activities, it offers little hope of long-term legitimate success. It carries the real dangers of drafting young people into the self-destructive worlds of drugs, crime, and sexual promiscuity. The notion of "peer solidarity" with its oppositional flavor, also suggests an anti-intellectual strain between the peers and the schooling experience. It should be emphasized, however, that it is more likely that the collectively negative schooling experiences of African-American youth produce this anti-school sentiment than the reverse, and that to whatever degree such a sentiment does exist within the culture, it is dependent upon the schools to produce the negative experiences that feed it new recruits.

In summary, given the presence of negative schooling experiences, the availability of positive peer experiences, and the inability of youth to perceive the long-term consequences of adolescent decisions, many of these youth can be said to be making what appears to them to be a logical decision in shifting from the school to the peers. In the long run, of course, they are disproportionately excluded from legitimate occupational success possibilities. They are also subsequently blamed, as adults, for the consequences of school-system-induced self-protection decisions made during adolescence. In this context, the rising crime, drug, and out-of-wedlock pregnancy rates among African-American youth may be seen as a consequence of the interplay of negative schooling experiences as provided by incompetent outsiders, a decline of parental control, and a significant rise in the independence of an attractive peer culture which offers positive strokes and ego-enhancement to a vulnerable population.

The Political Context

The political context in which these youth are found is quite different from what it was twenty years ago. The era of "black nationalism" and civil "rights" is not a conscious part of their experience and they are consequently deprived of the kinds of political socialization that was available to those of us who grew up prior to and during the era of Martin Luther King, Jr., and Malcolm X. They are more likely to blame themselves for their condition in the absence of political mentors, and less likely to understand the workings of the American social system. This knowledge void is further enhanced by youth attendance in schools we do not control in which they will more likely be taught "his-story" rather than "our-story." Since we provide no alternative structured ways for them to come to know, they are also likely to believe what they are taught. The absence of movements has also served to deny these youth the opportunity to develop the sense of community and "collective consciousness" that provided ego-protection enhancement and a sense of mission to many of us who were aware in the sixties. Such movements not only provided a shift from self-blame to system-blame, but also encouraged doing something about the group condition.

The consequences of the absence of such leadership and movements cannot be over-estimated, since such spokespersons and actions provide a "redefinition of the situation" to the population, along with increased racial pride, discipline, and willingness to work collectively toward problem resolution. Not only was this true in the political arena proper, but of other community-effecting institutions as well.

African-American music, for example, which used to give our youth such collective political messages as, "Say it loud, I'm Black and I'm proud," now instead provides such individualistic messages as "I'm bad, I'm bad, you know it." The African-American church, which has historically been a fertile source of child socialization, leadership, and moral development appears to have slipped in its ability to generate community solidarity and progressive leadership. African-American business remains largely what E. Franklin Frazier[17] described as an economic myth, as regards its ability to employ a significant number of African-American people, and willingness to play a philanthropic role in the community. The African-American press appears less willing to fill the information void regarding the true state of the community than it is in forwarding gossip and sensationalism. If the African-American church can be accused of deferrring gratification more than raising indignation, the African-American press can be accused of providing vicarious living experiences through the presentation of the lifestyles of selected "successful" African-Americans, most of whom are either athletes or enter-tainers.

This assessment is not intended to romanticize the sixties, but merely to describe the probable declines in community activism and responsibility and their likely effect on this coming generation.

On Mass Media Intrusion

This is an undeniable symbolic truth to George Orwell's prediction in *1984*. His error simply resided in direction when he predicted that "big brother" is watching you. The truth is that you are watching "big brother"! The average eighteen-year-old today has watched approximately 22,000 hours of television and 350,000 commercials. Aside from the exploitation of youthful insecurities by commercials, creating diseases to sell cures, such as perpetuating the need to "relax" one's hair, prevent chapped lips, and wear designer jeans, the tube serves to condition the population. Television tells youth what to want, whom to like, how to be, and what to think. It romanticizes greed, crime, infidelity, materialism, and individualism. Furthermore, it not only provides white America with distorted images of African-Americans and African-American commu-nities, but creates gross misconceptions of the world for African-Americans as well. While comic treatment of whites on the tube is counterbalanced by serious treatment, it is hard for a viewer to conclude that the African-American family, for example, is anything other than a joke. It creates people who confuse reality and illusion, desensitizes people to violence, and programs all populations to a pro-male, white, and upper-class imitation pattern.

To be sure the occasional presentations of serious African-American programs and sporadic appearances of uniquely talented African-American personalities do occur, but the dominant message to African-American youth remains illusionary possibilities of star status as through athletics or entertainment. For example, the futility of such programmed aspirations as star status in the NBA (National Basketball Association) or NFL (National Football League) was aptly indicated by sociologist Harry Edwards, when he noted that African-American youth were twice as likely to be hit by a star (a falling meteorite) as they were to become one in professional sports. For the less athletic and talented, even more bizarre possibilities, such as adoption by a nice rich white man are offered. One might wonder what such program exposure does to condition African-American children toward obedience to white men. Most importantly, however, one might simply wonder what else might have been done to, or for, a mind, had it not spent this amount of time (22,000 hours) sitting in front of the tube.

The point here is that, however subtle, television is the most massive programming and socializing instrument ever created, and cannot be expected to do anything more than deactivate our youth.

While it is probably true that television previously served to bring the news of marches, protests, and rallies, etc., into the home and the American conscience, it appears that the lesson has been learned and such events are intentionally being played down, if covered at all. The management of news has become more sophisticated and a shift from straight news to sensationalistic entertainment is evident. The danger of television raising consciousness is declining.

The American population generally, and the African-American population specifically, have yet to measure or understand the degree to which this new television generation has been affected. People have only begun to investigate, for example, the connection between television crime and street crime, and even less has been done to assess the long-term consequences of television addition for interaction skills or moral development. It is clear, however, that we do not control the tube and thus are surely giving strangers access to our children's minds when we fail to police their watching habits.

On Street Models

To the extent that role models are significant, poor African-American youth run a high probability of exposure to successful participants in what has been called "the underground economy." While short on doctors, lawyers, engineers, and other legitimized professionals to emulate, they are differentially exposed to numbers runners, drug dealers, pimps, prostitutes, and other assortments of creative and innovative characters with apparent money, cars, and fine clothes. To the extent that models of legitimate success become unavailable, and legitimate opportunities become scarce, these youth also become vulnerable to and recruitable to such activities. This becomes even more likely when one further considers that the professionals working in their communities such as teachers, police, fire fighters, etc., are not likely to live there, and that their local religious and political leaders are also less likely to have meaningful contact with them.

Thus African-American youth can be said to be in a community context that is simultaneously less effective in protecting, organizing, and socializing them, while more vulnerable to negative influences. The combined facts of mass media intrusion, an absence of control over local schools, and exposure to alternative lifestyles, provide increased opportunity for our youth to be programmed contrary to our, or their, interests.

The Psychology of Social Control

As pointed out long ago by Carter G. Woodson,[18] when you contol a man's thinking you do not have to worry about his actions. One does not have to accept the Grier and Cobbs[19] or Kardiner and Ovesey[20] arguments of self-hatred to acknowledge that *living under constant psychological and material abuse does have its price.* For example, some African-American people are successfully socialized into internalizing negative messages about themselves. Others are brought to believe what is said about the group is true, while viewing themselves as the exception. Still others, in over-zealous defense of the group, deny that there is any effect on any group members. Just as it would be unwise to claim nothing wrong with the lower-class African-American family, and thereby remove the system from any responsibility for the economic strains such families suffer, it would be foolish to fail to acknowledge the special pressures affecting African-American people. As indicated, rather than denying effects, we relocate the causes from the group to the system, while simultaneously recognizing both our responsibilities and societal responsibilities for change.

The combination of racism, an economically "deprived" and psychologically hostile enviornment, and negative schooling experience is bound to have profoundly negative effect on the psychological and academic adjustment of these African-American youth. Amazingly, however, they are also creative and talented in the development of survival skills, and in utilizing mechanisms to protect and enhance their self-imagery even if it means the reorganization of self-defintion. They are, therefore, capable of change and can be saved. It is toward this last capability that we must direct our energies. It is in this context that the following policy recommendations are offered.

POLICY RECOMMENDATIONS

(1) *Inform the African-American Communities* and others concerned of the true endangered status of the youth. In addition to meetings, utilization of mass media (television, press, radio, etc.) should be sought.

(2) *Work with Other Organizations, Community Groups, and Parents* to organize programs to assist the youth in developing:
- a stronger sense of self-worth and self-discipline and commitment to academic achievement.
- a stronger sense of commitment to family.
- a stronger sense of commitment to local community.
- a stronger sense of commitment to the general African-American community.
- a stronger sense of connectedness to all other oppressed people.

(3) *Work with African-American Business Persons, Politicians, Clergy, etc.* to provide opportunities for African-American youth to be exposed to mentors and role models, as well as to understand the workings of business, government, etc.

(4) *Provide Organized Collective Activities for Youth* the African-American church, for example, might prove an excellent location for the recreational, educational, and political socialization of our youth.

(5) *Develop Mechanisms of Accountability* for African-American professional business persons, politicians, clergy, etc.

(6) *Organize and Demand of the Federal Government:*
   a) Enforcement of our rights in general.
   b) Services delivery, such as health care, housing, employment, and child nutrition programs.
   c) Voting rights protection.
   d) Civil rights protection.

(7) *Organize and Demand of Local Government:*
   a) Quality education for our youth, as distinguished from but not as opposed to desegregated education.
   b) Services delivery, such as better drug enforcement, police service, sanitation service, fire protection, housing code enforcement, etc.

(8) *Organize, Register, and Vote.*

Such an analysis and action list is not intended to be all inclusive, but does represent a possible point of departure. It acknowledges our as well as the system's responsibilities, and suggests the need to move ahead collectively for ourselves, for oppressed peoples, and, most importantly, for our youth.

CONCLUDING REMARKS

Given the inequality-reproducing structure of the social system, there are limits to the amount of progress we can expect to make short of radical change. There are reforms, however, that can be pursued in order to decrease the probability that African-American youth will continue to suffer disproportionately as "class-plus" victims in a racist class system.

We must assist youth to organize, and in some cases to reorganize, in such a way as to maximize their self-image, self-discipline, and attainment. As previously indicated, it would seem that the African-American church would be an ideal site for the academic and political socialization of our youth. It is through such institutions that other ethnic groups have guaranteed the moral and political socialization of their youth necessary to the integrity and continuance of the community. This task becomes increasingly important for groups who are not in charge of the schools their youngsters attend. We must be aware, however, that to raise the expectations and efforts of African-American youth without also placing additional pressures on the institutions, agencies, and individuals (particularly teachers) who serve them would be grossly unfair. We must, in fact, seek better control of the environment in which our youth are located. If we do not, we may well not only have wasted human resources but also created an increasing population of embittered and dangerous adults.

NOTES

1. Samuel Bowles and Herbert Gintis, *Schooling in Capitalist America* (New York: Basic Basic Books, 1976).

2. *Crisis,* 93 (March 1986), entire issue on the topic, "Black Males in Jeopardy."

3. Walter Allen, "Family Roles, Occupational Statuses, and Achievement Among Black Women in the United States," *Journal of Women in Culture and Society* 4 (1979): 670-686.

4. Diane I. Lewis, "The Black Family: Socialization and Sex Roles," *Phylon* 36 (1975): 221-237.

5. Lorraine Mayfield, "Early Parenthood Among Low-Income Adolescent Girls," in Robert Staples, ed., *The Black Family: Essays and Studies* (Belmont, Calif.: Wadsworth Publishing, 1986).

6. *Brown V. Board of Education of Topeka,* 347 U.S. 483 (1954).

7. Bruce R. Hare, "Black and White Child Self-Esteem in Social Science: An Overview," *Journal of Negro Education* 46 (1977): 141-156; A. Wade Boykin, Anderson J. Franklin, and J. Frank Yates, eds., *Research Directions of Black Psychologists* (New York: Russell Sage Foundation, 1979) Margaret Spencer, Geraldine K. Brookins and Walter R. Allen, eds., *Beginnings: The Social and Affective Development of Black Children* (Hillsdale, N.J.: Lawrence Erlbaum Associates, 1985).

8. Aaron Cicourel and John Kituse, *The Educational Decision Makers* (Indianapolis: Bobbs-Merrill, 1963), pp. 136-137.

9. David Lavin, *The Predictions of Academic Performance* (New York: Russell Sage Foundation, 1963).

10. Irwin Katz, "The Socialization of Academic Motivation in Minority Group Children," in D. Levine, ed., *Nebraska Symposium on Motivation* (Lincoln: University of Nebraska Press, 1967).

11. Bruce R. Hare, "Self-Perception and Academic Achievement Variations in a Desegregated Setting," *American Journal of Psychiatry* 137 (1980): 683-689.

12. _____, "Development and Change among Desegregated Adolescents: A Longitudinal Study of Self-Perception and Achievement," in David E. Bartz and Martin L. Maehr, eds., *Advances in Motivation and Achievement,* Vol. 1 (Greenwich, Conn.: JAI Press, 1984).

13. _____, "Stability and Change in Self-Perception and Achievement Among Black Adolescents: A Longitudinal Study," *Journal of Black Psychology* 11 (1985): 29-42.

14. Louis A. Castenell, "Achievement Motivation: An Investigation of Adolescent Achievement Patterns," *American Educational Research Journal* 20 (1983): 503-510.

15. Scott Cummings, "Family Socialization and Fatalism Among Black Adolescents," *Journal of Negro Education* 46 (1977): 62-75.

16. Martin Maehr and A. Lysy, "Motivating Students of Diverse Socioculture Backgrounds to Achieve," *International Journal of Intercultural Relations* 2 (1979): 38-70.

17. E. Franklin Frazier, *Black Bourgeoisie* (Glencoe, Ill.: Free Press, 1957).

18. Carter G. Woodson, *The Mis-Education of the Negro,* 2nd Ed. (Washington, D.C.: Associated Publishers 1969).

19. William Grier and Price M. Cobbs, *Black Rage* (New York: Bantam, 1968).

20. Abram Kardiner and Lionel Ovesey, *The Mark of Oppression* (New York: Norton, 1951).

5

A Strategy of Responsible Militancy: A Template for Today's African-American Youth

Robert O. Washington

This article proposes a strategy of responsible militancy which is both a mind set and a tactic. As a mind set, the strategy is based on the individualized determination to excel on the part of youth, parents and the African-American community. As a tactic, responsible militancy incorporates the litigation, legislation and direct confrontation of harmful policies and practices of the past and presumes a high degree of positive self-determination. Recognizing the need for African-American youth to become effective citizens of tomorrow, the article offers a template for today's African-American youth. It calls for restoration of pride and stability to the African-American family, returning the streets and neighborhoods to the people who live there, parental commitment to join school officials in improving the quality of education in our schools, the creation of a national psychology of noblesse oblige, and maintenance of pressure upon the federal government to enforce affirmative action programs.

When today's African-American youth look toward the future, they see an illusion. On the one hand, they see a nation whose technology has enabled it to tame dreaded diseases, invent the most cunning machines, split and harness the atom, and hurl its rockets to the far regions of space. Then our youth also see a nation that has not learned how to curb racism, how to prevent hunger and deprivation, how to keep the human soul spiritually attuned, or how to fulfill the glorious promise of the Declaration of Independence.

As a world leader in science and technology, we have developed drugs and medical procedures that have potential to retard the aging process; we have spliced the gene and even talk about the potential of science to create new forms of life; and we have developed test tube babies and witnessed other forms of genetic engineering. However, we have not captured the secret for teaching today's African-American youth how to read, perform simple mathematical equations, or develop faith and confidence that the future holds more promises than the past. For more than 50 percent of today's African-

Originally published in *Centerboard,* Vol IV, No. 1, Spring 1986. Reprinted with permission of Southwest Center for Human Relations Studies.

American youth, life will be shorter; a quality basic education will be more elusive; and opportunities for an improved quality of life and higher paying jobs will be less available to them than to their White counterparts, and perhaps to their African-American counterparts of the past.[1]

As a panelist on the program "Young Black Males: An Endangered Species" at a recent New York City meeting of the National Association for the Advancement of Colored People (NAACP) Legal Defense and Education Fund conference, a California sociologist said 50 percent of young African-Americans are now unemployed, 25 percent under the age of 25 have never had a job, 1 in 6 has been arrested, and more than 10,000 African-American teenage males are killed in homicides each year. According to an article in the *Chicago Tribune* (June 3, 1985, p. 14), as a result of these high rates of unemployment, death, and incarceration, only 45 "marriageable" (economically stable) African-American males are available for every 100 African-American females aged 20 to 24. The question confronting African-Americans now in regard to their children is one with which they have been concerned in the past: How should African-American communities and individual African-American parents prepare their children for the future to avoid the problems revealed in the statistics presented above?

A STRATEGY OF RESPONSIBLE MILITANCY: A PARADIGM

Today's youth confront a chain of problems that can be overcome only by what I have chosen to call a strategy of responsible militancy. This strategy draws comparison with the "Black rage" of the 1960s when many African-American youth expressed their antagonism toward the "system" through alienation, estrangement, disaffection, and destruction. One need only pass through some of the fire-torn communities struck during the hot summers of the late 1960s to appreciate the residual of that era.

A strategy of responsible militancy is a mind set—a strategy based on an individualized determination to excel on the part of youth, parents, and the African-American community. It draws upon an inner strength of values and norms that gives order, meaning, and coherence to one's life. A strategy of responsible militancy is also a tactic. It incorporates the litigation, legislation, and direct confrontation of harmful policies and practices of the past and presumes a high degree of positive self-determination. This strategy recognizes the range of everyday, coercive patterns and social arrangements a racist society expresses through a web of rewards, sanctions, and other inducements which vary from patent racism to the most subtle forms of bigotry and discrimination.

A strategy of responsible militancy assumes that the battle for equality and social justice begins at home in the constructive way we treat our children and families, our neighbors and communities. It demands no less of ourselves than it does of others; it draws upon the use of self-help schemes and mutual-aid groups but rejects the notion that, by themselves, they are the salvation to the problems of African-Americans.

Self-Help—Necessary, but Not a Panacea

Without minimizing their importance as a major strategy or public policy, self-help schemes have their imitations in that most of them are developed by charismatic leadership and tend to be temporal in dimension. Also they tend to work better in situations that seek solutions to individual distress rather than solutions to systemic or institutional problems.

Researchers who have studied self-help groups and mutual-aid organizations have reminded us that we know very little about their global impact or how they gain acceptance in a community. What we do know, however, is that self-help schemes and mutual-aid organizations "can be best understood as one of several viable alternatives which need to be encouraged by policy makers, rather than as a panacea,"[2] And, if mutual-aid organizations are to serve large numbers of individuals over extended periods of time, they need stable financial support.

A strategy of responsible militancy demands that African-American males can no longer make babies, then walk away as if they just have conquered a tiger. Nor can "Black-on-Black" crimes continue to be ignored and condoned by the absence of protest, allowing the law of the jungle to prevail in African-American communities. But make no mistake, proponents of a strategy of responsible militancy are not bedfellows of those who proclaim ending racism tomorrow would have little effect on the plight of poor African-American children; nor do these proponents march to the same beat of those who argue that the primary sources of poverty in African-American communities lie in pathological cultural patterns.

Poverty—Still a Racial Issue

Poverty is, indeed, surreptitiously an issue of racism and inequality. The twin evils of poverty and racism in America have produced a system of social stratification that deprives African-Americans of opportunities to share equitably in the benefits and products of society. As a result, African-Americans are denied the same access Whites have to employment, money, education, contacts, power, and know-how, all essential to full participation in the economic and social mainstreams of society.

Poverty is one of the most pervasive correlates of being African in America. Poverty—not motivation—is the single most important source of the problems facing the majority of African-Americans in this country. Racism—not—indifferences—is the culprit that denies African-Americans equal access to economic and—political power; limits the franchise; sustains job discrimination and unemployment; permits unequal pay for similar work; tolerates inferior training of individuals for the workplace; restricts living to poorer housing and high-crime neighborhoods; and produces excessive health problems.

The strategy of responsible militancy does not naively blame the victim, but it does admonish African-Americans and other minorities not to make victims of ourselves. A strategy of responsible militancy rejects the notion that government social programs are necessarily counterproductive, discourage the work ethic, and foster dependency. Instead this strategy demands that the federal government provide for the social underclass ways out of poverty and the same protection it offers the corporate elite. The wealthy are protected by a "fiscal welfare" system of tax loopholes and tax codes as well as by an "occupational welfare" system of elaborate fringe benefit packages to corporate executives.[3] The poor are denied these significant advantages. Thus, they need a welfare system designed as a constructive set of ladders to climb out of poverty, not a system that maintains the status of poverty.

Before examining how a strategy of responsible militancy should be implemented, it is important to place it in a historical and ideological context.

A HISTORICAL PERSPECTIVE

Allison Davis and John Dollard studied the effects of caste and class discrimination upon eight African-American youth in Natchez and New Orleans. They published their conclusions in *Children of Bondage*.[4] *Negro Youth at the Crossways* reported the findings of E. Franklin Frazier's research, concentrating on youth and communities in Washington, DC and Louisville, Kentucky.[5] Charles S. Johnson's *Growing Up in the Black Belt* is a classic study on rural southern youth coming of age.[6] This study attempted to analyze socialization and maturation processes of youth in the rural South. W. Lloyd Warner collaborated with Buford H. Junker and an African-American psychoanalyst, Walter A. Adams, in a study of the personality development of African-American youth in the inner city of Chicago. They published the results in *Color and Human Nature*.[7]

The American Council on Education commissioned these studies to investigate the conditions, needs, and distinctive problems of "growing up Black in America." In addition, the studies sought to determine the effects of these factors upon the socialization and personality development of African-American youth between the ages of 16 and 24 and the ability of the youth to adapt in a hostile environment. Between 1935 and 1940, hundreds of thousands of American youth were unemployed, and when compared with the general population, the proportion of unemployed African-Americans was much greater.[8]

The findings from these studies showed that the American Dream—a symbol of society's definition of what is good and expected in American life—was as much an illusion for most African-American youth then as it is today. An underlying theme of this paper is: To achieve the American Dream, African-America must prepare itself and its youth to rise above historical, sociostructural barriers by helping them to develop the attributes discussed below:

Positive Self-Identity and Self-Esteem

We learn who we are and what we are like largely by carefully observing how other people, African-American and White—but especially, important other people—react to us. For underclass African-Americans, repression and discrimination coupled with lifelong poverty and social inequality give rise to feelings of powerlessness and victimization which curb the motivation needed to achieve their potential. Most frequently, the bottom line to African-Americans' feelings of powerlessness and victimization is poor education and unstable employment.

We live in a society in which a person's work is one of the factors others use in judging him/her and one of the more significant factors in self-evaluation. As one of the most important indices of social identity, a job is more than a "calling card." It is inexorably linked to self-esteem, and problems related to one's job—or the lack of a job—can create problems with one's self-esteem.

Sense of Control

Related to the notion of positive self-esteem is the idea of self-control. African-American youth must be imbued with the confidence that they have control over their futures. Such confidence is built through identification of youth with constructive role models. The four American Council on Education studies referred to earlier found that African-American youth who grew up to share the American Dream came from homes with strong family ties in which parents or significant others presented an image of self-respect and exhibited ambition and expectations for the children. Also, these families taught their youth that working hard and refusing to give up made achievement possible.

In order to realize a sense of control, youth need stability and permanence in their lives. However, for the 50 percent of African-American youth who live in homes where there are no stable male role models, a sense of self as well as a sense of control are difficult to maintain. A recent study reported by the Children's Bureau showed that of the 300,000 children in foster care in the United States, over 28 percent were African-American children.[9] All the major studies of foster care have shown that African-American children stay in foster care for longer periods than do White children—as much as four times longer.[10]

Faith in Democracy

Today, when general pessimism among African-Americans is growing, perhaps the most difficult challenge for African-America is to establish faith in democracy among its youth. A 1983 Gallup poll revealed that while 82 percent of Whites thought their personal lives were satisfactory, only 50 percent of African-Americans held this view. Also Whites indicated more satisfaction with the national conditions (39 percent) than did African-Americans (13 percent). The brighter side of this picture is that, compared with their parents, African-American teenagers expressed considerably more optimism about their own personal lives. The poll showed 76 precent reflected this optimism—not far below the 85 percent mark for White teenagers.

Moreover, the poll revealed a wide gap between White and African-American teenagers' satisfaction with trends in the nation. Twice the proportion of White youth (43 percent) compared with the proportion of African-American youth (20 percent) expressed satisfaction with national trends. Perhaps, these latter figures reveal a lack of optimism for the future among African-American teenagers. For today's youth, a steady decline in educational and employment opportunities may be even a tougher pill to swallow than it was for prior generations.

I am inclined to agree with Irving Kristol[11], the social critic, who insists that a free society which widely views the distribution of its wealth as unfair cannot long survive. I too raise the question: "Can men live in a free society if they have no reason to believe it is also a just soceity?"

PICKING UP THE GAUNTLET

If the future of African-America is in the hands of today's African-American youth, then the logical question is: How well equipped are they to pick up the gauntlet?

Overview

There are 28.6 million African-Americans in this country.[12] This represents 12 percent of the U.S. population with New York, Chicago, Detroit, Philadelphia, and Los Angeles having the largest African-American populations. About 60 percent of all African-American families live in central cities of urban areas. Cities in which the majority of the population is African-American include East St. Louis, Illinois (96 percent); Gary, Indiana (83 percent); Washington, DC (70 percent); Atlanta (66 percent); Detroit (63 percent); Newark (58 percent); Birmingham, Alabama (56 percent); Baltimore (55 percent); New Orleans (55 percent); and Richmond, Virginia (51 percent).[13]

There are 71,145,000 children in the United States between the ages of 1 and 19 (of whom 11 million are African-American).[13] These children live in families that have experienced a marked decline in disposable income since the election of the Reagan administration. A 1984 study of the Urban Institute revealed that African-Americans in every income strata, from the poorest to the most affluent, lost-ground and had a lower standard of living in 1984 than in 1980, and the key factors spurring this income loss were Reagan administration policies. The report noted: "Had Reagan administration policies not been followed, average Black disposable income would have been up slightly rather than down."[14] The median income for African-American families in 1984 was $15,887. However, 63 percent of all families earned less than $20,000.[15]

The wife in an African-American household typically contributes about 60 percent more to the family income than the wife in a White household. While there is growing disparity between the well-being of the middle-class African-American and the African-American poor, the African-American middle class is far more dependent than the White middle class is upon two earners for maintaining its standard of living. Unemployment among African-Americans remains high. As a matter of fact, the gap between African-American unemployment and White unemployment has widened during the past four years. For example, when the Reagan administration took office, African-American unemployment was 14.4 percent and White unemployment was 6.7 percent. In August 1984, White unemployment stood at 6.4 percent while African-American unemployment was around 16 percent.[16]

What all of this has meant is that the African-American child is almost three times as likely to be poor as the White child and can expect to spend more than five years of childhood in poverty. This picture has become even more distressful. Of the 11 million African-American children in the population, approximately 100,000 are without permanent homes. Although African-American youth under the age of 19 represent only 14 percent of the youth population, they comprise 33 percent of all children not living with their natural parents. In this country, 4 out of every 1,000 children lack a permanent home. However, among African-American children the number is 10 out of every 1,000—more than two times the national average.[17]

Education

There are roughly eight million African-American children in public schools throughout the United States. Yet 40 percent of them are functional illiterates. Standardized achievement test scores show that the average African-American child is roughly the equivalent of two grades behind the average White child at grade six, three years behind at grade nine, and four years behind at grade twelve.

This pattern of learning makes the school environment a very unfriendly place for the African-American child. The solution for many pupils, then, is to drop out before graduation. Many dropouts believe, given the current social and economic barriers to mobility, education will be of little benefit to them. Thus, dropping out of school seems a realistic and sound decision.[18]

The 1980 census data reported the high school dropout rate of 16 percent for African-Americans compared to 11 percent for Whites and 12 percent for all youths. A study of dropouts in the Waco, Texas school system revealed some rather startling information. This study found that while the dropout rate was 70 percent higher for African-American children than for Anglo children, the African-American dropouts had higher intelligence scores, as measured on a standardized IQ test, than those African-Americans who remained in school.[19]

The conclusion one may draw from the Richardson and Gerlach study is that African-American dropouts with higher intelligence scores (but lower educational aspirations and motivation) than those African-American pupils remaining in school sense impending futility and a lack of opportunity in American society for minority groups. Furthermore, they may not conceptualize the educational process as a way for them to improve their chances for economic success. These bright African-American youth tend to perceive American society as a closed system within which they will be unable to participate regardless of their educational background. In short, for many African-

American dropouts the concept of education as a ladder for social mobility simply seems inconsistent with what they perceive to be their opportunities for success in life.

Related to the African-American youth's feelings of hostility toward the school is the wholesale placement of African-American children in special education programs—frequently referred to as EMR (Educable Mentally Retarded). Three times as many African-American children as White children are placed in EMR programs, yet African-American children make up only 10 percent of the youngsters in gifted and talented classes.[20] The problem with the nationwide phenomenon of placement of African-American children in EMR classes is school officials expect so little of these students that few resources are devoted to quality programs.

A third educational problem is one of suspensions and expulsions of male African-American pupils. Most studies reveal that African-Americans are suspended and expelled from schools in disproportionate numbers to their population in the schools. The Children's Defense Fund found in its study that although African-American children accounted for only 27.1 percent of the enrollment, they represented 42.3 percent of the suspensions. Bennett and Harris found the extent of disparity of suspensions between African-American and White pupils related largely to the psychological climate of the school's attitudes and to the predisposition of the staff toward its African-American student populations.[21]

Census data have shown that African-American pupils finish high school at a higher rate than ever, in spite of high dropout rates, suspensions, and expulsions. Yet, a recent Rand Corporation study reported that although by the mid-1970s the percentage of African-American high school graduates enrolled in colleges had reached the percentage of White enrollment, African-American enrollment then declined in a pattern coinciding with the economic recession and a government freeze on the student-aid program.[22]

Employment and Unemployment

Despite the persistently high dropout rates among African-American youth and the relatively poor preparation many have for the world of work, most young African-Americans are committed to the work ethic and are willing to work. They also are more willing than Whites to take jobs at subminimum wages.[23]

Racism and discrimination are still barriers to employment for African-American youth, and African-American males generally earn 11 percent less per hour than do comparably educated White youth. Despite the fact that African-American youth seek employment as conscientiously as White youth,[24] one half of African-American youth are unemployed. In general, African-American youth are two and one-half times more likely to be unemployed than White youth.[25]

At present the heaviest concentration of African-Americans is in production jobs in the "smokestack industries," the jobs most threatened to become performed by robots. For example, in 1982 *Black Enterprise* predicted that by the end of 1985, 20 percent of the jobs in the automobile industry would be replaced by robots,[26] and current statistics substantiate this trend. The steel, textile, apparel, and leather product manufacturing industries expect similar decline in job opportunities for African-Americans. Already automation and computerization have advanced to the point that our semiskilled children will have fewer job opportunities than their parents have had.

Technology has created automated machines that mine coal, pick cotton, cast and finish engine blocks, sort bank checks, roll aluminum, grade oranges, weave cloth, and do myriad other things. Now computer technology performs traditional human tasks involving experience, memory, analysis, logic, and decision making. These robots diagnose symptoms for the physician, research a case for the lawyer, read envelopes for the postman, analyze market portfolios for the broker, design a plant for the architect, prepare war and defense plans for the military, fly missiles for the scientist, and keep inventory for the merchant. These machines "learn" to translate languages, compose music, play chess, transcribe speech, and "see" objects. Already they correct their own mistakes and identify trouble spots within their mechanisms.

The industrial robot, purchased at about $50,000, can be paid for and operated at less than $6 an hour compared with a minimum average cost of $20 an hour for a human worker. This fact alone suggests why forecasters are predicting that by the year 2000 a total of some 45 million factory and office jobs could be affected in some way by automation.[27]

The handwriting is on the wall for today's African-American youth. To be employable, productive citizens of the future, they must be educated and trained for jobs that are expected to expand and where there is room at the top; no longer can we prepare them merely for entry level positions or for jobs that will have short life expectancy.

A TEMPLATE FOR TODAY'S AFRICAN-AMERICAN YOUTH

Clearly today's African-American youth are not being properly prepared for a productive future in our society, and America, White and African-American, is left with the responsibility of answering the challenge of what strategies should be adopted and by whom to make what is "expected" in American life a reality and not an illusion for our African-American youth. The proposition has been made that much of the success of any strategy devised to bring more African-Americans into the economic and social mainstream of America rests with the future of African-American youth.

This article has tried to paint a picture of the status of today's African-American youth, and that picture conveys two images. On the one hand, we see a preponderance of today's African-American youth as disadvantaged, poorly educated, and poorly trained for a high-tech society. In effect, they are the symbol of a growing underclass. This image is spurred by an epidemic of teenage pregnancy and the twin package of high unemployment and high crime and death rates for males. Yet, we also see other African-American youth, who have embraced society's middle-class values, pursuing higher education in increasing numbers and fighting the odds imposed by social arrangements and the social structure of a racist, Social Darwinist society.

If today's African-American youth are to become effective citizens of tomorrow, then some imperatives must be achieved on their behalf that are neither debatable nor postponable! My conceptualization of these imperatives forms the strategy of responsible militancy which demands that we start with the basics.

Fundamentally, African-Americans as a group must recapture their sense of "peoplehood." This can be done by once again establishing coalitions. Churches must consolidate their fiscal resources and the social, economic, and political power their masses represent. Civil rights organizations must win back the confidence and support they once commanded and provide quality leadership in unifying African-Americans on local as well as national goals and action.

The efforts of the African-American media must be enlisted in promoting national goals, and in turn African-American community leaders must demand that merchants and businesses serving our communities support the media through advertisement and in other ways. With this financial backing, the African-American media should feel obligated to accept as one of its mandates the role of assisting in the mobilization of African-American coalitions to create local and national agendas for action.

RESTORATION OF PRIDE AND STABILITY TO THE AFRICAN-AMERICAN FAMILY

Social scientists regard the family as the critical social institution in our society. All societies depend upon the family for the socialization of children into adults who can then function successfully in that society. Yet, despite this essential function of socialization, the family itself has not fared well in this country over the last couple of generations. Part of the reason is it has not received the necessary societal and governmental support. Urie Bronfenbrenner, a respected authority, noted: "Our society does not treat families very well . . . it's been showing up in what's been happening inside families. It is most obvious that the family is breaking down, and . . . it is probably one of the most radical changes in a basic institution in our society to have happened outside a time of national crisis.[28]

In commenting about the breakdown of the family and its impact upon children and youth, the Joint Commission on Mental Helath of Children reported: "This nation, the richest of all world powers, has no unified national commitment to its children and youth."[29] The report charged that we lack a meaningful investment in children at the national, community, and personal levels, and as a consequence, millions of American children are "ill fed, ill housed, and ill educated."

This is a sad commentary about this nation and how it provides support for the most basic social institution in our civilization. Yet it is clear that the survival of African-Americans as a people depends upon the community taking special measures to strengthen and protect the family.

Our first obligation should be to stop excessive overglamorization of the African-American family's strengths and resilience. We must reject the argument that the provision of public social services necessarily interferes with the natural helping network of the African-American family and the community. Yes, indeed, the African-American family is strong. Since the days of Kunta Kinte, it has withstood abuse, exploitation, dislocation, and separation. But it is folly for us to continue to operate as if the African-American family is impervious to mounting poverty, idleness, escalating teenage pregnancy, and the increasing rate of drug abuse and crime among children. Neither African-American communities nor the nation can afford to neglect the growing incidence of child abuse or the reality that single parents have responsibility for rearing 50 percent of African-American children.

Social scientists who have cited evidence indicating that the support system of individuals sometimes more or less disappears when social agencies intervene carry, I believe, the interpretation of the data beyond its logical conclusion.[30] As Maya Angelou in *I Know Why the Caged Bird Sings* reminds us:

> Although there was always generosity in the Black neighborhood, it was indulged on pain of sacrifice. Whatever was given by Black people to other Blacks was most probably needed as desperately by the donor as by the receiver. . . .[31]

The lesson is this: African-Americans cannot allow the interpretation of some social scientists to be the alibi for the federal government to do less than it is required to do for the survival and strengthening of the African-American family.

A second obligation requires African-American communities to create a climate that coerces fathers who are out of the home to provide their share of child support on a consistent basis. African-American families and community leaders must instill in young males the conviction that poverty and human abuse created by neglect of their responsibility is intolerable.

Third, it is important to support legislation proposed by Congress that will form a foundation for establishing a viable family policy. The Family Economic Security Act of 1985, a bill proposed by Representative Harold Ford of Tennessee is an example. Also, we need to give assistance to those who seek equitable means for raising personal tax exemptions which would reduce the tax burdens of families with children.

Determination of Ways to Return Our Streets and Neighborhoods to the People Who Live There

Curbing crime, drug trafficking, and gangs on our streets is a high priority. A group called "Deacons of Christ" formed five years ago by members of the Christ Methodist Church in the Englewood section of Chicago is an example of what residents can do to protect their neighborhood.[32] The church has not been burglarized in five years, and during that time rapes, robberies, and other crimes have been reduced so dramatically that neighbors say they no longer fear walking around the block or sitting on their porches after the sun sets. In addition to working against crime, the Deacons of Christ group provides free food and clothing to poor area residents and recruits teenagers for volunteer church work to keep them out of gangs.

Parental Commitment to Join School Officials in Improving the Quality of Education in Our Schools

The current condition of our public schools tests our very morality and purpose as a people. If we cannot achieve nationwide consensus about the urgency of improving schools and marshal the will and resources to move forward quickly and adequately on the educational front, making things better for our children becomes an empty dream. Schools cannot escape the unique and major role they play in reducing anxieties, tensions, and frustrations of youth, which have their origins in poverty, racism, and the social structure of our society.

Dr. John H. Fischer, more than a generation ago, admonished us that public schools fail to meet the needs of African-American youth because of a restricted conception of what opportunity means:

> Even schools which open their doors freely to all comers often overlook the crucial truth that no situation is an opportunity except for those who can see its possibilities. The chance to learn means nothing to a child until he has been taught that learning can be rewarding for him. In children, as in adults, attitudes induced by the present environment and reinforced by centuries of repression are not reversed by the simple process of unlocking classroom doors.[33]

Also, parents and leaders must convey better than we have in the past the importance of an education that is in tune with our society as a way out of poverty. *Ebony Magazine* publishes each year a list of 100 influential African-Americans. During the past ten years, only two persons associated wtih education have been listed among our leaders. How can children be convinced that education is important when media do not use educators and other local achievers as role models?

Creation of a National Psychology of Noblesse Oblige

Those among us who have, must give more attention to those who have not! If African-Americans are to achieve the American Dream as a people, then African-Americans must be prepared, more than in the past, to carry on our shoulders those who require help to achieve the dream for themselves. We can do this in many ways. Churches can do a better job of combining their resources to build homes for our children and families. More African-American millionaire athletes must find collective ways to return some of their wealth to African-American communities. Some have performed nobly on this score. Others have done very little.

There is talk that one national civil rights organization has begun a campaign to bring pressure on top African-American recording artists and their record companies who have "almost entirely White operations" to hire more African-Americans for behind-the-scenes work.[34] It would be ironic if three-year-old African-American children who can sing the words to "What's Love Got to Do With It," "Purple Rain," "Thriller," and other songs that have reached the million mark in sales, could not hope for a job in the business of their idols.

Maintenance of Pressure Upon the Federal Government to Enforce
Affirmative Action Programs

I am not convinced of the declining significance of race in the labor market. I disagree with my African-American brothers who argue that affirmative action has hindered rather than helped the cause of social equality and social opportunity. William Wilson's argument[35] that the life chances of individual African-Americans in recent years have had more to do with their economic class position than with their day-to-day encounters with Whites is illogical. Separating racism, discrimination, and bigotry from class in this country is the same as arguing the chicken has no relatioship to the egg. And not associating progress among African-Americans in the marketplace with affirmative action is the same as arguing space exploration has no relationship to Einstein's theory of relativity.

Black Enterprise in a 1980 survey asked its readers if they believed their present jobs would have been available to them ten years ago.[36] More than 50 percent said no. More than 78 percent of the same readers believed that affirmative action had been effective and accounted to a large degree for the dramatic upsurge in the number of African-Americans in corporate management and the skilled trades. For example, in 1958, only 2.8 percent of African-American men were employed in managerial and administrative positions. By 1972, the percentage had doubled to 4.8 percent for men and was 2.3 percent for African-American women. By 1977, this number had increased to 6.4 percent for men. Today, that number is around 13 percent for men and women.[37]

One area in which minorities and women have made appreciable progress in capturing administrative positions is the public schools. A 1980 study[38] reported that since 1975 the proportion of minorities among administrators hired by schools was more than twice that of the national work force (11.2 percent) and the ratio of males to females (65:35) among recently hired administrators showed that female representation among administrative personnel was approaching the proportion of women in the national work force (42.5 percent). These data also indicated that African-American women were doing better than African-American men or White women in being upgraded into administrative positions. I disagree with those who contend that affirmative action is a useless doctrine that demeans African-Americans. Without it, African-Americans would suffer a greater degree of discrimination in the workplace. I hope it is here to stay.

CONCLUSION

I have tried to offer a relatively straightforward proposition in this article. The future of African America is inextricably tied to the hopes of African-American youth. The road to the American Dream for today's African-American youth is no more golden now than it was for previous generations. Racism, other social arrangements, and social structures have historically coalesced to impede the progress of African-Americans entering the social and economic mainstream.

However, we would make a serious mistake if we labored under the proposition that progress has been meager. Indeed, it has been dramatic and eventful. The closing of the income gap between African-American families of high school graduates and their White counterparts, the increasing number of African-American college graduates, and the dramatic increase in the SAT scores for African-Americans between 1976 and 1984 are *all* testimony to the growing value being placed upon education as a feasible way out of poverty.

Yet, there are still too many high school dropouts. Teenage pregnancies are epidemic, and crime rates on our streets are intolerable. We are losing too many bright minds to the scourge of drug abuse and alcoholism. Public education must be improved. And, those of us who have too often forgotten the have-nots must remember our obligations.

The imperatives are clear: We must restore vitality to the African-American family and reclaim its traditional values. We must support public education; demand consistent, fair, and well-defined discipline; and prepare our youngsters for careers where there is room at the top. We have to control hooliganism in our neighborhoods but not relieve governments of their responsibilities to insure life, liberty, and the pursuit of happiness. We must instill in our children hope. But we can do this only by believing that there is hope.

A nation flourishes, if it flourishes at all, through people who believe in something, care about something, and stand for something. No system of social arrangements, no matter how culturally entrenched, can be sustained when individuals coalesce around a set of beliefs and values in opposition to such social arrangements. The strategy of responsible militancy I have called for seeks to create such a coalition and a set of values for guiding action. The most important values we can believe in, care about, and stand for are those principles that impel us to make a greater investment in our children and to create a climate that persuades them that the American Dream is not a raisin in the sun.

NOTES

1. E.H. Grotberg (ed.), *200 Years of Children* (Washington, DC: Department of Health, Education and Welfare, Office of Human Development, Office of Child Development, Division of Research and Education, 1976), p. 7.

2. J. Rappaport, E. Seidman, P. Toro, L. McFaden, T. Reisfchl, L. Roberts, D. Salkem, C. Stein, & M. Zimmerman, *Finishing the Unfinished Business: Collaborative Research with a Mutual Help Organization.* Unpublished manuscript. (Champaign, IL: University of Illinois, School of Social Work, 1985).

3. M. Abramovitz, "Everyone is on Welfare: The Role of Redistribution in Social Policy Revisited," *Social Work* (November/December, 1983): 440-445.

4. A. Davis and J. Dollard, *Children of Bondage: The Personality Development of Negro Youth in the Urban South* (Washington, DC: American Council on Education, 1940).

5. E.F. Frazier, *Negro Youth at the Crossways: Their Personality Development in the United States* (Washington, DC: American Council on Education, 1940).

6. C.S. Johnson, *Growing Up in the Black Belt: The Negro Youth in the Rural South* (Washington, DC: American Council on Education, 1941).

7. W.L. Warner, B.H. Junker, & W.A. Adams, *Color and Human Nature: Negro Personality Development in a Northern City.* (Washington, DC: American Council on Education, 1941).

8. R.L. Sutherland, *Color, Class and Personality* (Washington, DC: American Council on Education, 1942), p. 15-16.

9. U.S. Department of Health and Human Services, Office of Human Development Services Administration for Children, Youth and Families, *Children's Bureau Initiatives for the Adoption of Minority Children* (Children's Bureau DHHS Publication No. OHDS 811-30300) (Washington, DC: Government Printing Office, 1981).

10. D. Fanshel and E.B. Shinn, *Children in Foster Care: A Longitudinal Investigation* (New York: Columbia University Press, 1978); and K.J. Snapper & J.S. Ohms, *The Status of Children* (Washington, DC: George Washington University, Social Research Group, 1975), (ERIC Document Reproduction Service No. ED 154 913.

11. I. Kristol, *Two Cheers for Capitalism* (New York: Basic Books, 1976), p. 262.

12. J. Thornton, "Rise of Minorities" *U.S. News and World Report,* March 9, 1984, p. 48.

13. U.S. Bureau of the Census, *Statistical Abstract of the U.S.: 1984* (104th ed.) (Washington, DC: Government Printing Office, 1984), p. 28-30.

14. J.L Palmer and I.V. Sawhill (eds.), *The Reagan Record: An Assessment of America's Changing Domestic Priorities* (Cambridge, MA: Ballinger, 1984), p. 329-30.

15. U.S. Congressional Budget Office, *The Combined Effects of Major Changes in Federal Taxes and Spending Programs Since 1981* (Washington, DC: Government Printing Office, 1984)

16. Center on Budget and Policy Priorities, *Falling Behind: A Report on How Blacks Have Fared Under the Reagan Policies* (Washington, DC: Center on Budget and Policy Priorities, 1984).

17. National Black Child Development Institute, *A Child Waits: Conference Report on Black Adoptions* (Washington, DC: National Black Child Development Institute, 1984), p. 5.

18. R.L. Richardson and C. Gerlach, "Black Dropouts: A Study of Significant Factors Contributing to a Black Student's Decision." *Urban Education* 14 (4) (1980): 489-494.

19. Ibid.

20. V. Wilson-Wesley, "Making America's Schools Work," *Black Enterprise* (September 1984): 36.

21. C. Bennett and J.J. Harris, III, "Suspensions and Expulsions of Male and Black Students," *Urban Education* 16 (4) (January, 1982): 399-423.

22. C. Page, "A Spiral of Falling Expectations." *Chicago Tribune,* Section 5, (April 18, 1985), p. 3.

23. M. Borus (ed.), *Pathways to the Future: A Report on the National Longitudinal Survey of Youth Labor Market Experience in 1979* (Columbus: Ohio State University, Center for Human Resource Research, 1981).

24. Ibid.

25. U.S. Bureau of Labor Statistics, *Handbook of Labor Statistics* (Washington, DC: Government Printing Office, 1983), Table 2175.

26. E Milne, "The Robots are Coming," *Black Enterprise* (January, 1982): 27-31.

27. Ibid., p. 28.

28. Yankelvich, Skelly & White, Inc., *Raising Children in a Changing Society* (Minneapolis, MN: General Mills, Consumer Center 1977), p. 22.

29. Joint Commission on Mental Health of Children, *Crisis in Child Mental Health: Challenge for the 1970s* (Report 1st ed), (New York: Harper and Row, 1970), p. 2.

30. N. Glazer, "The Limits of Social Policy," *Commentary* 52 (1971): 511-518.

31. M. Angelou, *I Know Why the Caged Bird Sings* (New York: Random House, 1969). p. 48.

32. R . Karwath, "Neighborhood Church Gives Crime the Devil," *Chicago Tribune,* (June 25, 1985), C1-2.

33. J.H. Fischer, "The Inclusive School," *Teacher's College Record* 66 (1) (October 1964): 1-6.

34. Lifeline, "Rock and Race," *USA Today* (July 4, 1985), D1.

35. W.J. Wilson, *The Declining Significance of Race: Blacks and Changing American Institutions* (Chicago, IL: University of Chicago Press, 1978).

36. E. Milne, "Employment," *Black Enterprise* (August, 1980): 64-69.

37. U.S. Bureau of the Census, *Statistical Abstracts,* 1984.

38. M. McCarthy and A. Zent, "Affirmative Action for School Administrators: Has it Worked, Can it Survive?" *Phi Delta Kappan* (March, 1982): 461-63.

6

Reading and Writing as Risk-Reduction: The School's Role in Preventing Teenage Pregnancies

Karen J. Pittman

In this article, the view is put forth that teenage sexual activity can be delayed and pregnancy decreased if teenagers have access to sexuality-specific information, counseling, and services. It is suggested that schools can play a major role by: (1) teaching family life and sexuality education and decision-making skills; (2) increasing the availability of individual and small group counseling; and (3) upgrading school health programs. But information and services alone are not enough. Students must see value in education so that they can become involved and do well. Thus, school involvement is seen as performing a pregnancy prevention role. It is, therefore, important for children to begin experiencing the positive impact of schools at the preschool and elementary school levels. Finally, for those teenagers who become pregnant and for teenage parents, the schools must develop alternate educational programs so they can complete their high school education.

In 1985, there were 467,000 births to teenagers: 178,000 births to those under 18 and 10,000 to those under 15. Each day 488 babies are born to young women who should be in school.[1] These numbers are undeniably sobering, especially in light of a recent study by the Alan Guttmacher Institute which found that while American teenagers are about as likely to be sexually active as teenagers in similarly developed countries, they are twice as likely as teenagers in France, England, Wales, and Canada and seven times as likely as teenagers in the Netherlands to experience pregnancy during adolescence.[2] Something must be done to help more of our young people delay pregnancy until they are prepared for the responsibilities of parenthood. But, what this should be, and what role schools play remain to be answered.

Ultimately, pregnancy prevention is achieved through only one of two means: abstinence or contraception. Schools have neither the mandate nor the capacity to monitor these personal decisions. But, a closer examination of the array of decisions, behaviors, opportunities, and beliefs that determine a teenager's ability to avoid pregnancy increases the possibility for school involvement and school leadership in pregnancy prevention.

The international data on teenage pregnancy rates make it clear that we urgently need to increase the capacity for all youth to delay sexual activity and pregnancy by increasing their access to sexuality-specific information, counseling, and services. Schools can certainly play a role in bolstering this capacity by: (1) examining and expanding their teaching of family life and sexuality education and decision-making skills; (2) increasing the availability of individual and small group counseling; and (3) upgrading school health programs (including but by no means limited to the provision of comprehensive school-based or school-linked clinic services.) Many school districts currently offer, or are exploring the possibility of providing, these kinds of programs and services (often with the assistance of other public agencies or community groups).

Pregnancy prevention is dependent upon more than the information and services that give teenagers the means to avoid pregnancy. Teenagers also need reasons to believe that delaying pregnancy is in their best interest. These reasons must be both positive and compelling because pregnancy and parenthood, unlike other frequently discussed youth problems, such as substance abuse and suicide, are not behaviors that are inherently negative. The issue here is timing. To convince teenagers that they should not be parents now, we have to convince them that there are other, more positive, activities in which they could be presently engaged.

School not only occupies teenagers' time in the present, but also determines how they may occupy their time in the future. If teenagers are involved in school and doing well, they have both positive and rewarding activities to occupy them for the present, and the promise of more to come. For these students, the schools are fulfilling a pregnancy prevention role whether or not they offer family life education or house a comprehensive health clinic. But what about those students at risk of failure in school and in the workplace?

Both conventional wisdom and a growing body of research suggest that those youth most at risk of early parenthood are those whose life options would have been limited with or without the added responsibility of children—i.e., poor teens with inadequate basic academic skills. Data from the National Longitudinal Survey of Young Americans (NLS) document the strong relationship between poor basic skills, limited life options, and teenage childbearing.[3] For example, young women and young men with poor basic academic skills, whether African-American, White, or Hispanic, are more than three times as likely as those with average or better basic skills to become parents (see Figure 1). Poor young women with below-average academic skills are almost six times as likely to be teenage parents as those with average or better basic skills (see Figure 2).

The feelings of competence and potential options that come with academic success have the same preventive effect on early childbearing for poor and minority teenagers as they do for nonpoor and White teenagers. Therefore, we have to be saddened by the fact that so few disadvantaged teenagers are acquiring the skills that would give them the feelings of hope, competence, and optimism that translate into delayed parenthood. Note the following: Poor teenagers are four times as likely to have weak basic skills as are teenagers with family incomes above poverty. More than half of the African-American 15- to 18-year-olds in the NLS survey and four out of 10 of the Hispanic teenagers fall in the bottom skills group, compared to 13 percent of the White teenagers. The level of basic academic skills makes a difference even among young adults with the same

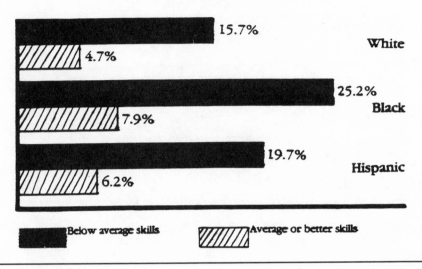

FIGURE 1
Parenthood by Basic Skills
Levels, 16-19 Year Old Men and Women, 1981

Source: Unpublished analyses of the National Longitudinal Survey, courtesy of Andrew Sum, Northeastern University

amount of schooling. High school dropouts with strong basic skills have average earnings more than twice as great as dropouts with weak basic skills.

Teenage pregnancy is not confined to poor and minority populations—almost two-thirds of teenage parents are White, non-Hispanic and non-poor.[4] But the connection between early parenthood and the limited life options implied by meager resources and limited skills suggest that the school's role in pregnancy prevention should be, first and foremost, to ensure a solid academic education. For disadvantaged and, increasingly for "advantaged" students, this must often translate into a comprehensive school program that addresses a broad range of developmental needs including, but by no means limited to, sexuality education and clinic services.

School-based pregnancy prevention strategies should certainly include efforts to increase teenagers' access to the sexuality-specific information, counseling, and services they need in order to delay sexual activity and avoid pregnancy. Many schools, working in consort with public agencies and private organizations are providing these much needed supports. Increasingly, data suggest that first and foremost, school-based pregnancy prevention efforts should focus on basic education improvement and dropout prevention.

WHAT SCHOOLS CAN DO

Broaden Their Approach to Educating At-Risk Youth

Schools alone are certainly not responsible for the developmental deficits found so widely among disadvantaged teenagers, and they should not attempt to correct these

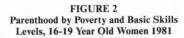

FIGURE 2
Parenthood by Poverty and Basic Skills
Levels, 16-19 Year Old Women 1981

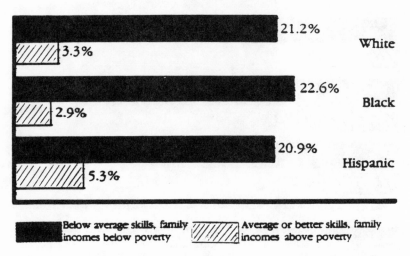

Source: Unpublished analyses of the National Longitudinal Survey, courtesy of Andrew Sum, Northeastern University

deficits alone. But there are three reasons that schools are essential in any effort to improve the life options of disadvantaged teenagers. In the first place, many schools are failing to educate these young people and to respond to their needs. Secondly, because of limited family and community resources, these adolescents urgently need schools that are committed to educating them well, and are responsive to their nonacademic needs that stifle their academic and social development. Finally, there is mounting evidence that well-designed schools and committed teachers and administrators can be responsive to the needs of disadvantaged students and can help them to achieve.

There are five areas in which children and youth need assistance in becoming self-sufficient adults who can form healthy families (see Figure 3). They are:

- Education—developing solid academic skills as well as sound decision-making and problem-solving skills.
- Work preparation—identifying and building work-related skills and getting exposure to a wide range of work experiences.
- Health—becoming and staying healthy, in addition to avoiding prevalent health-related risks in adolescence such as pregnancy, substance abuse, depression, and stress.
- Social responsibility/social awareness—developing a sense of connection with the community, and understanding its functionality and potential for change.
- Personal growth—developing an understanding of themselves and others, assessing their attitudes and values, and finding nonacademic avenues for success and growth.

FIGURE 3
Preparing Youth for Adulthood

	EDUCATION	HEALTH	WORK	SOCIAL RESPONSIBILITY/ AWARENESS	PERSONAL GROWTH
Information/ Decision-making Skills	—basic skills (verbal, writing...) —basic knowledge —problem-solving skills —learning skills	—education, understanding growth, development and health risks —value of regular health care	—understanding function and value of work —developing healthy work attitudes —exposure to variety of work environments, jobs, and adult workers	—understanding of individual's role in society and societal change —cultural awareness —social awareness	—development of self-identity, self-discipline, interpersonal skills and coping strategies
Assessment/ Guidance/Referral	—monitoring progress —assessing special educational needs —helping with school choices —curriculum/class choices	—identification of problem/need —assessment/ screening —counseling —locating affordable and appropriate health resources —understanding health systems	—defining criteria for choosing job/ assessing interests, skills, and goals —making job preparation plans —job search assistance —college choice assistance	—identification of antisocial behavior —recognition of socially responsible behavior	—assessment of talent, interests, potential —mental health screening
Direct Supports/ Opportunities	—formal instruction —informal instruction —homework assistance —tutoring —remedial instruction —special/alternative instruction	—preventive health care —general exams —mental health services —medical treatment for illness or injury —therapy	—post-secondary education —vocational training —on the job training/work experience —part-time work and summer employment —volunteer/paid jobs	—counseling/group homes —community group membership —community volunteer services —leadership opportunities	—counseling (indiv., family, group) —developmental education (sexuality, family life, relationships) —non-academic opportunities for success
Outcomes	—high school diploma/basic competencies	—good health	—job	—community involvement/ citizenship	—strong positive self-concept

Source: Children's Defense Fund.

In each of these areas, children and youth need basic information and support in building their decision-making potential. Across the board, these youth will need help in assessing their progress and making choices, as well as in identifying and linking up with needed supports and opportunities.

In moving beyond the narrow realm of basic education, schools, no doubt, will be forced to make choices. They will have to decide what needs are most pressing in the community and where the involvement of schools can have the greatest impact in helping to reduce teenage pregnancy. Unfortunately, the tension between these non-academic initiatives and the schools' responsibility for basic education is often exaggerated. Indeed, many seemingly "nonacademic" needs of disadvantaged youth prove to be essential elements of an effective strategy for improving their basic academic skills, as the work of Dr. James Comer and others makes clear.

During the school day, some schools offer much of the diverse programming that the community programs provide in the after-school and summer hours. Physical education, music, dance, creative writing classes, cultural arts programs, field trips to cultural institutions and work sites, family life education programs that include small group discussions, and student councils that provide opportunities for leadership are activities included in many middle and junior high schools during the regular school day.

In addition, many schools traditionally keep their doors open after school hours for a variety of sports, extracurricular, and remedial activities. After-school programs should not be the sole responsibility of community groups. While school-sponsored after-school programs may not be comprehensive, traditional extracurricular activities—sports, drama, orchestra and band, debating, and various academic clubs—are important in many adolescents' lives.

Unfortunately, in this era of tight funding and emphasis on "back to basics" education, schools, particularly those in low-income neighborhoods, often see academic instruction competing for scarce resources with nonacademic, extracurricular, or after-school activities. While academics are obviously important, ignoring the nonacademic needs of young adolescents thwarts efforts to develop well-rounded young people. Thus, bypassing extra opportunities for basic development undercuts the schools' educational achievement. By decreasing or eliminating nonacademic programs and classes, whether during or after school, schools may be eliminating the activities that can entice low-achieving youth into the school culture and toward learning and achievement.

Invest in Early Childhood Education

Efforts in elementary and secondary schools to both broaden and deepen the positive impact they have on at-risk children and youth are clearly needed and worth the investment. Further, few would disagree that a good preschool experience is vital for at-risk children.

The Children's Defense Fund is one of the many organizations that has recognized the value of a supportive early childhood development experience for low-income children. Head Start, of course, has been the model for such programs for over two decades. Because of the success of Head Start, parents from all income groups are increasingly seeking an early childhood development center or nursery school experience for their three- and four-year-olds. Due to the fact that poor families cannot afford to pay for preschool themselves, a two-tier system of care for our youngest children has emerged, which leaves low-income children at the bottom.

For example, while 67 percent of four-year-olds from families with incomes over $35,000 attended a preschool program in 1985, only 33 percent of those in families with incomes under $10,000 were in attendance. Moreover, 50 percent of three-year-olds in families with median incomes over $35,000 attended a preschool program, as opposed to 17 percent of those in families with incomes under $10,000.[5]

One answer to this problem is to build on proven success through increasing Head Start programs. A second, complementary answer is to have the public education system expand its preschool efforts. Twenty-seven states now invest some state funds in early childhood development programs, most of which are targeted to reach low-income children. States are taking varying approaches—from adding state funds to supplement Head Start to creating new programs through Departments of Education.

While the primary goal of Head Start and preschool programs must be to meet the developmental needs of the children, the programs also have to confront the reality of the family situations. One such reality is that the majority of preschool children have working mothers. Today, over ten million children under age six have mothers in the labor force.[6] Most employed mothers work full-time. Even when their youngest child is under three, about 66 percent of employed mothers are full-time workers. By 1995, two-thirds of all preschool children (and three quarters of school age children) will have mothers in the work force.[7]

The needs of those children are not being met, by and large, by new state preschool initiatives which only provide for a part-day program. A two-and-a-half hour day presents scheduling problems for parents working outside the home, as well as confusion for young children. While many parents are trying to patch together two or even three child care arrangements for their children, there is growing concern that multiple caregivers during a single day—especially two group- or center-type arrangements—may not be an optimal situation for youngsters. In short, more very young children need preschool, but they need some full-day arrangement.

The Act for Better Child Care Services, a comprehensive child care bill that was being deliberated in the 100th Congress, recognizes the important role the schools can play in child care. The bill would allow schools to use funds to operate child care programs, and to provide subsidies to low- and moderate-income families. In addition, the bill sets aside money to allow schools to extend the number of hours that part-day, preschool programs operate, to better meet the needs of working parents.

One final but critical question is program quality. Too many recent preschool initiatives have not yet included all of the following key criteria in their efforts. Elements central to a high-quality early childhood experience that must be addressed as new initiatives are as follows:

- Hiring staff with education, training and experience in working with young children (education does not necessarily mean formal academic credentials);
- Allowing existing child care and Head Start programs as well as school districts to operate the new and additional programs;
- Maintaining small child-to-staff ratios and small group size;
- Guarding against the implementation of eligibility guidelines that label young children as academically deficient;
- Creating a funding mechanism to operate a high-quality program that assures a per child reimbursement based on the real cost of providing quality care for four-year-olds, using kindergarten and first grade costs to determine funding levels;
- Involving parents in the planning and operating of the program;
- Operating in a manner that is sensitive to minority children and families with diverse cultural backgrounds;
- Utilizing the expertise of child care providers and early childhood professionals in planning and operating the program;
- Assuring that funds are not taken from the existing child care system to begin new preschool efforts;
- Providing an age-appropriate curriculum as opposed to simply adjusting the kindergarten program downwards.

The essentials require a solid financial commitment if they are to be combined into a quality program. Much of the growing interest of states in preschools has been spurred by the success of the Perry Preschool Project in Ypsilanti, Michigan. It would cost $5,000 per child to replicate the Perry Preschool program in 1985 dollars.

Help Build Teenagers' Capacity to Delay Pregnancy: Sexuality Education, Counseling, and Health Services

Expanding Sexuality Education. The idea that giving teenagers information about sex and sexuality is tantamount to giving them license is unfounded. This false perception has had unfortunate consequences. It has allowed opponents of formal sexuality education to imply that the bulk of what is being offered to young people is contraceptive education when, in fact, existing programs are far broader in scope, content, and goals. While reinforcing the premise that parents are the primary educators of their children, we must continue our efforts:
- to engage the full spectrum of individuals and agencies that reach youth in bolstering parent-child communication by providing instruction and support for both parents and children;
- to provide information and opportunities for discussion on a wide range of topics, including information about physical development, family and gender roles, parent-child communication;
- to have as a goal the development of healthy young men and women who can make informed decisions about this very important aspect of their lives.

Schools *should* be involved in helping parents provide timely and accurate information on sexuality and family life. But so should churches, youth serving agencies, health providers (including family planning agencies), and other adults who play a significant role in the lives of youth. A good classroom-based course can dispel a lot of myths and lay the groundwork for further communication and thinking. But even the best course is of limited use to the young teenager who has burning questions during the summer. Children need basic information. In addition, they need opportunities to discuss this information, as well as their general opinions and concerns, informally with groups of peers and adults. They also need opportunities to talk privately with adults when they have pressing concerns.

Linking Sexuality Education with Counseling. Community-based organizations such as Girls Clubs, Boys Clubs, YWCAs, YMCAs and churches as well as family counseling agencies and family planning service providers, are increasingly offering these kinds of opportunities to teenagers (and to their parents) off school grounds. Some of these groups, however, have linked with schools to provide these services during or after school hours.

For example, Inwood House, a New York City-based community agency serving young single women and their children, was invited to provide pregnancy prevention services in the New York City public schools in 1978. In 1986, their Teen Choice program was operating in two junior and five senior high schools in Brooklyn and Manhattan. Teen Choice offers information, counseling, and referrals on human sexuality, family planning, pregnancy, and parenting to teenage girls and boys through semester-long discussion groups and classroom presentations (as a voluntary alternative to physical education).

The staff encourages students to postpone intercourse as long as possible, to postpone parenthood beyond the teenage years, and to make informed, nonpressured decisions (which include using contraceptives if choosing to be sexually active). Teen Choice social workers are also available for individual counseling and are consulted not only for sexuality and pregnancy-related concerns, but also for general mental health evaluation and counseling, suicide prevention, family problems, and general social service referrals.

In other programs, sexuality education and counseling or discussion groups are being built into school-linked programs that address other developmental needs. School-based health clinics (or adolescent clinics linked to schools through staff-sharing arrangements) provide both counseling and clinic services. Their counseling efforts are often overlooked in discussions about their effectiveness. While there are no independent data on the effects of the education-counseling combination on sexual activity and pregnancy, it is clear that clinic providers see counseling as an essential part of their work. This explains their heavy emphasis on individual and group counseling, and primary educational program components.

Linking Teens with Health Service. There has been tremendous growth of interest in comprehensive school-based clinics over the past few years. However, school-based clinics, as examples of strong health programs, stand in sharp contrast to what normally exists in public schools. School health programs, like school counseling programs, have suffered as a result of funding cuts and changes in funding priorities. Many programs have been scaled back and some have been eliminated completely. Only about $1 billion of the estimated $102 billion national annual school budget is spent on school health services—that is, about $25 per child per year. A 1981 survey found that 42 states required health instruction in the school curriculum, but only 13 required a health room or clinic in each school.

Expanding the use of school-based nurse practitioners would be an important step toward upgrading school health services. At present, only about 1,000 of the 45,000 registered nurses working in schools are nurse practitioners.[8] Nurse practitioners can—under the supervision of a physician—diagnose and treat a broad range of illnesses, conduct health assessments, and follow established protocols (including writing some kinds of prescriptions). Studies comparing school nurse practitioners with school nurses found that practitioners spent twice as much time caring for patients; had three times the number of daily contacts with parents to discuss physical, emotional, or learning problems, and, because of their ability to give on-site treatment, sent home from school about one-half as many pupils. A large demonstration program sponsored by the Robert Wood Johnson Foundation found that expanded school health programs could be managed successfully. Annual costs per student ranged from $43 to $83.[9]

School-based clinics can now be found in more than 61 schools in 27 communities in 17 states across the country, as reported by the Support Center for School-Based Clinics.[10] An almost equal number are in the planning stages, and while there is not an exact count, there are probably an equal or greater number of clinics across the country that are not on school grounds but are linked with schools, recreation centers, or other community organizations that serve youth. These clinics, located primarily in schools in low-income neighborhoods where general access to health care is limited and unmet health needs are great, offer comprehensive primary health care to teenagers at a cost that averages between $100 and $150 per teenager per year. Comprehensive care is important because teenagers, especially poor teenagers, have a very wide range of unmet health needs.

For instance, the Robert Wood Johnson National School Health Services Program found that 83 percent of the problems detected when school children were examined were previously unknown, and many were significant. While school health workers were able to treat nearly all of these problems, many could have resulted in long-term health problems if left unresolved.[11] Moreover, school-based clinics often provide the *only* access to health care for children. Nearly 16 percent of children in New York have no health insurance and poor children are even more dramatically uninsured. A conservative estimate of the health problems among school children in New York City found that one in ten had a referrable vision condition and one in fifteen required treatment for a hearing problem.[12]

A comprehensive adolescent health clinic, located on or near school grounds, serves a dual purpose. It is a response to high levels of unmet general health needs among teenagers with poor access to medical services, and it maximizes the effect of a first-rate family life and sexuality education program. For example, studies show that reproductive health services account for only a fraction of clinic visits. An estimated 80 percent of the visits are for nonreproductive primary health needs.[13] (Student use of these clinics for general or reproductive health care is always dependent upon written parental consent.) Even within the area of reproductive health, it is important to understand that these clinics do much more than dispense contraceptives.

Clearly not every school needs a school-based clinic. Equally important, not every low-income school or every school with high pregnancy rates needs a school-based clinic; and not every clinic needs to dispense contraceptives. Accessibility, not location in a school, is the issue. In addition, it is recognized that not every school that should house a clinic will be able to staff one in the near future. Thus, certain aspects of successful model programs that can be applied less expensively should be implemented in a variety of settings.

Keep Pregnant Teenagers and Teenage Parents in School

For teenage parents to succeed in their efforts to achieve self-sufficiency, they must have solid academic skills, as well as sound decision-making and problem-solving skills. These attributes will help them to compete in the labor market and cope with other demands of adult life. Schools, and other educational programs are, therefore, essential parts of a self-sufficiency strategy for teenage parents.

Too often, however, it is assumed that pregnant teenagers and teenage parents are representative of the in-school population, when in fact there may be significant differences between these groups. Pregnant teenagers, it is commonly acknowledged, face high risks of dropping out of school. Half of the teenage parents younger than 18 have not obtained their high school diploma by the time they are in their twenties, and four out of ten teenage women leaving school cite pregnancy or marriage as the reason for leaving.[14] However, these low rates of school completion typically are attributed to the demands and difficulties of pregnancy and parenthood rather than to underlying educational deficits of youth who become parents at an early age.

Until recently, relatively little attention has been paid to the possibility that teenagers who become parents may have been doing poorly in school before they became pregnant. Data now suggest that this is a very strong possibility. For example, data from the National Longitudinal Survey of Young Americans show that three out of four 14- to 15-year-old mothers had basic skill deficiencies in reading and mathematics that ranked in the bottom one-fifth of all girls in their age group. Further, analyses of the High School and Beyond data collected by the National Center for Education Statistics show that more than one-fourth of the teenagers who dropped out of school and had a child between their sophomore and senior years had dropped out before they became pregnant.[15]

Because teenagers' basic academic skills shape, to a considerable degree, both their likelihood of bearing children out of wedlock at an early age and their future employment prospects, education is vital in preventing welfare dependency. Analyses of the National Longitudinal Survey data conducted by Andrew Sum of Northeastern University, indicate that young women (ages 18-24) with poor basic reading and mathematics skills are four times more likely to receive benefits from the Aid to Families with Dependent Children (AFDC) program than are those with average basic skills (undoubtedly, in part, because of their increased risk of early parenthood).

Educational goals for teenage parents, including those on AFDC, must be established through individualized assessments of their strengths and needs. Those who have already graduated from high school should be encouraged to explore options for college-level courses. Others who have dropped out before graduation should be able, with appropriate child care and other supports, to return to their regular high school programs and obtain their diplomas. But many will need special help to strengthen their basic skills, including remedial education tailored to their individual abilities and the supportive services necessary to keep them moving toward graduation or completion of a GED.

The common expectation that teenage mothers should continue in, or return to, their regular school shortly after delivery ignores the needs of many teenage parents. They have special educational needs as well as those specifically related to parenthood. Few schools can provide the additional supports that teenage parents often require to cope with the demands of parenthood. Further, many schools are not equipped to serve teenagers who have fallen far behind their peers academically. For these reasons, requiring teenage parents to return to their regular schools—without recognizing their individual needs or the capacity of these schools to respond to them—can be a sure prescription for failure.

In response to the needs of teenage parents and other at-risk youth who do not fare well in the traditional school environment, more flexible programs have been developed to allow students to work at their own pace with the individualized attention they need to succeed. Examples of such nontraditional approaches include the following:

- The Bridge Program in Boston established its own program of high school equivalency courses because it found that pregnancy and parenting adolescents often did not do well in existing GED programs, which had little experience with their needs. The Bridge Program employs two teachers and a remedial education specialist and holds special graduation ceremonies each year. Follow-up is also provided by job development and career guidance counselors.
- The Comprehensive Competencies Program developed by the Remediation and Training Institute in Washington, D.C., offers a state-of-the-art system for individualized, self-paced instruction that can be used by schools or community-based organizations to improve the basic skills of teenagers who do not get the help they need in traditional classrooms. With support from the Ford Foundation, the Comprehensive Competencies Program has been tested in nearly 200 sites serving 10,000 learners,

including teenage parents, other teenagers at risk of school failure, as well as adults with poor basic skills.

While it is very important that we recognize the fact that teenage mothers and fathers fall heavily in the bottom of the basic skills distribution, it is equally important that we do not allow early parenthood to close the academic gates on those teenagers who could benefit from college or long-term post-secondary education. Obviously, teenage parents have immediate income needs that press for a quick end to their education and employment training, but it is often short-sighted on their part (and often on our part) not to see the long-term benefits of continued education and training. The immediate needs for income must be balanced against the long-term needs for above minimum-wage earnings.

Schools, then, must take care to neither overestimate nor underestimate the educational potential of pregnant teenagers and teenage parents. Realizing that these young people's future needs for employment and earnings have become present needs, schools must make every effort to maximize their opportunities for learning. In many states, the Carl Perkins Act is being used to offer pregnant teenagers and teenage mothers training for nontraditional careers.

Any educational programs targeted toward pregnant teenagers and teenage parents, however, must recognize the needs teenage parents have for health care, child care, transportation, counseling, housing and income support services. Schools obviously cannot and should not take on these responsibilities alone. But it is clear that if they are not addressed these immediate needs will quickly overwhelm many young parents and force them to leave school.

Research, for example, has found lack of adequate child care to be the teenage parent's greatest single barrier to participation in educational programs.[17] Where possible, on-site or easily accessible child care should be arranged so that parents can be involved in the care of their infants and toddlers.

The Teenage Pregnancy and Parenting Project (TAPP) in San Francisco is a fine example of how schools and public agencies can coordinate efforts to assist pregnant and parenting teenagers. TAPP is currently in three high schools and also has a primary site for teenagers who are in other schools or who are no longer enrolled in school. The backbone of the project is the "Continuous Counselor" who provides personal counseling and case management to the teenagers. The counselor serves as the primary contact, personalizing the relationship between the client and the service network. The network consists of a variety of agencies that come to the schools or to the primary TAPP site to provide special education, health services, nutritional information, and counseling to the teenagers and their families. The program is open to all teenagers regardless of their school enrollment status or income level. The results attributed to TAPP include reduction of the incidence of low birthweight babies born to teenagers, an increased rate of school completion, and a significant reduction of repeat pregnancies.

On-site or coordinated health care, child care, and case management services are obviously an ideal way to help pregnant teenagers and teenage parents stay in school while dealing with the increased complexity of their lives, but there are other ways. We would strongly recommend that, at the state and district levels, policies and procedures that stand as real or potential barriers between these teenagers and their education should be identified and analyzed. Often, even trivialities such as the regulations governing who can ride the school bus stand between a teenage parent and school completion.

In an era of demands for improved academic achievement and educational reforms at state and local levels, the demands on our public schools are great. School officials are being asked to raise standards and promote academic excellence while at the same time ensuring that lower-achieving students are not left behind. Schools also are called upon to respond to a host of other national ills ranging from alcohol and drug abuse to teenage suicide and juvenile delinquency.

How can schools reconcile efforts to address the adolescent pregnancy problem with this array of competing demands? In part, schools and others who are concerned about teenage pregnancy must recognize that success is the schools' central mission. Thus, the development of basic academic skills in itself makes a major contribution to adolescent pregnancy prevention. A foundation of sound basic skills in childhood and early adolescence is essential to the future achievement, self-esteem, and life options that encourage disadvantaged youths to delay pregnancy.

Virtually all schools offer some nonacademic courses, activities or services in response to the broader needs of youth. These efforts reflect a recognition that the strongest academic programs can be rendered ineffective by students' personal problems or low expectations for future success. They also reflect an awareness that responding to adolescents' other needs can yield significant dividends in academic achievement. Few schools have the resources to address all of the diverse needs of their student bodies. Yet schools have managed—often by collaborating with parents, community groups, businesses, and universities—to tackle a wide array of problems and mount effective responses to specific needs.

A fifteen-year-old junior high school student in a very depressed area of Detroit offered this sentence in response to a question about her aspirations: "To go to school and finish my schooling without getting pregnant."[18] Helping this student realize her dream will take nothing short of a comprehensive effort. Sexuality education, yes. School-based clinic services, perhaps. But without broad-based dropout prevention efforts in school and after school, this student will not meet her goal. Schools clearly cannot do all of this alone, nor are the needs of every student as great as has been depicted. But pregnancy prevention and preparation for adulthood must go hand in hand, and schools, because of the pivotal role they play in the development of the life options of youth, will remain at the hub of these efforts for the foreseeable future.

NOTES

1. National Center for Health Statistics (NCHS), *Advance Report of Final Natality Statistics, 1985,* 36 (4), Supplement 14, July 17, 1987.

2. Elise Jones et al., *Teenage Pregnancy in Industrialized Countries* (New Haven, CT: Yale University Press 1986).

3. Information on the relationship between basic skills levels, teenage parenthood, and poverty are based on analyses of the National Longitudinal Survey of Young Americans (NLS) conducted by Andrew Sum in conjunction with the Children's Defense Fund. See Children's Defense fund, *Preventing Adolescent Pregnancy: What Schools Can Do* (September 1986).

4. Unpublished analyses of the NLS by Andrew Sum and analyses of data from the National Center for Health Statistics by the Children's Defense Fund.

5. Unpublished estimates from Sheila Kamerman and Alfred Kahn of Columbia University, based on data from the U.S. Department of Education's Center for Statistics.

6. Sandra L. Hofferth and Deborah Phillips, "Child Care in the United States, 1970 to 1995," *Journal of Marriage and the Family* (September 1986).

7. Ibid.

8. Margaret A. Kohn, *School Health Services and Nurse Practitioners: A Survey of State Laws,* Center for Law and Social Policy (April 1979).

9. Robert Wood Johnson Foundation, *National School Health Services Program,* Special Report #1, 1985.

10. Sharon R. Lovick and Wanda R. Wesson, *School-Based Clinics: Update,* Support Center for School-Based Clinics of the Center for Population Options (1986).

11. Ibid.

12. New York City Department of Health, "Report of the School Health Assessment, Planning, and Evaluation Project (SHAPE)" (February 1984).

13. C.A. Bachrach and W.D. Mosher, "Use of Contraception in the U.S., 1982," *Advance Data,* National Center for Health Statistics #102 (December 4, 1984).

14. Frank L. Mott and William Mavsiglio, "Early Childbearing and Completion of High School," *Family Planning Perspectives* 17 (5) (1985): 234-237; and unpublished analyses of the High School and Beyond Survey conducted by Samuel Peng of the U.S. Department of Education.

15. Stephen Barro, "The Incidence of Dropping Out: Descriptive Analysis." Unpublished analyses of the High School and Beyond Survey, 1984.

16. Unpublished analyses of data from the NLS by Andrew Sum in conjunction with the Children's Defense fund.

17. Helen Wallace, John Weeks, and Antonio Medina. "Services for, and Needs of, Pregnant Teenagers in Large Cities of the United States, 1978," *Public Health Reports* (97) (1982):583-588.

18. Wall Street Journal, "Grim Anniversary: Detroit's Racial Woes Persist Two Decades After Devastating Riot," June 17, 1987, p. 1 and 16.

7

African-American Male Responsibility in Teenage Pregnancy: The Role of Education

Stanley F. Battle

After tracing the current educational and occupational status of adolescent fathers, this article describes a number of community-based programs that were developed for these youth as well as for those who are not yet fathers. The programs are designed to empower adolescents to take charge of their lives and to avoid early parenthood. The expected outcome of these programs is to enhance the self-esteem of these youth, help them find meaning and value in the educational process, and become responsible adults. The article concludes that male responsibility can be perpetuated if African-American adolescents are allowed to experience success in school and at work. In addition, African-American adult males must provide social support for our youth by serving as role models.

The United States is experiencing many changes in her social fabric. One important change affecting the family is an increasing delay in marriage and childbearing. However, at the same time, there has been an increase in the number of adolescent parents. Until recently, parenthood in adolescence was considered solely as a woman's issue, with the adolescent father being viewed as a "shadowy unknown figure, more a culprit than a potential contributor to either the mother or his offspring.[1] Moreover, traditionally the father's role irrespective of his age, has received little attention from social scientists, the legal profession, health care professionals, and policy makers. The quote from Margaret Mead put this issue in perspective, "Fathers are not only a biological necessity but a social accident," and bears witness to this neglect.

To a significant extent, services and research in areas of sexual behavior, pregnancy and parenting have concentrated on teenage females. There is evidence that successful pregnancy prevention programs for adolescents must include males.[2] Recent surveys of cities regarding service programs for pregnant teenagers showed that a majority of cities in the United States have some special programs for pregnant teenagers, but only one fourth of these programs provided services to their male partners.[3] In an extensive review, Earls and Siegel have pointed out the paucity of research available around teenage fatherhood.[4] Significant gains in research on teenage fathers have been achieved, however, since the Earls and Siegel review.[5] The purpose of this article is to present current knowledge about teenage fathers, describe new innovative educational programs, detail how African-American men can participate in this process and suggest policy recommendations for program development.

CURRENT KNOWLEDGE

In 1983, there were more than 1.1 million pregnancies to women 20 years of age and younger resulting in 499,038 births accounting for 14 percent of all births in the United States.[6] Eighty-five percent of teenage mothers keep their infants rather than place them for adoption.[7] Based on statistical data from the 1983 Urban League report, there were an estimated 1.3 million children living with 1.1 million teenage mothers.[8] In 1977, 143,000 live born infants were fathered by men younger than 20 years of age. The number of births per 1,000 in unmarried 15- to 19-year-olds was over six times greater among non-Whites than Whites.[9] The risk of becoming an adolescent father is higher in African-American and Hispanic males due to higher prevalence of sexual activity and lower use of contraception.[10] Some studies are available on White teenage males who become fathers, but the literature indicates adolescent fatherhood appears to be synonymous with minority, especially African-American males.

Usually a teenage father and his partner are approximately the same age, and in most instances the father of the baby is no more than 4 years older than the mother.[11] The average age of the father in a New Haven study of pregnant girls 17 years of age and younger was 18.5 years, with 66 percent of males in the 17- and 19-year range.[12] In Hendricks' study, 50 percent of the males were 17 years of age or younger when they became fathers,[13] whereas in a descriptive study of 26 teenage fathers from Charlotte, North Carolina, the fathers' mean age was 18.7 years.[14] In most studies, a majority of the adolescent fathers are described as unmarried at the time they became fathers. A majority of them come from low-income families. They are often not in school, frequently work part-time at low wages, or are unemployed. Unemployment among African-American adolescent males in urban areas is approximately 50 percent.[15]

Minority fathers and mothers generally face significantly less favorable occupational opportunities than do majority workers. In general, African-American workers tend to be concentrated in lower-paying, less prestigious occupations. In 1980, only about 33 percent of African-American males were employed in high paying male occupational categories (professionals, managers, salesmen, and craftsmen), while 59 percent of White males were employed in these categories. Similarly, while 32 percent of White women were employed in professional, managerial, and sales categories, only 19 percent of African-American women were so employed.

Educational competence and access to meaningful employment opportunities play a major role in expectations of the adolescent minority fathers.[16] Teenage fathers obtain substantially less education, lower income levels and demonstrate lower academic abilities. In a New Haven study, basic information on fathers was obtained from 180 pregnant girls. Fifty percent were employed, 40 percent were enrolled in school, (nearly 50 percent of those in school also worked), and less than 10 percent were out of school and unemployed.[17] In Hendricks' study of 21 African-American adolescent fathers and 21 controls, fathers were less likely to attend any type of school and more likely to be employed.[18] Due to the cross-sectional nature of some studies, however, obtaining information at one point in time in regard to school or employment is likely to lead to an erroneous impression. Overwhelmingly, the evidence suggests that given appropriate support, teenage fathers are anxious to find jobs and finish their education.

The task of parenting and taking on adult responsibilities is a challenging one. Generally, the literature on teenage parenting has focused on three areas: (1) actual behaviors toward the child; (2) knowledge of child development; and (3) attitudes toward parenting.[19] Throughout the literature, two underlying themes emerge. The first is that teenage mothers exhibit parenting practices that differ from those of older mothers. The second is that teenage fathers are not completely willing or prepared to assume a responsible parenting role.[20] Some fathers generally assume marginal roles in rearing their children. However, there is evidence that supports the theory that adolescent fathers want to participate in the parenting experience but are at a disadvantage because of lack of age appropriateness, income, and educational attainment. Family considerations also play a significant role in how the adolescent deals with responsibility.

The elements that seem to be missing for adolescent fathers are access to services, limited understanding on the part of society, and access to appropriate education as a means of prevention. Adolescent fathers who choose to stay involved with their children face a Catch 22 dilemma. For young fathers who drop out of school, it is difficult to support their family without an education. Current data reveal that one-half of African-Americans and one-quarter of Whites who do not have a high school education are unemployed. Thus, it is clear that education and services are important needs of this population.

THE ADOLESCENT FATHER'S ROLE: COMMITMENTS AND CONCERNS

The father's role is important to the psychological development of both the mother and child. Henderson describes several aspects of this role which include genetic input, facilitation of the real world for the mother during pre- and post-natal periods, role modeling for boys in the pre-Oedipal period of development, separation-individuation process in the child, development of the superego during the Oedipal period, role modeling in post-Oedipal identification, shaping and helping socialization, and cognitive-maturational development.[21] Some providers have speculated that if fathers are given greater opportunities to be involved with their infants in the early neonatal period, they will participate more in infant caretaking in the post-hospital process. This type of interaction is even more important for adolescent fathers.[22]

There are no large scale systematic investigations regarding parental behaviors of adolescent fathers. In many situations, the adolescent male is discouraged from continuing the relationship, thereby creating a perception that he abandoned the expectant mother. A teenage father's absence leads to a common misconception of noncaring among health care providers, who often perceive adolescent fathers as irresponsible, deserters of their children, and not being part of the "teen family."

The divorce rate for teenage parent is five times higher than that of the adult population.[23] However, in a five-year follow-up study of 404 first time pregnant adolescents, Furstenberg found that 21 percent of the fathers were still residing with their children five years after the birth of the child, while 20 percent of the fathers visited their children irregularly.[24] An association was found between naming patterns of the children, and the frequency of paternal contact and child support. In cases where parents were not married but the father visited his offspring at least once a week, 48 percent of the male children had their father's forename and surname. However, in cases where the father did not visit his offspring regularly, only 14 percent of the children had their fathers' names. Children named after their father and having regular contact with him were also more likely to receive financial support.[25]

In the Bank Street College Project at the end of a two-year observation period, 82 percent of approximately 400 teenage fathers had daily contact with their children and 74 percent contributed to the child's financial support.[26] In that same project a longitudinal study of 180 teenage mothers was conducted. It was found that 46 percent were either married to or dating the father of the baby 26 months after delivery, and 64 percent of the mothers were receiving financial support for the infant 3 and 15 months post-partum.[27] In a descriptive study of 26 teenage fathers in the Bank Street Project, approximately 67 percent of the fathers reported maintaining regular contact with the mother of the child.[28] Although the length of the period over which this contact was maintained is not specified in this study, the percentage maintaining contact compares favorably with Furstenberg's study.[29]

INTERVENTION PROGRAMS FOR ADOLESCENT PARENTS

Some steps have been taken to address the needs of adolescent parents. There are ambitious programs like The Hub in New York's South Bronx. This program was designed five years ago by Planned Parenthood of New York City as a one-step "life options" center to help teenagers take charge of their lives and futures and ultimately avoid early pregnancy. The Hub is a health center as well as a learning center. There are social activities; computer, karate and cooking classes; peer tutoring programs; college and career counseling; and work experience programs. Workshops are also offered for families in sexuality and family values.

The Hub tries to build self esteem in adolescents so that they can make independent decisions about sex. The program has been quite successful helping adolescents understand that sex is a quality of life issue, not a reproductive issue. The program involves teenagers as well as parents, and offers weekly sessions in family life and sex education which link sexuality not just to intercourse but to intimacy, social roles, and feelings. The program's success has been encouraging. Out of 140 adolescents enrolled in the program in over three years, there have been only two pregnancies.

Another program, The nonprofit Comprehensive School Age Parenting Program (CSAPP), provides counseling on health care, nutrition, day care, home tutoring, financial aid, employment and housing. Developed ten years ago at English High School in Boston, Massachusetts, the program is now affiliated with more than twenty hospitals and health centers, and last year received $204,000 from the school board, state, and private grants.

The program was designed to help students juggle parenting and school work. Of the 197 students participating in the program last year, 87 planned to return to school this year, 30 dropped out, 41 graduated, 12 transferred to other schools, and 27 who were uncertain of their school plans, moved out of town or were enrolled in programs to earn their high school diploma.

In 1982, the Chicago chapter of the African-American fraternity Alpha Phi Alpha was working to get teenage males to think about the responsibilities of fatherhood before they became fathers. Alpha projects have been developed in several parts of the country. These projects have been sponsored jointly by the Alpha Phi Alpha Fraternity and the March of Dimes. They provide young African-American men who have demonstrated some leadership potential an opportunity to particpate in intensive weekend training sessions. One approach focuses on life issues and value formation and is designed to provide intensive, educational sessions on human sexuality, parenting responsibilities, and appropriate decision making.

The Bank Street Project was a large scale project that involved community organizations in eight United States cities. Funded by the Ford Foundation and coordinated by the Bank Street College of Education in New York, the project offered vocational services, counseling, prenatal and parenting classes to approximately 395 teenage fathers and prospective fathers in eight cities. At the end of the two-year program, 61 percent of the previously unemployed teenage fathers were employed and 46 percent of those who had dropped out of school resumed their education.[30]

The Urban League of Eastern Massachusetts (ULEM) developed the Positive Futures Program, a pregnancy prevention program based on the cognitive-behavioral approach. This approach assumes that many pregnancies occur not because teenagers lack information, but because they do not have the behavioral skills necessary to utilize such information. Thus, Positive Futures is designed to provide young adolescent males from single parent families an opportunity to interact with positive role models who will help them explore options for the future.[31] These adolescent males are not fathers and the adult mentors do not moralize upon them. Instead, they try to instill values and skills which will enable the young men to succeed in school, avoid irresponsible sexual behavior, and resist involvement in crime. The program methods are designed to maximize the influence of community institutions in shaping the future of participants over a period of two years.

A CHALLENGE TO AFRICAN-AMERICAN MEN

The chances of African-American adolescent fathers surviving in America are slim to none if they do not receive support from family, peers, and most importantly, from other adult African-American males. The National Center for Health Statistics can only approximate the number of teenage fathers because it relies solely on birth certificate information to identify them. In 1984, more than 106,000 males under age 19 were listed as fathers. During the same year, 479, 547 babies were born to females under 19. Of those babies, 60 percent had teenage fathers.

The lack of accurate national statistics is due also to the reality that teenage fathers rarely attend health clinics and generally do not trust providers. Dr. Leo Hendricks, a Washington-based consultant, who has devoted eight years to the study of teenage fathers, points out that society has borne the high cost of out of wedlock births, but is still reluctant to commit full resouces to research.

Young adolescent fathers feel the brunt of society's frustration. They are seen as the "perpetrators" and the young mothers as the "victims." In reality, all adolescent parents are victims. But to some extent that is one of the reasons the adolescent father population is a mystery.[32] Teenage males who become fathers are 40 percent more likely than nonparents to drop out of school to seek work, but high paying jobs often elude dropouts. Frequently, they turn to the street to earn easy money.

Much has been written about the context of the African-American family and the important role that African-American men play in providing nurturing, and emotional stability in the family. The most important commodities that African-American men can provide to African-American adolescent fathers are their time, energy, and attention. Several programs exist that provide innovative services to African-American adolescent males, but they are generally limited. On the whole, however, services for African-American adolescent fathers are poor in quality and serve a very small percentage of the eligible population. Most of these programs lack one important commodity; that is, sufficient participation from adult African-American men.

A CURRICULUM FOR ADOLESCENT FATHERS

Education is one of the most important factors to success for these young men. With this view in mind, the leadership of the Comprehensive School Age Parenting Program (CSAPP) at English High School in Boston, Massachusetts has developed a curriculum for adolescent fathers.[33] The overwhelming majority of the fathers in the program are African-American (98 percent) and the male counselors in the program are African-American. This is the first time that CSAPP has offered a program geared specifically to males, and the curriculum is the first of its kind in Massachusetts.

Information shared in this course enables the young men to express their feelings candidly. Moreover, it helps them to understand that their feelings are not unique. Thus, it is expected to enhance peer support and help them to appraise their role in society realistically. The course makes accessible vital community resources that will aid in the personal and educational growth of these youth. In addition, many participate in employment and mentor relationships that have a life-long impact on their self-esteem. The young fathers participate in day-long activities with their children and are involved in peer support groups. They utilize both the employment resources and most importantly, the educational programs at English High School. The course is offered in the high school for credit and students can enroll through the normal enrollment procedures.

The course consists of 15 sessions with a pre/post test design built into the curriculum. The following areas are adressed:

A. *Effective Social and Environmental Living.* The central focus of this section is on developing an understanding of self. Lectures, group processes, and role playing are utilized to explore peer structure and environmental factors (i.e. home and the community).

B. *Relationship with significant other/partner/girlfriend.* The focus is on communication and responsibility for actions, attitudes, and behaviors. Males also have an opportunity to interact with adolescent females during these sessions.

C. *Coping with stress.* Various techniques in stress management are utilized to help participants develop appropriate coping skills. Questions addressed will include: What is stress? How is stress defined? What are the consequences of stress? Trained professionals assist with these sessions.

D. *Male responsibility and parenting.* Fathers and nonfathers are exposed to bonding with the newborn, developing an appropriate helping relationship during infancy, and the elements of day to day parenting (e.g., importance of a doctor's appointment, shopping for the infant, emotional and psychological support).

E. *Facilitating positive child health and development.* Fathers will be involved with parenting for two full days in a supportive environment with other adolescent fathers. A nurse and pediatrician participate in these sessions. Through direct participation, the young fathers will learn the importance of nurturing their child. The key to these sessions is responsibility.

F. *Importance of personal development.* Sessions focus on traditional versus nontraditional educational programs. Emphasis is placed on the value of a high school or college education.

Overall, the curriculum focuses on decision making and responsibility. A variety of professionals are utilized to assist the young men in the course. The most important feature is direct input from other adult males.

ENFORCING THE CYCLE OF MALE RESPONSIBILITY

The National Urban League has produced a series of posters aimed at fostering responsibility among teenage fathers. One poster shows an African-American man tenderly holding a young child, and above it is a line from a Billie Holiday song: "God Bless The Child Who's Got His Own." It is hoped that such positive images will help African-American male adolescents to reject the notion of invisibility which makes them feel irrelevant.

The sociocultural reality of the African-American extended family and the reaching out by African-American adults to youth has been misunderstood by some observers to be a character flaw among African-Americans. In fact, it has been suggested that it

promotes unacceptable social behavior among adolescents, including teenage pregnancy. Notwithstanding, African-American adults must be aware of the attitudes and
messages they transmit to African-American children concerning sexuality, pregnancy
and parenting.

One area an adolescent male can count on to test his masculinity and experience is
his sexual conquests. Moreover, a baby is often a symbol of pride for the mother and
father. But the reality is that many males cannot support these babies financially, and
often their emotional support is missing. Such behaviors cause myths and fallacies to be
perpetuated. For example, in 1987, CBS aired a documentary on adolescent pregnancy,
the "Moyers Report," which projected the stereotype of adolescent pregnancy in the
African-American community as the norm.[34] Fallacies that young girls get pregnant to
receive a welfare check and that young people are promiscuous and irresponsible were
reinforced.

For years, African-American scholars have done research on the family. Organizations such as the National Urban League and African-American sororities and frater-
nities have been trying to address many of these problems with limited exposure.
Recent research indicates that many adolescent fathers are involved with their children.
Their involvement varies from making financial contributions to their children, to
spending time with their childen.

RECOMMENDATIONS AND CONCLUSIONS

There are no "quick fixes" and we cannot afford to moralize upon adolescent parents.
A concerted effort is required to address the needs of pregnant and parenting teenagers.
However, attention must also be paid to the total population of teenagers at risk.
Solutions must be realistic and focus on how society addresses the needs of adolescents
and children. Senator Daniel Patrick Moynihan proposes that we develop a national
policy that would treat families with children (including teenage parents) the way we
treat the elderly; that is, with provisions for income indexing and tax breaks. But our
track record with the elderly has been poor, and young people do not have a strong
political base to ensure that they would fare any better.

Education, prevention and community responsibility are the key ingredients to dealing with the needs of African-American adolescent fathers. Such education must include parents, teachers, community members, and teenagers. Prevention goes hand in
hand with exposure to appropriate information that includes sex education, accessibility to contraceptives, educational and career options, and access to appropriate
role models. Adult males who work 40-60 hours per week and provide for their families
are excellent role models. One does not have to be a movie star or professional athlete to
be a role model. We must utilize the many strengths that exist in the African-American
community.

Community health care clinics can play an important role in providing education
and counseling in sexuality, family planning, health/nutrition, and life options. Further,
community groups can assist with career counseling, employment training, and job

placement. Success is measured in terms of education and a job. Thus, with appropriate exposure, teenagers will be able to make appropriate decisions and become self-sufficient.

The following recommendations focus on the adolescent father, but they can be applied to the needs of the mother as well:

A. Recognizing the needs of fathers does not imply competition with the mother or separation. It is important to instill RESPONSIBILITY in the father so he can fulfill his emotional and financial obligations. Based on a review of the literature on adolescent fathers, the following areas have been identified for further research:

1. Longitudinal studies with large sample sizes are needed to assess the psycho-social and personality characteristics of adolescent males that may be predictive of behavior on becoming a father.
2. The importance of sexual attitudes, contraceptive knowledge, and behavior of teen males must be explored.
3. Information is needed regarding teenage couples' commitment to each other and the factors in their decision-making process that influence the use of contraception and the continuation of a pregnancy.
4. A better understanding is needed of gender differences in regard to expectations of parenting responsibilities and exploration of the meaning of competent functioning for adolescent males.
5. A better understanding is needed regarding the teenage father's direct and indirect involvement in the mother-infant-father triad.

The absence of sufficient research on adolescent fathers has left a void in our understanding of the male's role in parenting. Thus, we are attempting to provide services to this population without fully understanding their psychological makeup. Research can lead to greater understanding and this work can be directed by African-American scholars.

B. In the area of services, male involvement in family planning, infant health maintenance and development must be encouraged. Frequently the male determines whether he or his partner will use birth control. It is, therefore, important that African-American males understand the implications of RISK and CONSEQUENCES. Information can be provided through the home, community services, health clinics, schools, and the church. The print media are also an excellent avenue for this information, but discussion and direction are needed to make this material useful. Other than the parent and community, the school is probably the most accessible agency to educate adolescent fathers about their responsibility. For instance, many young fathers are totally uninformed of their legal obligation (paternity adjudication and child support).

C. Schools should adopt curricula that are culturally sensitive. They should address family planning and sexuality, and provide access to comprehensive health care services in the community. Support must be provided for adolescents who wish to abstain from sexual activities, and provisions must be made for those who are sexually active to receive contraceptives on a referral basis. Professional counseling and peer interaction are vital to this plan. The Center for Population Options in Washington, D.C. has developed a Life Planning curriculum designed to address the interrelatedness of sexual decision making and future vocational options. The Lanier High School Adolescent Health Education Program in Jackson, Mississippi provides comprehensive health education and a clinic health program in which parents and grandparents are encouraged to participate. (As of April 1985, there were 31 clinics in 18 cities with some 25 more in various stages of development. These centers provide access to services and hopefully better understanding, leading to change in knowledge, attitudes, and behavior.)

D. Existing programs that offer parenting training for fathers in communities should form a network alliance so that services can be better coordinated. Expectant fathers should participate in prenatal and parenting classes so as to be informed about fetal development, the birth process, and child care needs. It is important for African-American males to work with these young fathers. Indeed, direction and guidance from them are critical. In addition, pre-vocational and employment counseling should be provided routinely by agencies servicing young fathers.

E. Hospital maternity wards should provide opportunities for teenage fathers to learn and practice basic child care skills during the early postpartum period. Adolescent fathers should be given paternity leave, counseling around pertinent issues, and information about child development and child care. This can be achieved through training classes in infant development and caretaking. Surrogate grandmothers could assist in facilitating these classes with support from child care facilities and community day care programs.

In the final analysis, the plight of adolescent parents and the particular needs of the father are community responsibilities. In all fairness, though, the issue of adolescent pregnancy cannot be solved solely in the African-American community because it is related to systemic problems of employment, schooling and discrimination. However, the African-American community does need to assume local responsibility. In this regard, the African-American church and fraternal and sororal organizations have taken giant steps and are making a difference. Yet, more information is needed about fathers in regard to parenting and developmental skills.

African-American adult males can act as role models to help strengthen and support adolescent fathers. In addition, each segment of the African-American community must become involved in teaching responsibility and the importance of group identity to males. Our resources for the future rest with our young people. Access to education is the key and direction from African-American adults is the solution.

NOTES

1. R.D. Parke, T.G. Power, and T. Fisher, "An Adolescent Father's Impact on the Mother and Child," *Journal of Social Issues* 36 (January 1980): 88-106.

2. E. Brann, L. Edwards, and H.T. Callico, "Strategies for Prevention of Pregnancy in Adolescents," *Advantages of Planned Parenthood* (1979): 14-68.

3. H.M. Wallace, J. Weeks and A. Medina, "Services for Pregnant Teenagers in the Large Cities of the United States 1970-1980," *Journal of the American Medical Association* 48 (August 1982): 2270-2273.

4. F.J. Earls and B. Siegel, "Precocious Fathers," *American Journal of Orthopsychiatry* 50 (July 1980): 469-480.

5. See, for example, L.E. Hendricks, C.S. Howard and P.P. Caesar, "Help Seeking Behavior Among Select Populations of Black Unmarried Adolescent Fathers: Implications for Human Services Agencies," *American Journal of Public Health* 71 (1981): 733-735; L.E. Hendricks, "Unmarried Black Adolescent Fathers' Attitudes Toward Abortion, Contraception and Sexuality: A Preliminary Report," *Journal of Adolescent Health Care* 2 (March 1972): 199-203; R.L. Barret and B.E. Robinson, "A Descriptive Study of Teenage Expectant Fathers," *Family Relations* 31 (July 1982): 349-352; A.B. Elster and S. Panzarine, "Teenage Fathers: Stresses During Gestation and Early Parenthood," *Clinical Pediatrics* (October 1983): 700-703; L.E. Hendricks, T.A. Montogmery, and R.E. Fullilove, "Educational Achievement and Locus of Control Among Black Adolescent Fathers," *Journal of Negro Education* 53 (February 1984): 182-188; and F.P. Rivara, P.J. Sweeney, and B.F. Henderson, "Black Teenage Fathers: What Happens When the Child is Born? *Pediatrics* 78 (July 1986): 151-158.

6. National Center for Health Statistics, "Advance Report of Final Natality Statistics, 1983," *Monthly Vital Statistics Report,* 34 (6) Supplement. September 20, 1985 (Washington, DC: Department of Health and Human Services).

7. J. Skar and B. Berkov, "Teenage Family Formation in Post-War America," *Family Planning Perspectives* 6 (April 1974): 80-9021.

8. J. Williams. *The State of Black America, 1983* (New York: National Urban League, Inc. 1983; and National Center for Health Statistics, "Advance Report of Final Natality Statistics: 1979," *Monthly Vital Statistics Report.* 30 (6) Supplement 2 (Washington, DC: Department of Health and Human Services, 1981).

9. National Center for Health Statistics, "Natality Statistics," *Monthly Vital Statistics Report* 27 (11) Supplement (Washington, DC: Department of Health and Human Services, 1979).

10. L.B. Johnson and R.E. Staples, "Family Planning and the Young Minority Male: A Pilot Project," *The Family Coordinator,* (1979): 535-543; M.L. Finkel and D.J. Finkel, "Sexual and Contraceptive Knowledge, Attitudes and Behavior of Male Adolescents," *Family Planning Perspectives* 7 (November/December 1975): 256-260; and M.M. Brown-Robbins and D.B. Lynn, "The Unwed Fathers: Generation Recidivism and Attitudes about Intercourse in California Youth Authority Wards," *Journal of Sex Research* 9 (November 1973): 334-341.

11. H.M. Babikian and A. Goldman, "A Study in Teenage Pregnancy," *American Journal of Psychiatry* 128 (December 1971): 111-116; and M. Howard, Improving Services for Young Fathers," *Sharing* (Spring 1975).

12. M.E. Lorenzi, L.B. Klerman and J.F. Jekel, "School Age Parents, How Permanent a Relationship?" *Adolescent* 35 (April 1977): 13-22.

13. Hendricks, Montgomery and Fullilove, "Educational Achievement and Locus of Control."

14. Barrett and Robinson, "A Descriptive Study of Teenage Expectant Fathers."

15. C. Casale Rivera, L.V. Klerman, and R. Manela "The Relevance of Child Support Enforcement of School-age Parents," *Child Welfare* 63 (November/December, 1984): 521-532.

16. Williams, *The State of Black America, 1983.*

17. J.J. Card and L.L. Wise, "Teenage Mothers and Teenage Fathers: The Impact of Early Childbearing on the Parents' Personal and Professional Lives," *Family Planning Perspectives* 10 (July/August, 1978): 199-205.

18. Hendricks, Montgomery, Fullilove, "Educational Achievement and Locus of Control."

19. J. Brooks-Gunn and F. Furstenberg, "The Children of Adolescent Mothers: Physical Academic and Psychological Outcome," *Development Review* (1986): 225-251.

20. Ibid.

21. J. Henderson, "On Fathering: The Nature and Functions of the Father's Role," Part II: Conceptualization of Fathering, *Canadian Journal of Psychiatry* 25 (August 1980): 413-431.

22. R.D. Parke and S.E. O'Leary, "Father-Mother-Infant Interaction in the Newborn Period: Some Findings, Some Observations and Some Unresolved Issues," in *The Developing Individual in the Changing World,* eds. K. Riegal, and J. Meachon, Social Economic Issues, Vol. II, The Hauge, Mouton.

23. L. Connolly, "Boy Fathers," *Human Behavior* (January 1978): 40-43.

24. F.F. Furstenberg, "The Social Consequences of Teenage Parenthood," *Family Planning Perspectives* 8 (1976): 148-164.

25. F.F. Furstenberg and K. Talvitie "Childen's Names and Parental Claims," *Journal of Family Issues* 1 (March 1980): 31-57.

26. J. Sander, *Working with Teeenage Fathers: A Handbook for Program Development* (New York: Bank Street College of Education—Ford Foundation, May 1986).

27. Ibid.

28. Ibid.

29. Furstenberg, "The Social Consequences of Teenage Parenthood."

30. Sander, *Working with Teenage Fathers.*

31. Positive Futures was developed by the Urban League of Eastern Massachusetts; Project Director, Hal Phillips; President Donald Polk, 1987.

32. S.F. Battle, *The Black Adolescent Parent* (New York: Haworth Press, 1987).

33. The Adolescent Fathers Curriculum was developed by S. Battle, and M. Stiles, Comprehensive School Age Parenting Program, 1987.

34. Bill Moyers, "The Vanishing Family: Crisis in Black America," CBS Television Documentary, January 25, 1987.

8

Responsibility of the African-American Church as a Source of Support for Adolescent Fathers

Althea Smith

This article traces the African-American church's traditional role as a source of social support for the African-American community. It notes that the African-American church has served as a channel through which responses to issues in and outside the African-American community were made. For African-American men, the relationship with the African-American church has been supportive and nurturing on the one hand, and restrictive and irrelevant to their life style on the other. Unfortunately, the African-American church has been conservative on the issue of adolescent pregnancy, in general, and on African-American adolescent fatherhood, in particular. As fathers, African-American men need the church to advocate for their social needs, and to offer family and parenting services to support their roles as partners and as fathers. Moreover, African-American men need to take positive and active roles as members of the church.

The African-American church has traditionally played a crucial role in the lives of African-American families and the African-American community. It has been a mainstay of social support and cohesion for the African-American community in general, and African-American men in particular.[1] As used here, "the African-American church" refers to the way African-American people live and celebrate "organized" religious life. More specifically, it refers to church doctrine, such as liberation theology, which was the link between activism and morality, and spirituality and actions against oppression. It is the social culture of church members, the choir, the deacon boards, fraternity- and sorority-affiliated organizations, the lay members of the church, and the clergymen. As such, it includes all denominations, including Catholics, Pentecostals, Muslims, as well as storefront churches, television ministries, and mosques.

In the current discussions on teenage pregnancy, however, the African-American church has been shockingly silent or has espoused Victorian morality as the solution to soring teenage births. It has taken a conservative one-sided approach to leadership on this issue, which is not representative of the full range of opinions in the larger African-American community. For example, in September 1985, thirteen African-American clergymen from the south side of Chicago, along with others, filed a lawsuit against the

DuSable-Bogan Health Clinic housed in the DuSable High School. The charges were as follows:

- violation of students' privacy because of the questions about sexual activity;
- failure to warn parents of the risks involved in the use of certain birth control devices;
- invasion of parents' rights to instruct their children; and
- violation of a Supreme Court ruling requiring school neutrality on issues involving religion.

These clergymen continued to voice their opposition although most parents and students were strongly supportive of the clinic.

Yet, the African-American church is not categorically opposed to family planning or sex education programs. The contention here is that given the extensiveness of the issues surrounding teenage pregnancy, the African-American church must play a larger, more prominent role. Before discussing more fully the crucial role of the church, however, a brief examination will be made of some of the factors that impact on African-American men as fathers, the needs of adolescent fathers, and the relationship that African-American men have had with the church.

FACTORS IMPACTING ON AFRICAN-AMERICAN MEN AS FATHERS

Family instability, early sexual activity, tension in male and famale relationships, increased sexuality, and changing sex roles are social forces which have affected African-American men in specific ways and raise special issues for African-American men in the parenting role. A number of conditions in the social structure influence the African-American adolescent, particularly with regard to the role of parenthood. Some of these are lack of stability and support for the family, changing sex norms, and the lack of role models engaging in positive male-female relationships. Moreover, pressures for economic survival have increased the need for both full- and part-time employment, multiple jobs, and for families to change residence. These pressures have had devastating effects on African-American families. For instance, when parents have to take on two jobs, it greatly reduces the amount of time they can spend with their families to give advice, support, and child care. Thus, in many instances, there has been erosion of the family. Although many African-American families may still rely on each other for help, support is made more difficult by the physical distance of their residence.

Another factor impacting on African-American males is the change in sexual attitudes and behaviors that resulted from the "sexual revolution" of the 1960s and 1970s. Being sexually active has become acceptable as a part of the "normal" dating process. Traditional family values against premarital sex are no longer popular. Young men are expected to be sexually active before marriage. Music and videos with sexually suggestive lyrics, clothing fashions, and dances give a clear message to even the youngest listener or viewer to be sexually aggressive. Soap operas and night time dramas also portray sexually explicit themes. Pre-adolescent children are exposed to adult images of sexuality and sensuality which encourages their sexual curiosity and exploration. In addition, sexism has played a role in the heightened sexual activity. Specifically, the popular myth of "machismo" put great pressure on men and boys to be sexually active as a sign of their masculinity.

Another related issue is the nature of the relationships between African-American men and women. One researcher, Karenga, describes four types of "connections" that reflect exploitation between African-American men and women. The first is the "cash connection," which focuses on financial resources by at least one member of the pair. Thus, men and women are seen in terms of their cash assets—car, house, bank account. The second connection, the "flesh connection," is based primarily on the interest in sexual pursuits. Karenga describes this as a mechanistic sex that is usually without passion or love. Thirdly, the "force connnection" is based on violence and a "macho" mentality with the illusion of ownership. Here, the male is characteristically possessive and jealous claiming exclusive rights to "his" woman. The fourth connection, the "dependency connection," stems from one or all of the three connections above. Usually the woman becomes so attached to the man that she will not leave him no matter what happens.[2]

Finally, the parenting role of African-American males has been impacted by the changing roles of women. As women become more economically independent and socio-politically active, they are less likely to accept the more traditional, passive, deferential relationships with men. These changing roles have led to tension in the relationships of African-American men and women. The tension is reflected in fewer long term, committed relationships, higher divorce rates, fewer marriages, and a growing number of African-American singles.[3]

NEEDS OF ADOLESCENT FATHERS

Until recently, much of the debate on teenage pregnancy focused on the behaviors of teenage mothers. Society, for the most part, blamed the teenage girl exclusively for her pregnancy, poverty, and single parenthood. In fact, one author can be quoted as saying, "the behaviors that were said to lead to teenage girls becoming mothers were nonmarital coitus, failure to use effective contraceptives consistently, nonuse of abortion, decision not to place child for adoption and decision not to marry."[4] When the adolescent father was mentioned, it was often in a negative manner, and pointed to his lack of formal education and poor vocational success. In fact, almost all of the intervention programs recruited young pregnant women and neglected the teenage fathers.[5] Fortunately, there are a variety of programs that currently help African-American teenage fathers.

Recently, several researchers have documented the importance of including the adolescent father in all program activities. For instance, Allen-Mears suggests that during the prenatal stage, adolescent fathers should be consulted in all aspects of decision-making and encouraged to act as advocates for the new family-to-be. Further, in the postnatal phase, the father-newborn relationship can be encouraged emotionally and behaviorally with child care skills training. In addition, Allen-Meares points out that the father should be included in the family planning, sexuality and birth control decisions of his family.[6]

Other needs of adolescent fathers were highlighted in a study conducted by Elster and Panzarine. These young men reported four categories of stressors in their lives. They were (1) vocational-educational concerns; (2) concerns about the health of the mother and/or baby; (3) concerns about future parenthood; and (4) problems with their relationship with the partner.[7] Similar findings were reported by Hendricks in his study of 95 unwed fathers. Hendricks' sample of fathers reported concerns about fathers' rights, sex education, information on the role of the father, and consumer education.[8] The results of these studies clearly indicate that the needs of teenage fathers are those of other new fathers in many ways. There are, however, additional needs associated with African-American manhood and youth that require special attention.

AFRICAN-AMERICAN MEN AND THE CHURCH

The African-American church has been a source of institutional support generally, for African-American men in their roles as fathers.[9] Although in many ways the African-American church is undeniably a female institution (based on the gender of its membership and its most active members), most of the positions of authority are held by a few select men.[10] In addition, many African-American men have benefited in a variety of important ways from their association with the church and its social action programs. For example, the church has provided support and spiritual strength to many African-American men, enabling them to fight addiction to alcohol or drugs. Moreover, the African-American church has helped these men to change their lifestyles from illicit street life to legal, productive, stable lives. In addition, the African-American church has provided leadership skills training within the organization, as well as in the external political and educational arenas. The church has historically been a place where debates and plans about the relationship between African-American religion, political, economic, educational, cultural and social life took place. The days of Garveyism and civil rights activism are examples.[11]

Indeed, the African-American church has been one of the few places where African-American men have learned the behaviors necessary to succeed in the White world.[12] Further, the African-American church encouraged the male authoritarianism found in the Bible and advocated for it in the home.[13] In addition, the church has occasionally provided job opportunities for African-American men as merchants, carpenters, plumbers or maintenance men for the church and church-owned projects, or as ministers, pastors, deacons, teachers and the like. In short, the church as an institution has been the wellspring of a variety of activities, positive experiences, and resources for African-American men.[14]

Although the church has been a benefactor in many ways to African-American men, it has failed to recruit large numbers of men as members. As a matter of fact, many men remain apathetic or even hostile toward the church. In his work on African-American men and the African-American church, Tinney offers several possible explanations for this apparent contradiction.[15] One explanation, Tinney notes, is that there are few roles for laymen in the church. Most denominations of the African-American church do not empower their laity or parishioners. Thus, the male role models are the older, long-standing male church members. There is often no role for young vibrant men who might want to participate in the leadership of the church.

Another explanation is that the church encourages and requires passivity among men. For instance, in many of its messages the African-American church advocates nonviolence and pacifism. Moreover, the male image of Christ seems naive in the competitive, urban, exploitative world of many African-American men. In addition, sermons that put prohibitions on behaviors that are associated wth masculinity, like "don't drink," "don't smoke," are restrictive and Victorian in tone. Finally, the African-American church is reported to be lacking significant outreach programs in places where there are large numbers of African-American men, such as colleges, universities, prisons, and the military.[16]

In summary, African-American men have had a mixed relationship with the church. In order to strengthen this relationship, the church must be willing to change and grow, and incorporate the varied needs of men. As one of the few institutions providing a positive, supportive and nurturing environment for African-American men, it is important for the church to develop new strategies to reach out to men.

THE CHURCH AND ADOLESCENT PREGNANCY

A number of policy and program issues need to be addressed in discussing of the role of the African-American church and adolescent pregnancy. To date, no concerted efforts have been made by persons in authority to systematically involve the African-American church in policy issues relative to teenage pregnancy. At the same time, the church itself has not been proactive in coordinating an agenda for adolescent pregnancy that should be developed in the African-American community.

Researchers, practitioners and others interested in teenage pregnancy have written on various aspects of the problem. Some have written about legalities of privacy rights regarding contraception and abortion.[17] Others interested in education have explored the curriculum needs for pregnant and parenting teenagers.[18] In addition, state, regional and national planning bodies have met to examine implications for welfare, health, and nutrition policy.[19] The debaters, researchers, policymakers, and community planners have not agreed on what should be addressed in teenage pregnancy programs.

Thus, a number of questions have been raised concerning the focus of such programs. For instance, should the priority be pregnancy prevention programs, prenatal and postnatal health programs, or family planning and functioning programs? More specifically, it is not clear whether the primary issue is related to premature sexual activity, limited educational, employment and/or career life options, or limited sex education. Similarly, it is unclear whether the teenage pregnancy problem is due to limited knowledge of contraceptives, a shift in the African-American family structure, or deterioration in African-American male-female relationships. All of these factors are perceived to be related to adolescent pregnancy. It is, therefore, important for the African-American community to take the leadership role in identifying the priority issues and addressing them with vigor.

In the absence of any comprehensive community effort, various states have initiated programs. Thus, it is difficult to assess progress and to evaluate the most effective programs and most salient issues. In the state of Massachusetts, for example, there are several models of school-based pregnancy programs. Some programs offer individual services at locations physically outside of the school. Other programs are full-functioning health clinics complete with child-care centers. Depending on the key issue, however, the school-based programs may or may not be the most effective model.

It seems appropriate that the African-American church should become the community representative clarifying the issues related to teenage pregnancy. There are a variety of roles that the African-American church can take with respect to the issue of teenage pregnancy. For example, the church can take the leadership role in identifying and setting priorities as representative of the African-American community. Historically the African-American church has taken responsibility for fostering family solidarity. It also served as the meeting place for planning strategies on such actions as the boycotts, demonstrations, and sit-ins in the 1950s and 1960s during the civil rights movement. If such strategies were restored, the African-American church could be invaluable in setting an African-American agenda.

Another role the African-American church can play is to take steps to attract more young people to its congregation and to engage in open dialogue about sex and sexuality. The Pentecostal and some smaller store front churches have been responsive to the changing needs of their membership. The doctrines of some of these churches have been forward thinking on questions about birth control, premarital sex, and equality in gender roles. In order for African-American churches in general to regain community support, they should look to some of their more progressive competitors for guidance and leadership. Perhaps all churches cannot advocate for the more liberal social viewpoints. However, even the most conservative churches can play a more facilitative role.

Some innovative programs focusing on strengthening African-American family life have been supported and sponsored by a few African-American churches around the country. For instance, a church in Illinois offers a sex education program that promotes open communication about sexuality between teenagers and parents. It does not encourage teenage sexual activity, merely open discussion. Although it may seem to be a contradiction for the church to be involved in sex education, it is necessary for the church to play a role in encouraging sex education and responsible sexual behavior for preteens, teenagers and adults. In this regard, one of the more active church groups is the Catholic church. It provides information on fertility awareness, human sexuality, and natural family planning.

By providing a support system for all families—traditional and so-called nontraditional—the church is helping to restore the sanctity of the family as the building block of the African-American community. African-American Muslims and other groups have tried to foster a very traditional model of two-parent African-American family life.

However, other family forms also need to be given a strong base of support from the African-American church. For example, parenting programs for fathers who decide to raise their children alone should be offered through the church. In addition, parenting programs offering family counseling, family life education, and child abuse prevention designed for families that may not be legally married or that are made up of two separate families should be designed and offered through the church.

The church needs to create opportunities for active participation by African-American men to help them develop positive self-images. Too many African-American men are disappearing in the criminal justice systems, to drugs and alcohol, homelessness, and unemployment. The church should take the moral responsibility to advocate against the oppression of these African-American men. Further, it should be instilled in the African-American community that church participation is a civic responsibility as well as an individual spiritual mission.

Finally, the church should sponsor workshops and training designed to build positive African-American male-female relationships. The clergy are often consulted for advice on marital problems and should use these opportunities to be a resource for African-American men and women while at the same time benefiting the church. Emphasis should be on more supportive and less oppressive relationships between African-American men and women. In other words, church-based programs should promote more egalitarian and less sexist, rigid, and exploitative male-female relationships. In this regard, the church can offer liberal, updated, practical guidelines for building and maintaining successful relationships.

SUMMARY

It seems that an important contribution the African-American church can make is to be more vocal by taking a leadership role in identifying pertinent issues related to teenage pregnancy. Although the African-American church has traditionally been very conservative on many of the related issues (i.e., abortion, contraceptives, premarital sex), there are more liberal roles the church can play. The church should not steer away from this issue simply because it is controversial. We need the strength and voice of our African-American churches and we need them now!

NOTES

1. E.F. Frazier, *The Black Bourgeoisie* (New York, NY: The Free Press, 1957).
2. M. Karenga, *Beyond Connections* (Los Angeles, CA: Kawaida, 1978).
3. J. Hare, "Black Male-Female Relationships," *Sepia* (November, 1979); and J. Jackson, "But Where Are the Men?" in *The Black Family: Essays and Studies*, ed. R. Staples (Belmont, CA: Wadsworth, 1978).
4. C. Chilman, "Feminist Issues in Teenage Parenting." Special Issue: Toward a Feminist Approach to Child Welfare. *Child Welfare*, 64(3) (1985): 225-234.
5. A.B. Elster and M.E. Lamb, "Adolescent Fathers: A Group Potentially at Risk for Parenting Failure," *Infant Mental Health Journal* 3(3) (1982): 148-155; and A.B. Elster and S. Panzarine, "Teenage Fathers: Stresses During Gestation and Early Parenthood," *Clinical Pediatrics* 22(10) (1983): 700-703.
6. P. Allen-Meares, "Adolescent Pregnancy and Parenting: The Forgotten Adolescent Father and His Parents," *Journal of Social Work and Human Sexuality* 3(1) (1984): 27-38.

7. A.B. Elster and S. Panzarine, "Teenage Fathers."

8. L. Hendricks, "Suggestions for Reaching Unmarried Black Adolescent Fathers," *Child Welfare* 62 (2) (1983): 141-146.

9. J.S. Tinney, "The Religious Experience of Black Men," in *Black Men*, ed. L. Gary (Beverly Hills, CA: Sage, 1981).

10. D. Brown and R. Walters, *Exploring the Role of the Black Church in the Community* (Washington, D.C.: Institute for Urban Affairs and Research, Howard University, 1979).

11. R. Barnett, *Black Redemption: Churchmen Speak for the Garvey Movement* (Philadelphia: Temple University Press, 1978).

12. E. Liebow, *Tally's Corner* (Boston: Little Brown, 1967); and J. Young, *Major Black Religious Leaders Since 1940* (Nashville, TN: Abington, 1979).

13. E.F. Frazier, *The Negro Church in America* (New York, N Y: Schocken, 1964); L. Russell, "A Feminist Looks at Black Theology," in *Black Theology II: Essays on the Formation and Outreach of Contemporary Black Theology*, ed. C. Bruce and W. Jones (Lewisburg, PA.: Bucknell University Press, 1978).

14. Gary, *Black Men*.

15. Tinney, "The Religious Experience."

16. Ibid.

17. S.F. Battle and J.L. Rozie-Battle, *Adolescent Sexuality: Cultural and Legal Implications* (New York: Haworth Press, 1987).

18. Ibid.

19. National Research Council, *Risking The Future: Adolescent Sexuality, Pregnancy, and Childbearing* (Washington, DC: National Academy Press, 1987).

9

Adolescent Pregnancy:
A Medical Concern

John M. Taborn

Medical problems associated with adolescent pregnancy and motherhood in the United States are common across cultural and racial boundaries. These problems are, however, exacerbated for the African-American adolescent. This article examines the importance of maternal and infant mortality, low birth weight, and the social implications of these for health practitioners. Inadequate pre and postnatal medical care are seen as more problematic for teenage parents than for older parents. Some reasons cited for the inappropriate use of medical care by adolescents are their contemporary lifestyles, the inaccessibility of health care, and their reluctance to seek prenatal care.

Adolescent pregnancy and parenthood among African-Americans in the United States is neither a unique nor recent phenomenon. Indeed, during slavery African-American slave girls frequently became mothers by the age of 13. Once the fact of their fecundity was established, these same girls were often used to bear even more children. In the "peculiar institution" of slavery, these female "breeders" were highly sought after and accorded special significance due to their ability to contribute to the slaveholders' labor pool. Following slavery, in an agrarian economy, girls tended to marry young and their early childbearing contributed to the family's survival by supplementing the farm labor force whether they were landowners or sharecroppers.

Obviously in the 1980s, teenage childbearing no longer has economic utility. National shifts from a rural-agrarian to an urban-industrial economy, coupled with a concomitant extension in the length of schooling have drastically altered the public's evaluation of African-American teenage pregnancy from that of a "blessing" (in earlier times) to that of a "problem" (today).

The economic implications of the "problem" are far-reaching—socially, economically, and morally. Too often, unwed adolescent mothers do not complete high school, do not seek (or find) employment, are likely to experience a subsequent pregnancy, and have a decreased likelihood of establishing a traditional American nuclear family lifestyle with financial independence. The heightened public concern with the issue of adolescent pregnancy has been generated, in part, by the publication of statistics which demonstrate that among African-Americans, the rate of unwed adolescent pregnancy and childbirth approximate 237 per 1,000 births, compared with 71 per 1,000 for White teenagers.[1] This rate, as well as the racial differential between such rates is alarming. It should be noted with caution that the rate among African-American adolescents appears to have reached its peak (and is indicating a slight decline), while the rate among White adolescents is increasing. In 1983, the absolute number of American White teenage parents was more than double the number of African-American teenage parents (1,567,555 to 342,283).[2]

The increased national focus on teenage pregnancy and parenting has accentuated the professional focus on health issues associated with adolescent pregnancy and parenthood. There are concomitant health issues associated with teenage pregnancy which appear to be the norm in that population. The incidence of these adolescent health issues correlates, in part, with race, age, and socioeconomic status. The common difficulty of sorting out the relative cause-effect contributions of age (teenagers), race (African-American), and socioeconomic status (poor) is, at best, difficult.

Currently, there are two conventional, opposing, "wisdoms" concerning the consequences of adolescent pregnancy and childbearing.[3] The first, which seems most pervasive and acceptable, posits that teenage parenthood is negative because it is the source of myriad physical, social and psychological problems for both mother and child.[4] A second, opposing view, (held prominently during the past) posits that the younger the woman's age when she bears a child, the better off (physiologically) she and her child will be. Youth, according to this perspective, is associated with strength, resilience and health of the younger woman compared with the older women.[5] Studies which have supported the second view have also discovered that while high health risks do prevail for girls age 15 years or younger, they do not necessarily prevail for those 16 and older.

As a consequence for these two views, it is probably worth considering that while adolescent pregnancy may be biologically advantageous (for those 17 and over), it is clearly socially disadvantageous. This consideration reflects recent findings that the health-related issues of poor nutrition, quality and quantity of prenatal care, inadequacy of preparation for childbirth, and low quality of postnatal care appear to be more related to the subsequent medical problems of adolescent mothers and their children than age and physical immaturity alone. In a related sense, deficits in those four health areas tend to be associated with adolescents' (especially the poorer ones) behaviors and lifestyles. Whatever the cause for medical problems in adolescent mothers and their children, whether biological or social, the fact remains that medical issues do exist for these populations. And the solutions to these problems are the responsibility of health care professionals.

A pregnant adolescent mother and her unborn child represent a complex and highly interdependent system. Bolton observed:

Any alteration in the biological and psychological composition of this experience for one member of this pair has nearly immediate and frequently intense influences upon the well-being of the other.[6]

The potential for complications with pregnancy which lead to medical problems for both the mother and child is exceptionally high for adolescents. Some medically-related complications associated with the pregnancy of adolescent women include maternal mortality, iron deficiency anemia, pregnancy-induced hypertension, and maternal toxemia. For numerous biological and social reasons, African-American adolescents are more at risk than their older counterparts to experience health-related complications during and after pregnancy, for both themselves and their children. These mother-child health risks begin at conception and may continue (unless abated) throughout the child's life. The basis for assignment of an "at risk" status can be found in the adolescents' biological immaturity, their social/cultural environment and lifestyle, their attitudes toward pregnancies, and their underuse of health services.

While medical problems associated with adolescent pregnancy and motherhood in the United States are common across cultural and racial boundaries, these problems are exacerbated for the African-American adolescent. Acknowledgement of this becomes critical when designing programs. Too often, the strategies for prevention and intervention are based upon research findings that consider adolescent mothers to be a homogeneous group. One practitioner noted:

> Clearly, the awareness of the cultural and historical context of which the adolescent is a part provides knowledge to the practitioner about her needs, resources and obstacles to health care.[7]

MATERNAL MORTALITY

Death of the mother (maternal mortality) is one of the most serious consequences of adolescent pregnancy. Complications (other than illegal abortions) most commonly leading to maternal mortality include toxemia, hemorrhage and infections. Studies of incidence rates for these complications indicated that low-income African-American adolescent mothers are at a disproportionately higher risk than older (ages 20-24) African-American mothers and adolescent White mothers. According to Hollingworth et al.,

> The high rates of pregnancy-induced hypertension, anemia, prematurity, and perinatal mortality in teenagers with a low gynecological or chronological age were documented in reports from urban clinics with 72 to 100 percent African-American patients. In sharp contrast, reports from more economically advantaged clinics with 67-91 percent White teenagers did not show an increase in medical complications in teenagers 16 years or less or their newborn infants.[8]

Nationally, the death rate among non-Whites is 3.2 times that of Whites.[9] Between 1968-1975, African-Americans under the age of 15 had a maternal mortality rate of 43.7 per 100,000. For whites, it was 23.0 per 100,000. In the 15-19 year-old age group the rates were 27.6 for African-Americans and 9.7 for Whites per 100,000.[10] These proportional differences provide more than ample evidence that pregnant African-American adolescents are significantly "at risk."

INFANT MORTALITY

Infant mortality (infant death during the first year) is obviously the most serious consequence of medical complications that may arise with the offspring of adolescent mothers. Infant mortality is more likely to occur among the infants of teenage mothers in the United States. Many studies have revealed a strong relationship between young maternal age and increased risk of low birthweight and infant mortality.[11] In a related sense, however, the infants of teenage mothers are more frequent among the socioeconomically disadvantaged segment of the population. This is important since the survival and quality of life of an infant during its first year is a result not only of its heredity (nature), but also of its social, economic, health, and maternal environment (nurture).

In 1975, the infant mortality rate for African-Americans was 26.8 per 1,000, compared with 14.1 per 1,000 for Whites.[12] Similarly, in 1984, the infant mortality rate for African-Americans was 18.4 per 1,000 compared to 9.4 for Whites. The racial disparity in infant mortality rates remains relatively constant in spite of medical advances. For example, among African-Americans over the age of 14, neonatal mortality rates are remarkable for their relative uniformity in comparison with White rates. African-Americans in their teens and mid- and late-20s have rates of short gestation, low birthweight, and neonatal mortality higher than those of White teenagers over age 14.[13] Many factors contribute to infant mortality, but most studies suggest that the strongest predictor is low birthweight.

LOW BIRTHWEIGHT

Low birthweight (less than 2500 grams or 5.5 pounds) is associated, in part, with prematurity. However, low birthweight (independent of prematurity) has been found to be associated with the mother's prepregnancy weight, her weight gain during pregnancy, and the length of gestation.[14] In her research, Helen Chase clearly shows that babies of low birthweight represent a significantly higher proportion among African-American adolescent mothers.[15] Relatedly, in a study of New York babies, Clarke reveals an increasing incidence of low birthweight with lower ages of parenthood.[16] Clarke's data also indicate that the rate of low birthweight among African-American adolescents exceeded that of White adolescents.

As in the case of maternal health, inadequate prenatal care has been singled out as one of the more important determinants of both prematurity and low birthweight.[17] In discussing low birthweight infants, Geronimous summarizes:

> ... low birthweight may result from a variety of physiological consequences of their environmental disadvantage, not primarily from inherent and intractable biological developmental limits.[18]

POSTNATAL MEDICAL PROBLEMS

In considering medically-related issues that might arise for the adolescent mother and child after birth, several problems become apparent. A study conducted in Canada revealed that adolescent mothers tended to visit their physicians for alleviation of specific medical complaints such as feeding problems (interventive). Adult mothers, on the other hand, tended to see their physicians for well-baby care (preventive).[19] Earlier studies discuss the appearance of later mental subnormality as well as multiple neurological difficulties in children born prematurely (high among adolescents).[20] In more recent studies, though, the association between adolescent parenthood and later problems of their children (e.g., intellectual development) appears to be related to the quality of interaction between the young mother and her child.

The relationship between early parenthood and later cognitive development may be summarized as follows:

> The effects of parental age are apparently not biological; instead they are due chiefly to the impact of sociodemographic factors and the tendency for young mothers, especially African-Americans, to be overrepresented in the low socioeconomic groups and in female-headed households.[21]

Similarly, Card and Wise, who conducted an extensive follow-up study of boys and girls born of parents who were 15-17 years of age state:

> Significantly low scores for children of adolescent mothers tend to become minimal when appropriate controls are instituted for adverse effects of poverty, racism, and family hardship. Sons of adolescent parents may be more adversely affected than daughters in respect to cognitive development and educational achievements.[22]

SOCIAL IMPLICATIONS

Recent studies that analyze the causes for many of the mother/child health-related problems commonly associated with teenage pregnancy tend to find that most problems could be decreased with proper health care.[23] These causes are deemed to be:

1. remediable or preventable given the adolescent mother has adequate prenatal care;
2. preventable or remediable if the deleterious environment (effects of poverty and racism) can be decreased; and
3. remediable or preventable if antecedent situations (before conception), including mother's prepregnancy weight, use of alcohol or drugs, and poor nutritional habits are modified by exposure and adherence to positive health care regimens.

Teenage maternal mortality risks are much lower in some other societies (where medical services are more readily available to all citizens). In England and Wales, for example, the maternal mortality rate for teenage mothers is even lower than that for 20- to 24-year-old mothers in the United States. An analysis of two Scandinavian studies found no additional maternal mortality risks for adolescents compared with mothers in the 20- to 24-year-old group.[24] These findings and other studies have demonstrated that early access to, and continuing use of prenatal care by the pregnant adolescent is the strongest factor contributing to decreasing maternal mortality.

A study of births in Denmark reveals that children born to adolescent mothers experienced lower rates of stillbirth and neonatal mortality than those born to adult mothers.[25] Similarly, in the United States, researchers associated with the large Collaborative Perinatal Project (where the subjects were followed for several years, thereby receiving continuous pre- and post-natal monitoring) found perinatal mortality to be lowest for the children of young white adolescents.[26]

Thus, it is generally agreed that the quality of prenatal care impacts the relationship between the adolescent mother and risk to the newborn, in terms of birthweight, parent weight gains, and prematurity.[27] Yet, being an African-American, poor, pregnant, adolescent female in America is highly predictive of the likelihood of receiving inadequate prenatal health care.

FACTORS IMPACTING PREGNANT ADOLESCENTS' APPROPRIATE USE OF MEDICAL CARE

Contemporary Adolescent Lifestyles

Compared with their older counterparts, there is a tendency for pregnant teenagers to seek prenatal care later, to have poorer nutrition, to stay unmarried longer, and to experience a decline in socioeconomic status (and education). Part of the problem is associated with the typical behaviors of contemporary adolescents. Solutions to this pervasive attitudinal problem may lie in increasing the emphasis on proper health care through education and public forums.

Accessibility of Health Care

One of the factors that differentiates the United States from some other industrialized countries is the degree of accessibility of the health care system. Accessibility in the United States is related, in part, to cultural, economic, and racial variables. Bolton found that the effort necessary to solicit and receive adequate prenatal care may be beyond the capacity of many adolescents, particularly those of low income.[28] Some typical problems include transportation limitations, getting time away from work to go to the doctor, long waiting lines in public clinics, perceived laissez-faire attitudes on the part of some health care professionals, and for many adolescents, a desire to conceal or deny the pregnancy. Health care professionals must continue to find ways to decrease or eliminate these logistical hindrances.

Reluctance to Seek Prenatal Care

Adolescents are often reluctant to seek prenatal care. For many adolescents, public acknowledgement of their pregnancy may not occur until the second trimester. A visit to the physician may not occur until the third trimester. In 1983, more than half (54 percent) of all pregnant adolescents received no first trimester medical care and nearly 20 percent did not receive an initial evaluation until the third trimester.[29]

The stress of revealing their pregnancy to parental or other authority figures is often considered deterministic in the reluctance of adolescents to seek prenatal care in a timely manner.[30] Pregnant adolescents undergo significant psychosocial stress from negotiations with parents, revelations to the unborn child's biological father, peer rejection, leaving school, and fear. The anticipated perceptions of insensitivity of health care professional toward her pregnancy may also be stressful to the adolescent. Coddington's research reveals that pregnant adolescents experience significant stress which could negatively impact their physical state if it went unmanaged.[31]

IMPLICATIONS FOR HEALTH PRACTITIONERS

There is no question that African-American adolescent pregnancy in the United States is a health concern. Thus, health professionals and other interested persons need to increase their involvement with this problem's solution. The following are some suggested ways for involvement:

1. Health care workers need to consider the critical impact of cultural, racial and socioeconomic factors when formulating their strategies for implementing prevention/intervention programs. Such considerations will increase the responsiveness of health care systems to the unique needs of the African-American pregnant adolescent population.
2. Given the reluctance of teenagers to seek prenatal care until late in pregnancy, barriers to conducting effective outreach must be removed at the policy and practice levels. Further, outreach efforts must receive more funding and be tailored to appeal to this "at risk" population.
3. Limitations impacting the accessibility to pre- and postnatal health care must be removed through creative options (e.g., portable delivery, provision of transportation, and programs of family support). Health care professionals need to make cultural awareness an integral part of their formal preparatory, as well as on-the-job, training and education. The African-American pregnant adolescent's reluctance and heightened sensitivity to rejection make it critical that health care delivery strategies include processes to overcome these problems.

4. National policies concerning abortion reduce the likelihood that poorer pregnant adolescents will be able to afford that option, if desired. Thus, more African-American adolescents will be carrying their babies full term. This means that increased availability and accessibility to family planning for contraceptive information and provision is needed.
5. Recent national welfare guidelines make it financially advantageous for adolescent mothers to move away from home, thereby disrupting the African-American extended family. This also increases the difficulty of providing well-baby health care, postnatal information and other medical follow-up to adolescent mothers who tend to perceive medical attention as something to seek only when there is a "problem," not as prevention. New accessible program models must, therefore be developed to overcome these increased logistical and attitudinal barriers.
6. Public health and family planning services need to establish more culturally and economically relevant sex education programs for all age levels (from kindergarten through college).

Marian Wright-Edelman summarizes elements of the cost effectiveness of increasing our health care delivery to pregnant adolescents as follows:

- It costs $68 to provide family planning services to a sexually active teen, but $3,000 to provide that teen and her baby prenatal care and delivery under Medicaid.
- It costs $600 to provide a mother with comprehensive prenatal care to facilitate the growth of healthier babies, but more than $1,000 per day to keep low birthweight babies alive through neonatal intensive care.
- It costs $495 per year to provide infant care through the supplemental food program for Women, Infants and Children (WIC), while it costs an average of $12,000 to save a tiny newborn with neonatal intensive care.[32]

Comprehensive preventive health care initiatives that begin to meet some of the unique needs of pregnant African-American adolescents should include the following elements:

- An emphasis on risk identification and reduction;
- An emphasis on expanded health education;
- Increased access to prenatal care;
- Focus on the African-American adolescent as "high risk" in the delivery of prenatal care;
- Intensified assessment of premature delivery risk;
- Increased provision of prenatal supplementary health programs (e.g., nutrition, smoking, and chemicals);

- Intensified professional coordination with involved health care organizations (HMOs, Medicaid, hospitals, health insurance carriers) to insure that the African-American adolescent population gets access to necessary information and services;
- Promotion of research efforts that will emanate from a broader philosophy of health to include more antecedent environmental conditions impacting on pregnancy (e.g., stress, racism, and poverty).

NEED FOR COLLABORATION AND LEADERSHIP

The African-American community needs to collaborate with its health/medical professionals to aggressively pursue and maintain involvement with comprehensive health planning agencies, community health services, and health education organizations. Concurrently, new ways must be developed to motivate African-American adolescents to seek preventive rather than episodic health care. Finally, there must be continued pressure to receive more funds to support health maintenance, increased training of health care practitioners, and a more proportionate distribution of accessible health care centers, particularly in central cities. As with all programs, there must be continuous monitoring, evaluation, and dissemination of results. In particular, those programs that appear to be successful in meeting the needs of the African-American adolescent population should be publicized and replicated in other areas.

In conclusion, Edelman aptly summarizes the "mission" as follows:

> This surge of Black community energy and commitment is essential because we will have to reach many of our vulnerable children, teens and parents on a one-to-one basis. It is also essential because the Black community knows far better than anyone else . . . knows in its bones and in the hard school of experience . . . that without its own strong leadership now, as in the past, too little can be expected from government or other institutions.[33]

NOTES

1. J.M. Taborn and S. Battle, *Working With the Black Adolescent Parent* (Minneapolis Survival Skills Institute, Inc., 1984).

2. M.W. Edelman, *Families in Peril: An Agenda for Social Change* (Cambridge: Harvard University Press, 1987).

3. M. Konner and M. Shostak, "Adolescent Pregnancy and Childbearing: An Anthropological Perspective," in *School-Age Pregnancy and Parenthood*, eds. J. Lancaster and B. Hamburg (Hawthorne, NY: Aldine DeGruyter, 1986).

4. Alan Guttmacher, *Teenage Pregnancy: The Problem That Hasn't Gone Away* (New York: The Alan Guttmacher Institution, 1981).

5. P.B. Rothenberg and P.E. Varga "The Relationship Between Age of Mother and Child Health and Development," *American Journal of Public Health* 71 (1981).

6. Frank G. Bolton, *The Pregnant Adolescent* (Beverly Hills: Sage Publications, 1980).

7. Alva P. Barnett, "Sociocultural Influences on Adolescent Mothers," *International Journal of Pediatric Social Work* 3(4) (1985).

8. D.R. Hollingworth, J.M. Kotchen and M.E. Felice "Impact of Gynecologic Age on Outcome of Adolescent Pregnancy," in *Premature Adolescent Pregnancy and Parenthood* ed. E.R. McAnarney (New York: Grune and Stratton, 1983).

9. M.H. Rudov and N. Santangelo, *Health Status of Minorities and Low Income Groups* (U.S. Department of Health, Education and Welfare, Publication No. (HRA) 79-627, 1979).

10. R.W. Rochat, "Maternal Mortality in the United States of America," *World Health Statistics Report* 34 (1) (1981).

11. J. Menken, "The Health and Demographic Consequences of Adolescent Pregnancy and Childbearing," in *Adolescent Pregnancy and Childbearing*, ed. C. Chilman (Washington, D.C.: U.S. Government Printing Office, 1980).

12. Rudov and Santangelo, *Health Status of Minorities.*

13. Arline T. Geronimous, "The Effects of Race, Residence and Prenatal Care on the Relationship of Maternal Age to Neonatal Mortality," *American Journal of Public Health* 76(12) (1986).

14. R. Frisancho, J. Matos and W. Ballettino, "Influence of Growth Status and Placental Function on Birthweight of Infants Born to Young Still-Growing Teenagers," *American Journal of Clinical Nutrition* 40 (October 1984): 801-807.

15. Helen C. Chase, "Trends in Prematurity: United States, 1950-1967," *American Journal of Public Health* 60 (1967).

16. Mildred I. Clarke, "Black Teenage Pregnancy: An Obstetrician's Viewpoint," *Journal of Community Health* 11 (1) (Spring 1986).

17. Menken, "The Health and Demographic Consequences."

18. Geronimous, "The Effects of Race."

19. J.M. Hendry and J.A. Shea, "Pre and Post Natal Care Sought by Adolescent Mothers," *Canadian Journal of Public Health* 71 (1980).

20. Howard J. Osofsky, *The Pregnant Teenager* (Springfield, IL: Charles C. Thomas Publisher, 1968).

21. E.M. Kinard and L.V. Klerman, "Effects of Early Parenthood on the Cognitive Development of Children," in *Premature Adolescent Pregnancy and Parenthood*, ed. E.R. McAnarney (New York: Grune and Stratton, 1983).

22. J.J. Card and L.L. Wise, "Teenage Mothers and Teenage Fathers: The Impact of Early Childrearing on the Parents' Personal and Professional Lives," *Family Planning Perspectives* 10(4) (1978): 199-205.

23. Rochat, "Maternal Mortality."

24. J.P. Deschamps and G. Valantin, "Pregnancy in Adolescence: Incidence and Outcome in European Countries," *Journal of Biosocial Science*, Supplement 5 (1978).

25. B. Mednick, U. Brock, and R. Baker, "Infant Caretakers: In Praise of Older Women." Paper presented at the annual meeting of the Western Psychological Association, San Diego, CA, April 6, 1979.

26. J. Osofsky, D. Osofsky, N. Kendall and R. Rajan, "Adolescents as Mothers: An Inter-Disciplinary approach to a Complex Problem," *Journal of Youth and Adolescence* 2 (1973).

27. T.O. Scholl, W.K. Miller, R.W. Salmon, M.C. Dofsky and J. Shearer, "Prenatal Care Adequacy and the Outcome of Adolescent Pregnancy: Effects on Weight Gain, Preterm Delivery and Birth Weight," *Obstetrics and Gynecology* 69 (3), Part 1 (March, 1987).

28. Bolton, *The Pregnant Adolescent.*

29. Robert D. Shaw and Norma J. Hirsch, "Infants of Teenage Mothers: The Black Children's Hospital Experience, 1984," *Seminars in Adolescent Medicine* 2 (3) (1986).

30. Edelman, *Families in Peril.*

31. R.D. Coddington, "Life Events Associated with Adolescent Pregnancies," *Journal of Clinical Psychiatry* 40 (1979).

32. Edelman, *Families in Peril.*

33. Ibid.

10

Factors that Adversely Affect the Health and Well-Being of African-American Adolescent Mothers and Their Infants

Alva P. Barnett

The purpose of this article is to describe some of the health consequences associated with African-American adolescent pregnancy and motherhood. This includes the impact of age, inadequate nutrition, family income factors, and the lack of available and accessible quality health care services. Within the context of cultural and structural considerations, this article briefly discusses several strategies for effective and relevant service interventions. These intervention strategies are likely to positively impact the disabling process, thus increasing the functional capacity and optimal ability of these mothers and their infants.

This article is intended to contribute to the understanding of health problems and needs of the African-American adolescent mother and the health effects associated with adolescent pregnancy and motherhood. Selected antecedent factors that adversely affect the health and well-being of the African-American adolescent mother and her child will be discussed. These antecedent factors are: age; inadequate nutrition; family income; changing family structure; and the lack of available and accessible quality health care services. If uncorrected, these factors could have far-reaching implications for the functional capacity and optimal ability of these mothers and their infants, as well as serious consequences for future generations.

Quality health should be available to every individual. It is necessary regardless of the race, ethnic identity, social status or economic circumstances of individuals or groups.[1] As Clark reminds us, "Youth is the foundation on which quality health is built. If America is to be free and offer fulfillment to its people, it must guarantee every teenager a healthy body, a sound mind and a decent environment."[2]

This guarantee is a noble gesture that—no matter how profoundly we hope, desire and believe it to be—simply flies in the face of reality. This contention is supported by facts that are disturbing and warrant the full attention, and understanding of all adults,

Originally published in *Pediatric Social Work,* Vol. 3, No. 4, 1988. Reprinted with permission of Eterna Press.

practitioners and most importantly, African-Americans. Some of the present conditions that affect the health and well-being of African-American families, children and youth include the steady growth of single parent households; alarming rates of infant mortality; growing numbers of poor persons and those below the poverty level as defined by the U.S. government; higher fertility rates, especially among younger adolescents; an increasing percentage of out-of-wedlock births, unemployment and increasingly low levels of family income. These facts strongly suggest a crisis situation for several reasons.

First, the effects are multiple and will negatively impact at least two subsequent generations. Secondly, adequate and effective intervention-prevention techniques have not been utilized to any measurable degree. The descriptive literature and statistical reports have not focused significantly on understanding the interactive, multidimensional nature of the situation that impacts especially on African-American lives. These include structural barriers to opportunities, cultural values, and individual coping and adaptive patterns relative to survival and individual development.

PRESENT CONDITIONS

In 1982 over forty-seven percent of African-American families with children under the age of 18 years were single mother households; this represents an increase of nearly 40 percent since 1950 when the incidence was 8 percent. During this same time, white single mother households increased 12 percent, from 3 percent in 1950 to about 15 percent in 1982.[3],[4] These figures show that differences between African-American and White family structures are widening. It is particularly devastating that single mother households constitute the majority (56 percent) of the nation's poor. It is estimated that 44.9 percent of African-American children under 18 years of age live below the poverty line.[5]

The gap between African-American and White infant mortality rates is widening at a steady pace. In 1978, the African-American infant mortality rate was 86 percent higher than the White infant mortality rate. Four years later, the African-American infant moratlity rate was 95 percent higher than that of Whites. According to Rice, the federal government's goal to reduce African-American infant mortality to no more than 12 infant deaths for each 1,000 live births by 1990 will not be realized if this emerging trend continues.[6] Directly related to infant mortality is the high percentage of underweight babies being born, inadequate nutrition and poor health care.

The most seriously underweight babies have disproportionately been born to African-American mothers. For example, in 1981, 6 percent of all White infants were underweight at birth while 31 percent of all African-American babies were underweight at birth.[7]

There are many other related facts that have an impact on the health and well-being of African-American adolescent mothers and their infants. Two of these are the higher fertility rates and percentages of out-of-wedlock births. Also included are higher unemployment levels and lower family income (see figures 1-4).

The data presented here disclose the continued lack of parity and in many instances the widening gap that exists between minority and majority group circumstances that adversely affect the health and well-being of African-American children and youth. The social, health and structural conditions of which these facts are representative, are ultimately surrounded by the issues of wealth and income opportunities.

CURRENT KNOWLEDGE

Over the past two decades, the occurence of adolescent pregnancy and motherhood has continued to receive an enormous amount of national attention from a variety of disciplines and professional audiences. The steady attention given to adolescent pregnancy and motherhood has resulted in a plethora of descriptive literature and statistics.

Many of the studies have identified such related issues as: health risks associated with adolescent pregnancy, childbearing and the infant; the incidence of adolescent pregnancy and childbearing; and the negative economic social and emotional consequences of adolescent motherhood affecting the quality of life.[8,9,10] Descriptive information has been important in learning about the prevalence of problems related to adolescent motherhood and aggregate statistics are a significant part of the literature. As Resnick indicates, these types of statistics tend to hide more than they reveal, particularly the patterns and functions of behaviors. Some of the questions that arise from these areas that have not been greatly explored are: What are the cultural patterns that must be understood in light of the structural barriers to opportunities afforded African-American adolescents? What are the meanings of certain values and beliefs that influence functional behaviors that help to maintain family and community support of African-Americans in light of numerous stresses, such as minimal economic resources? What are the adaptive patterns toward optimal functioning of African-American youth given the structural nature of various environmental systems of subsystems in which African-American adolescents interact? Have these socio-cultural, and structural issues been adequately addressed from an African-American perspective and incorporated into the programs that provide services to African-American adolescent mothers and their infants?[11]

PROGRAM ISSUES

Over three hundred programs have been developed to address these issues associated with adolescent pregnancy and motherhood, especially within the age group under 15 years. This growth in program development has occurred since the period of greatest increase in adolescent motherhood, 1960-1974.[12]

Many of these programs have been characterized as inadequate in meeting the diverse and multiple needs of the pregnant adolescent and young mother, in part due to the unidimensional aspect of the programs.[10,13] For example, frequently a biological or physiological education approach to intervention is taken without priority being given simultaneously to socio-economic needs. The inaccessibility of programs and services has been clearly documented, especially in low income areas where inadequate public transportation, lack of child care services, and geographical distance to services represent barriers to the equal access of services.[14,15,16,17] The anticipated outcome goals of these programs are: to reduce the incidence of adolescent pregnancy; to minimize the impact of aspects that affect the quality of life associated with adolescent motherhood, which include morbidity and mortality rates, limited educational gains and employment skills.[18] These expected goals with the general objective of improving the health and well-being of the adolescent mother and her child have not been realized in any appreciable measure.[19]

This lack of goal attainment is evidenced by the increasing birthrate since 1960 among adolescents younger than 14 years of age and the steady increase in births among adolescents 14 to 17 years of age.[20,21] In 1980, nearly 600,000 babies were born to adolescents under 20 years of age and over 10,000 of these births were to adolescents 14 years of age and younger.[22] Fifty seven percent of all babies born to adolescents under 15 years of age are African-American. For the African-American adolescent female, the birthrate remains disproportionately higher than for White adolescents. For example, one out of every four American babies is born to an African-American adolescent while one out of every seven American babies is born to a white adolescent.[23]

As indicated, there has been an enormous amount of concentrated attention to the growth rates of our young who are having children and choosing to rear them. There has been an increase in the descriptive studies and statistics and numerous programs have been developed in hopes of reducing the number of babies that are born to adolescents. Moreover, the overall objective of these intervention strategies over the last few decades has been to improve the health and well-being of these youth and their infants. These efforts have been worthy and for some they have even been effective. However, for the African-American adolescent mothers whose babies have consistently had the highest mortality rates, minimal access to services, and disproportionately higher birthrates, these intervention efforts have not significantly altered the impact of adolescent pregnancy and motherhood.

Given this state of affairs, the question is raised as to why program goals and activities have not significantly improved the health and well-being of the population of adolescents who become pregnant and choose to rear their infants. There may be several reasons attributed to this problem. However, only two major reasons will be discussed with alternative suggestions.

The first major reason that contributes to the stated goals not being fully realized could be that adolescent pregnancy and motherhood is viewed as an epidemic of a physical nature rather than an epidemic of a social problem. This perception does not view the total structure of the problem, thus limiting targets for intervention. In recent years this view has been discussed and debated.[24] Many have called into question the extent to which the incidence of adolescent pregnancy is a disease process which places emphasis on symptomology and the individual as the problem rather than broadening their perspective and priority to include the need for understanding antecedent causes that have severe consequences for the adolescent who becomes pregnant and chooses to rear her child, particularly the African-American adolescent.[25] For example, Klerman states that:

> This country is not faced with an epidemic but rather a continuing problem which will fluctuate with the size of the population at risk . . . no magic bullet will solve the problem; rather its underlying causes must be examined and appropriate intervention designed.[24]

The second reason that contributes to the failure to accomplish the identified program goals is the tendency to view adolescent mothers as a homogeneous group.[26] For the African-American adolescent, this view can mean the difference between prevention and chronic or intractable health and socioeconomic problems. Clearly, the awareness of the cultural and historical context of which the adolescent is a part, provides knowledge to the practitioner about her needs, resources and obstacles to health care. It allows the practitioner to move beyond categorizing or compartmentalizing behaviors and lifestyles. Appreciating and accepting the uniqueness that allows the adolescent mother to functionally adapt, the practitioner can intervene and advocate appropriately and in ways that positively impact existing adverse circumstances.[27]

Taking into account the need for effective programs to minimize the effects and consequences of adolescent pregnancy and motherhood, the following statement acknowledges issues that must be addressed:

> We need a new philosophy of health—nothing less. It must be seen in the context of a larger societal whole and the interactions between the person and the environment. Thus, if a better basic income or environment will produce a healthier individual or family, they should be part of the health strategy.[38]

In further support for minimizing the impact of these areas that affect the quality of life of adolescent mothers and their infants, Fox has suggested that "the success of a program in promoting well-being must be reflected in the life experiences of its members."[29]

THE IMPACT OF MORBIDITY AND MORTALITY

Maternal Effects

Research has shown that pregnant adolescents who choose to have their babies are more likely to experience an increased incidence of health problems than their older counterparts. For example, adolescent mothers between the ages of 15 and 19 years are twice as likely to die from hemorrhage and miscarriage than mothers over 20 years of age.[24] For this adolescent age group, the maternal death rate from pregnancy and its complications is 60 percent higher than for mothers in their early twenties.[21]

Similarly, these younger mothers are 23 percent more likely to experience a premature birth with complications such as anemia, prolonged labor and nutritional deficiency; and 92 percent more likely to have anemia than mothers in their twenties.[22,31,32] Toxemia, hemorrhage and infection have been identified as major medical determinants of maternal mortality.[33]

For the African-American adolescent who chooses motherhood, the risk of health problems and medical complications is even higher when adverse antecedent factors are present. These factors are largely due to the lack of equitably distributed resources and have been identified as inadequate nutrition, the lack of opportunity to secure training, employment, and adequate housing facilities. The factor that places African-American adolescents in an extremely high risk group for medical complications is inaccessible, quality health care (prenatal and postnatal) services.[22,34,35] For example, in a study by Rothenberg and Varga, the health and development of children born to adolescent mothers were not disadvantaged when compared to the children of older mothers, if the socio-economic backgrounds were similar.[36]

Age, associated with biological immaturity, is being given less attention as an independent risk factor for pregnant adolescents and mothers over 15 years of age.[7,24] Death rates for these mothers are 60 percent higher than for female counterparts in their early twenties; one in five adolescents in this age group receive late or no healthcare as compared to one in ten pregnant adolescents in all age groups.[37]

It is apparent that the risk of material morbidity and mortality to African-American adolescents is disproportionately higher than to the majority population. It seems that the adverse antecedent factors significantly contribute to these differences. As Antonovsky points out, class and race do affect the life chances of an individual.[38] In order to improve the life chances of the African-American mother who is at greatest risk, active attention toward change will need to be given to the structural inequities that negatively impinge upon the functional capacities of these young lives who are capable of becoming successful contributing adult citizens.

Infant Effects

Health, security and the opportunity to enter a world in which one can develop to maturity in the best possible state of health is considered a right of every child.[39] The measures most frequently used in regard to infants include: rates of stillbirth; birthweights and birth lengths; neonatal and infant mortality.[36]

Infant mortality is considered the rate most sensitive to differences in health care and is inextricably related to social and economic factors. As a result, it is often described as a social indicator or measure determining the level of health. There has been a decrease in infant mortality rates over the past twenty years; however, the gap between African-American and White races has not narrowed. In fact this widening gap in rates of infant mortality is said to potentially undermine the slow progress in reducing the nations's infant mortality rate. In the past five years, almost 20,000 African-American infants died during the first year of life who, according to Anderson, would not have died had their chances for health care been equal to that of White infants.[40] Statistics from the Bureau of the Census indicates that the cities with the highest infant mortality rates have majority or near majority African-American populations.

In 1979, the African-American infant mortality rate was 21.8 deaths under the age of one for every 1,000 births while the infant mortality rate for Whites was 11.4; in 1982, the rate of African-American infant mortality was 95 percent higher than the rate for Whites. This represented a 9 percent increase within a four year period.[41] If this emerging trend continues it is likely to adversely affect the goal of the federal government to reduce African-American infant mortality by 1990.

Prematurity and low birthweight are the most frequently cited problem conditions of babies born to young mothers.[36] Premature babies are generally underweight and their mortality rate is high. In a study done at Johns Hopkins, it was found that increases in low birthweights and prematurity were attributable to adolescents under 15 years of age.[42] Two factors that have been frequently associated with premature infants are inadequate prenatal care and inadequate nutrition received by adolescent mothers. Some of the potential risks of low brithweight are epilepsy, cerebral palsy, other disabilities and death.

Given such possible outcomes as these, it is clear that a combination of intervention strategies is needed. Some of the strategies needed are: health care that is responsive to the needs of the infants and their mothers; an aggressive outreach program that will familiarize young mothers with services as well as provide educational information and demonstration in such areas as nutrition and infant stimulation skills; accessible and adequate health care services; an adequate number of health care and social service providers whose attitudes about adolescent mothers and their infants are acceptance, high expectations and encouragement toward self-sufficiency; the modification of attitudes, policies and practices in social welfare services to provide options and resources based on individual needs and acknowledge the diversity of lifestyles and cultural values; program policies that automatically include family members and other natural support systems; and sufficient income for basic needs while providing opportunities for young mothers to gain self-sufficiency through job training and placement services.

The problems associated with adolescent pregnancy and its prevention are not so much internally generated as they are resultant from interactions with a variety of systems. Therefore, we must understand the individual dynamics within primary systems as well as institutional dynamics that interface with a diverse group of people. Then, there is a need for commitment to prevention intervention along with a commitment to helping adolescent mothers become self sufficient and self-determining and thus contributing members of society.

NOTES

1. C. Zastrow, and L. Bowker, *Social Problems: Issues and Solutions* (Chicago: Nelson-Hall, Inc., 1984).

2. R. Clark, *Voices of Concern: America Speak Out for Teenage Health Services Pamphlet* (Georgia: Emory University Family Planning Program, Grady Memorial Hospital, 1978).

3. W. Raspberry, "New Interest in an Old Problem," *Chicago Tribune*, 1984; February 6, pg. 1, Sect. 1.

4. U.S. Bureau of the Census. *Statistical Abstract of the United States 1984.* (Washington, D.C.: U.S. Department of Commerce. 1983).

5. W. Mathey, and D. Johnson, America's Black Population: 1970 to 1982. *The Crises,* December 1983, Vol. 90, No. 10.

6. D. Rice, A report from the National Center for Health Statistics in: *National Leader,* January 1984, 19.

7. Avery, B. The Status of Black Women's Health. *Congressional Black Caucus Foundation.* Spring 1984.

8. E. Ogg, *Unmarried Teenagers and Their Children,* Public Affairs Pamphlet, No. 537, 1976.

9. L. Klerman and J. Jekel, *School-Age Mothers Problem, Programs and Policy.* Connecticut: The Shoe String Press, Inc., 1973.

10. S. Brown, "Early Childbearing and Poverty: Implications for Social Services." *Adolescence,* Summer 1982; 17 (66): 397-408.

11. M. Resnick, "Studying Adolescent Mothers' Decision Making About Adoption and Parenting." *Social Work,* January-February 1984).

12. W. Baldwin, "Adolescent Pregnancy and Childbearing: Growing Concern for American," *Population Bulletin,* 1976; 31: 3-21.

13. P., McKenry, L. Walters, & C. Johnson, "Adolescent Pregnancy: A Review of the Literature." *The Family Coordinator,* January 1979; 17-28.

14. C. Chilman, *Adolescent Sexuality in a Changing American Society: Social and Psychological Perspectives.* (Washington, D.C.: U.S. Government Printing Office, 1980).

15. G. Shannon, et.al. "The Concept of Distance as a Factor in Accessibility and Utilization of Health Care." *Medical Care Review,* February 1969, 26: 143.

16. Health, Eudcation and Welfare. *Health Status of Minorities and Low Income Groups.* Maryland: Office of Health Resources Opportunity, 1980).

17. Congressional Budget Office. *Health Differential Between White and Nonwhite Americans* (Washington, D.C., 1978).

18. D. Russ-Eft, M. Springer, & A. Bearver, "Antecedents of Adolescent Parenthood and Consequences at Age 30'. *The Family Coordinator,* April 1979: 173-178.

19. F. Bolton, *The Pregnant Adolescent.* (California: Sage Foundation, 1980).

20. Guttmacher Institute. *Eleven Million Teenagers: What Can be Done About the Epidemic of Adolescent Pregnancies in the United States* (New York: Planned Parenthood Federation of America, 1976).

21. D. Boque, (ed.). *Adolescent Fertility.* (Chicago: University of Chicago Community and Family Study Center, 1977).

22. M.W. Edelman "Remembering Our Youngest Mothers," *The Omaha Star,* May 10, 1984, p. 3.

23. L. Meriwether, "Teenage Pregnancy." *Essence,* April 1984.

24. L. Klerman, "Adolescent Pregnancy: A New Look at a Continuing Problem. *"American Journal of Public Health,* 1980; 70 (8): 776-778.

25. J.D. Butts, Adolescent Sexuality and Teenage Pregnancy from a Black Perspective, in: Ooms (ed.) *Teenage Pregnancy in A Family Context.* (Pennsylvania: Temple University Press, 1981); 305-307.

26. R. Falk, M. Gispert, & D. Baucom, Personality Factors Related to Black Teenage Pregnancy and Abortion. *Psychology of Women Quarterly,* 1981; 5 (5): 737-746.

27. Litsitzky. *Four Ways of Being Human.* (New York: Viking Press, 1956).

28. McNerney. Quoted in Somers and Somers *Health and Health Care: Policies in Perspective,* (Maryland: Aspen Systems Corporation, 1977); 411.

29. K. Fox, *Social Indicators and Social Theory.* (New York: J. Wiley & Sons, 1974).

30. Planned Parenthood. Teenage Pregnancy: A Major Problem for Minors, *Zero Population Growth.* (California: Planned Parenthood Association of San Diego, 1979).

31. Guttmacher Institute. *Teenage Pregnancy: The Problem That Hasn't Gone Away* (New York: Alan Guttmacher Institue, 1981).

32. C. Cooke, & S. Dworking, *The Ms Guide to a Woman's Health,* 1980.

33. D. Minkler, Pregnancy an the Prevention of Undersirable Consequences. In: R. Jackson, J. Morton M. Sierra-Franco (eds.), *Social Factors in Prevention,* (California: University of California, School of Public Helath, 1979): 3-15.

34. A. Somers & H. Somers, *Health and Health Care: Policies in Perspective,* (Maryland: Aspen Systems Corporation, 1977); 411-417.

35. M. Peoples, R. Grimson, & G. Daughtry, "Evaluation of the Effects of the North Carolina Improved Pregnancy Outcome Project: Implications for State-Level Decision-Making" *American Journal of Public Health,* June 1984; 74 (6): 549-554.

36. P. Rothenberg & P. Varga, "The Relationship Between Age of Mother and Child Health and Development," *American Journal of Public Health,* August 1981; 71 (8).

37. Children's Defense Fund. *America's Children and Their Families* (Washington, D.C.: Children's Defense Fund, 1982).

38. A. Antonovsky, Class and the Chance of Life. In: Rainwater (ed.) *Equality and Justice* (Chicago: Aldine Pess, 1974).

39. Department of Human Resources. *Children: The Resource of the Future.* Washington, D.C., November 1974).

40. D. Anderson, Study: Black Infant Mortality Rates Not Declining. *National Leader,* January 19, 1984; 5.

41. John Reid. Black American in the 1980's, *Population Reference Bureau, Inc.* 1982.

42. F. Battaglia, T. Frazier, & A. Hellegers, "Obstetric and Pediatric Complications of Juvenile Pregnancy." *Pediatrics,* 1963; 32: 902.

11

The African-American Adolescent Male and School-Based Health Clinics: A Preventive Perspective

Robert C. Evans and Helen L. Evans

The problems of adolescent health and childbearing are often researched and discussed from the standpoint of the adolescent female because the male's responsibility in adolescent pregnancy and childbearing is often ignored. Based on the high rates of adolescent pregnancy and sexually transmitted diseases, this article suggests there is a need to provide services to African-American adolescent males. Data obtained from two school-based health clinics in Chicago's inner city show that these clinics are effective in encouraging adolescents to develop positive and informed attitudes about their health, including values about responsible sexual behavior. Contrary to expectation, African-American adolescent male students are heavy users of the clinics.

AFRICAN-AMERICAN MALES AND SCHOOL-BASED CLINICS

A recent search of journal articles published in the last five years utilizing four data bases (ERIC, Med-Line, Sociological Abstracts, and Psychological Abstracts) produced one journal article that discusses the use of health clinics by African-American adolescent males. The problems of adolescent health and childbearing are often researched and discussed from the standpoint of adolescent females because the male's responsibility in adolescent pregnancy and childrearing is often ignored. However, the high rates of adolescent pregnancy and sexually transmitted diseases suggest a need to focus on the health-seeking practices and knowledge of African-American adolescent males.

Clark and his colleagues report that 87 percent of the African-American adolescent males in their sample of 660 junior and senior high school students were sexually active. Thirty percent of the sexuallly active males reported that they or their partner had not used a contraceptive at the time of last intercourse.[1] Forty-one percent of those who used a contraceptive at last intercourse used the condom. This suggests that the male is assuming more responsibility in pregnancy and disease prevention than is generally thought. In the study by Clark et al., it also was found that 41 percent of all the males had impregnated a girl one or more times. This information seems to indicate a need to programmatically focus on helping males to be better users of contraceptives.

The low-income African-American male adolescents in Clark et al.'s study reported the following sources of information about sex and birth control: parents (32 percent), friends (21 percent), books and other printed materials (19 percent), schools (9 percent), clinics (3 percent), and 'other' 16 percent. Even though a majority of the respondents identified their parents as a major source of information, a large percentage stated that their parents would not disapprove of sexual intercourse with a girl, and a smaller percentage indicated that their parents would not care if they got a girl pregnant. With these factors in mind, and given the other sources of information, school-based clinics might be the best source of information available to low-income African-American adolescents.

Zabin et al. found that the younger African-American adolescent males in their study were more likely than older males to use the birth control clinic.[2] If this finding is generalizable and males are more motivated at younger ages, then school-based clinics should target junior high school males (grades 7-8). Sonenstein reports that males are not responsive to the medical model of service delivery.[3] Patricia Davis-Scott, Director of Toward Teen Health with the Ounce of Prevention Fund in Chicago, Illinois, observes that African-American males come to their school-based clinics for health care and information.[4] The clinics provide a safe place for them to talk, and frequently serious health problems unknown to the adolescent might be diagnosed. The latter points to the need for school-based clinics in low-income communities.

AFRICAN-AMERICAN MALE DEVELOPMENT

There are several critical factors in a male's development that will influence his decisions regarding sexual activity, use of contraceptives by himself and his partner, and general health care behaviors. The factors that seem most important are community, family and the male adolescent himself.

The community provides a sense of values which the adolescent uses as part of his decision-making process. It is important that the community values open communication regarding sexual behavior and contraceptives. The Chicago school-based health clinics operated by The Ounce of Prevention Fund were formed with the support of the local communities. The clergy, medical community, schools, city government and parents had some say in the clinics' program design. These community leaders recognized that the critical health issues of low-income African-American adolescents that were of primary concern were: (1) high infant mortality; (2) high teenage pregnancy (at one of the schools, one third of the females were pregnant during the year prior to the clinic's opening); and (3) the tremendous lack of pediatric health services.

The overall life goals and values of adolescents are tied to the resources available to them in their community. Health is one of these very important resources. The kind of life goals the adolescent has will influence his decision to become an adolescent father. His life goals also are influenced largely by role models (for boys, male models are critical). In order for older males to provide effective models, they must find and/or create resources within their community. The involvement of the assortment of male community leaders in the development of the Chicago school-based clinics demonstrated that there were positive value-oriented older males that the younger males could strive to emulate.

The family provides physical care, emotional care, social support and practical life knowledge to young males. In this regard, the family influences the kinds of things the male will or will not do. Clark et al. found that males who talked with their parents about sex, countraceptives and teenage fatherhood were more likely to use birth control.[5] The reinforcement that parents provide to males for their behavior shapes the adolescent's actions, goals and attitudes. More importantly, adolescents learn from the example set by their parents. In the final analysis, the adolescent male himself must ultimately be clear about his values, especially those regarding sexual activity and fatherhood.

DUSABLE AND ORR HIGH SCHOOL ADOLESCENT HEALTH CENTERS

In Chicago, the school-based clinics are an important method for encouraging African-American males to develop positive values about their health, including values about responsible sexual behavior. The Ounce of Prevention Fund administers school-based health clinics in three Chicago high schools. Since the clinic at Richard Crane High School opened in the Fall of 1987 and year-end statistics were not available at the time of this writing, the discussion will be limited to DuSable and Orr clinics that were opened earlier. Both of these clinics require parental permission for students to receive service unless there is a medical emergency. The clinics provide a comprehensive array of services; such as:

Immunization Series	Health Maintenance
Diagnosis of Sexually Transmitted Diseases	Acute General Medicine
Family Planning	Chronic General Medicine
Pregnancy Diagnosis	First Aid
Prenatal Care	General Gynecology
Postpartum Exams	Mental Health
Psychosocial Screening	Health Education
Child Abuse Screening	

DuSable's Katherine Bogan Health Center opened in June of 1985. It serves currently enrolled students, who must have a permission slip signed by their parents on file in the clinic. DuSable's student population as of September 1986 was 1,955 (female—966; male—989); of this total, 1,399 (female—737; male—662) had signed permission slips on file in the clinic. During the 1986-87 academic year, there were 4,320 visits (female—3,030; male—1,290), made to the clinic.

TABLE 1
Health Services Provided for Students at DuSable
School Years 1985-86 and 1986-87
(Number of Students Served)

	June 30, 1986	June 30, 1987
Immunization Series	101	76
Diagnosis of Sexually		
Transmitted Diseases	169	158
Ongoing Family Planning		
Female	120	361
Male	198	155
Diagnosis of Pregnancy	61	50
Comprehensive Prenatal Care	44	20
Deliveries	11	23
Psychosocial Screening	420	305
Child Abuse Cases Filed	11	2

Number of Clinic Visits by Type of Service
School Years 1985-86 and 1986-87

	June 30, 1986	June 30, 1987
Acute General Medicine	1,494	1,716
Chronic General Medicine	251	354
First Aid	292	97
(includes some students without permission slips on file)		
Health Maintenance	1,145	678
General Gynecology	484	329

Table 1 shows the DuSable service data for the 1985-86 and 1986-87 academic years. It can be seen that the largest number of clinic visits were for acute general medicine. In the 1985-86 academic year, the first year of the clinic, there was a sizeable number of health maintenance visits representing physical examinations and preventive health care services. The latter might reflect the high initial need for health care services in the medically underserviced community. The clinic also offers a comprehensive set of services including mental health (1,324 participants in 1986-87) which are not shown on Table 1.

The above data from DuSable indicates that males are just as likely as females to be enrolled in the clinic. However, females made more clinic visits in both years and males accounted for slightly more than one quarter of such visits. Given the generally low rate of utilization of medical and family planning clinics by African-American adolescent males, this figure seems encouragingly high. With regard to family planning, males made more than one-half and close to one-third of the total visits in 1985-86 and 1986-87 respectively. This is very positive and suggests that the program offers an appropriate approach to service delivery.

Orr's Adolescent Health Center opened in August 1986. It, too, serves currently enrolled students who have written parental permission. In September 1986, the school's total enrollment was 1,894 (females—900; males—994); 1,129 (females—554;

males—575) had signed permission slips on file in the health clinic. There were 3,485 clinic visits (females—2,592; males—893) in the 1986-87 academic year. As can be seen in Table 2, most of the visits were for acute general medicine and health maintenance. Many students received family planning services and immunizations (many students needed these to continue in school). In addition, there were 1,528 mental health visits and 1,309 health education participants which are not shown in Table 2.

The Orr data are similar to DuSable's in that males are just likely as females to be registered with the clinic. However, while males only account for slightly more than one-fourth of Orr's total clinic visits, they represent a little less than one-third of the family planning visits, which is very encouraging. As was true for DuSable, Orr's students are in serious need of general health care. Students with general health concerns are helped to understand how to take better care of their health. Interestingly, first aid is not a high service need for either school. This seems somewhat surprising but might indicate that more serious kinds of health issues predominate among low-income African-American high school students.

At both Orr and DuSable, there are a large number of clinic visits for mental health and health education. Both of these services are very central to the service model of the clinics. Every student is offered individual and group counseling on a variety of health issues (i.e. nutrition, hygiene, sexuality, substance abuse, birth control, etc.). The psychosocial screening process has identified many troubled student situations that caused or had the potential of producing stress for the students. These persons are helped individually and in groups.

TABLE 2
Health Services Provided for Students at Orr
School Years 1986-87
(Number of Students Served)

	June 30, 1987
Immunization Series	356
Diagnosis of Sexually Transmitted Diseases	42
Ongoing Family Planning Services	
Female	246
Male	108
Diagnosis of Pregnancy	66
Comprehensive Prenatal Care	40
Deliveries	25
Psychosocial Screening	442
Child Abuse Cases Filed	12

Number of Clinic Visits by Type of Service
School Year 1986-87

	June 30, 1987
Acute General Medicine	1,074
Chronic General Medicine	111
First Aid	82
Health Maintenance	1,222
General Gynecology	460

The staff at Orr and DuSable Health Centers are basically the same. They include a medical director, an administrative director who also serves other clinics, a pediatrician, an obstetrician/gynecologist, an internist, a nurse practitioner, a counselor/social worker, a medical assistant, a health educator, and a secretary. All of the services and medicines are free of charge. Each student who registers with the clinic is seen as soon as possible for a complete physical examination and psychosocial evaluation.

DISCUSSION

In the school-based clinic, the teenagers receive comprehensive health care services at no cost. The services are easily accessible and the adolescents clearly are taking advantage of them. Most of the clinic visits (75 percent) are for health needs unrelated to family planning. Having a clinic that serves only enrolled students encourages school attendance, which benefits the students and the schools. While providing good health care, it increases the students' availability for learning as well as the school's daily per-pupil allowance from the state of Illinois. Moreover, those students who have sexual concerns have ready access to health care services and counseling. In addition, the pregnancy outcomes of female students have been enhanced by the availability of continued health care. More importantly, parents demonstrate their interest and sense of responsibility by giving written permission for their children to utilize the clinic's services.

Clark et al. indicates that a significant number of African-American adolescent males in their study were willing to tolerate unprotected intercourse and were embarrassed to buy any kind of birth control substance or device in a store. Additionally, the respondents in the same study valued having children at an earlier age more than they did marriage. Each of these attitudes points to the need for the education provided by the clinics regarding the problems of teenage parenthood and the available alternatives.[6] DuSable and Orr High School Clinics provide a great deal of counseling and educational services. However, it is important that all junior and senior high school students have, at the least, health education and counseling services available in their schools. This might help them to learn appropriate problem-solving and decision-making skills about teenage sexual involvement.

Patricia Davis-Scott (Director of School Clinics) noted that the focus of the school clinics was on the "unwellness" states of the adolescent population which might be associated with school dropout, teenage pregnancy, depression, and violence. Moreover, the clinics provide a place for the students to go and talk about their problems. While some students might come to the clinic for minor health reasons, sometimes they also have serious health and emotional problems which are diagnosed and treated.

For the most part, male students are as concerned about diseases and information as female students. Many of the males who use the school clinics do so independently of their girl friends. Mostly, they come for physical examinations for sports, and to request condoms. In this regard, the clinic provides a safe place where they can get factual, reliable information. The males have been able to trust this. They are empowered by the clinic to make decisions about their health care, thus increasing their self-esteem and sense of control. Males ages 14-19 in grades 9-12, are described by Davis-Scott as being very sensitive about health problems and how they might impact their female friends. Education and counseling helps in this regard.

Davis-Scott notes, however, that the male users of the clinic do not comply with follow-up health care when they feel better. Nonetheless, the participatory environment of the clinics seems to be conducive to maintaining male involvement. In summary, it is emphatically reiterated that educating African-American male adolescents about their responsibilities regarding contraception and fatherhood are necessary services and should be provided to all junior and senior high school students.

NOTES

1. S.D. Clark, L.S. Zabin, and J.B. Hardy, "Sex, Contraception and Parenthood: Experience and Attitudes Among Urban Black Young Men," *Family Planning Perspectives* 16 (March-April 1984): 77-82.

2. L.S. Zabin, M.B. Hirsch, E.A. Smith, R. Streett, and J.B. Hardy, "Evaluation of a Pregnancy Prevention Program for Urban Teenagers," *Family Planning Perspectives* 18 (May-June 1986): 119-126.

3. F.L. Sonenstein, "Risking Paternity! Sex and Contraception Among Adolescent Males," in *Adolescent Fatherhood,* ed. A.B. Elster and M.E. Lamb (Hillsdale, NJ: Lawrence Erlbaum Associates, 1986), pp. 31-54.

4. The Ounce of Prevention Fund is located at 188 West Randolph, Suite 2200, Chicago, IL 60601.

5. Clark et al., "Sex, Contraception and Parenthood."

6. Ibid.

12

Dispelling Myths About Teenage Pregnancy and Male Responsibility: A Research Agenda

Betty J. Watson, Cyprian L. Rowe, and Dionne J. Jones

The growth in poverty has been linked with the issue of teenage pregnancy and male irresponsibility. This article presents evidence to dispel many commonly held beliefs about the nature and magnitude of poverty, and its relationship to teenage pregnancy. It challenges the popular view that poverty is caused by the values or lack of values of young males and females. The advancement of this position has resulted in a shift away from seeking systemic socioeconomic solutions, to more person-oriented solutions. That is, the focus is on the value system of teenagers instead of on advancing full employment policy and antipoverty strategies. While we do not question the worthiness of an intact value system, we believe that more concerted efforts need to be placed on systemic solutions to the problem of teenage pregnancy. Thus, the article concludes with suggestions for a research agenda.

Over the last few years, teenage pregnancy has been given considerable attention by the media. Bill Moyer's show, "The Vanishing African-American Family," Leon Dash's seven-part series in the *Washington Post* and Charles Murray's book, *Losing Ground,*[1] have collectively transmitted to the public a broad set of misconceptions relative to: (1) the nature and magnitude of the teenage pregnancy "problem" and (2) the relationship of teenage pregnancy to poverty. The public has been saturated with a set of ideas that shift the causes of poverty to the behaviors and values of young males and females. Indeed, the linkages between poverty, teenage pregnancy, male responsibility, the "underclass," constitute an entire system of thought which is used to explain stagnation in African-American socioeconomic development.

Using this intellectual structure, public policy advocates have retreated from systemic socioeconomic solutions to more person-oriented ones. Specifically, attention has been turned away from a full employment policy, and residential and educational integration. Instead, policy-makers have embraced public and private efforts toward a "national family policy" as an antipoverty strategy. In accordance with such reasoning, then, various congressional committees have studied welfare reform and other federal programs and policies in order to formulate new strategies that address not only poverty, but also the dysfunctional behavioral problems of the poor and disadvantaged. An example of this is the new welfare reform bill hurriedly passed in September 1988 entitled "The Family Support Act of 1988." This legislation effectively maintains families on below-poverty-level benefits as long as they provide community services. More effective strategies for combating poverty would be to provide education, training, and placement of these families in jobs with real wages.

In some respects, these efforts were misguided for they came out of a basic misunderstanding of the relationship between teenage pregnancy and poverty. Even more distressing, existing misinformation continues to forestall and preclude the creation of programs and policies that could intervene into the *total* process by which adverse socioeconomic forces are transformed into behavioral dysfunction at the individual level. This article presents evidence that modifies and/or dispels many commonly held beliefs about the nature and magnitude of poverty and its relationship to teenage pregnancy. It also examines the relationship between beliefs about poverty, teenage pregnancy, and intervention programs.

THE NATURE AND MAGNITUDE OF TEENAGE PREGNANCY

At the first level there exists confusion relative to basic statistics about teenage pregnancy. Part of the confusion arises out of interpretations of the raw data. There is also an absence of clarity regarding research in this area. In many instances, interventions are not based upon research findings. Thus, it becomes critical to examine theory and data regarding teenage pregnancy and poverty.

Myth #1: Teenage pregnancy is increasing. An assertion often made is that teenage pregnancy is increasing. Teenage pregnancy is not increasing, but is actually decreasing. In 1960, there were 594,000 births to women under age twenty. In 1984, there were 480,000 births to such women. By 1986, this number had decreased to 472,081 births.[2]

Myth #2: Teenage pregnancy is the major source of out-of-wedlock births. Teenage pregnancy is not the major source of out-of-wedlock births. In 1986, approximately 65 percent of all births to unmarried women were to those twenty years of age and older. In contrast, women over age twenty comprised only 59.5 percent of out-of-wedlock births in 1960.[3]

Myth #3: African-American teenagers constitute the majority of out-of-wedlock births and teenage pregnancies. Historically, the *level* of out-of-wedlock births in the African-American community has exceeded the *level* in the White community. However, the White community has experienced a greater *increase* in out-of-wedlock births than has the African-American community. In 1960, 63.2 percent of all out-of-wedlock births were to African-American and "other" race unmarried women. In 1986, this proportion had decreased to 48 percent. The African-American proportion of all *teenage* pregnancies is even lower. In 1986, *less than 30 percent* of all teenage pregnancies were to African-American teenagers.[4]

Myth #4: Teenage pregnancy is the major cause of the large number of female-headed households among African-American Americans. Fewer than 38 percent of African-American out-of-wedlock births are to teenagers. Thus, teenage pregnancy is not the major factor in the formation of single-family households by African-American females. Moreover, in 1986, more than 60 percent of African-American female heads of households were comprised of separated, divorced, and/or widowed females rather than never-married women.[5]

Myth #5: Female-headed households are the major causes of the recent increase in poverty. Family structure is related to poverty. However, the increase in female-headed households does not, by itself, explain the post-1979 increase in poverty. Indeed, a greater proportion of female-headed households were poor in 1959 than in 1986.[6] Furthermore, the greatest increase in poverty since 1980 has been among White male-headed households. Thus, analysts must be careful when making such linkages.

Myth #6: Teenage pregnancy poses a significant financial burden for the country. Considerable attention has been directed to the "financial burden" of teenage mothers and their children upon all levels of government. However, a 1986 hearing by the House Ways and Means Committee reported that in 1979 only 3.8 percent of AFDC payments were to mothers age 18 or under. By 1983, this percent had decreased to 3.3 percent.[7] Furthermore, fewer than half (46.5 percent) of 1982 AFDC recipients were persons who had not been married to the father of their child.[8] Recent studies have estimated that nationally, teenage pregnancy cost the state and federal government $16.65 billion in 1985.[9] But studies have failed to point out that this amount constituted less than two-tenth of one percent of total *direct* state and federal government expenditures in 1985. If indirect expenditures are included, the proportion becomes even smaller.

Myth #7: Teenage pregnancy leads to the formation of an underclass through permanent welfare dependency. The linkages between teenage pregnancy and welfare dependency are far from "proven." Furthermore, the permanence of welfare dependency has been exaggerated. The concept of the underclass implies the emergence of a social group for which socioeconomic mobility is virtually impossible. Again, however, empirical data does not fully support this conclusion. Indeed, the proportion of AFDC recipients who stay on AFDC for six years or more have actually declined since 1975. In 1975, 25.6 percent of all AFDC recipients had received payments for six or more years. In 1982, this proportion had fallen slightly, to 24.1 percent.[10] Disaggregated by race, African-American females have a 19 percent probability of remaining on AFDC for four years or longer in comparison to a 7 percent probability among White females.[11]

Myth #8: Teenage pregnancy is related to an increase in the proportion of children, and particularly African-American children, living in poverty. First, the proportion of children living in poverty has actually decreased. In 1959, 26.9 percent of related children under 19 years existed in poverty. This percentage decreased to 13.8 percent by *1969*. From 1969 to 1979, it increased slightly, to 16 percent. In *1986*, the proportion had risen to 20.1 percent. This increase, however, has been greatest among White, not African-American children. In 1959, 66.7 percent of related African-American children under 18 years of age were in poverty. This proportion fell to 40.3 percent in 1979 and increased to 45.1 percent in 1986. It is important to note that while the figures are high, there are fewer African-American children in poverty today (both absolutely and relatively) than 25 years ago.

Myth #9: Teenage pregnancy and out-of-wedlock births are an indication of low self-esteem of the female. Popular sentiment holds that low self-esteem is a causal factor in teenage pregnancy. However, a study by Linda Held, "Self-Esteem and Social Network of the Young Pregnant Teenager," contradicts this assertion.[12] Held administered the self-esteem inventory test to a sample of 62 pregnant teenagers. She found that the African-American teenagers who chose to keep their babies scored higher in self-esteem while simultaneously rating the pregnancy as unacceptable social behavior.

Myth #10: Children of female-headed households are more likely to engage in delinquency and other antisocial behaviors. Several studies have indicated that female-headed household status *alone* is not the most critical determinant of socially dysfunctional behavior among children. Indeed, research by Sheppard Kellam on African-American family structure in the city of Chicago indicated that African-American children in mother/grandmother family structures are no more likely to engage in antisocial behaviors than are children in mother/father families.[13] Kellam's research also revealed that children from two-parent households which included a step-parent, exhibited approximately the same level of antisocial behavior as children in single parent households. Further, research by Robert Hill which used data from the National Urban League's Black Pulse Survey, indicates that the total life experience of African-American children from one and two parent households may be more similar than different.[14] For example, Hill indicates that nearly the same proportion of African-American children go to college from one-parent low income families as from two-parent low income families.

TEENAGE PREGNANCY, MALES, AND FAMILIAL RESPONSIBILITY

In addition to the described erroneous presuppositions about the magnitude and nature of teenage pregnancy, there are a related set of misconceptions about the role and behavior of teenage fathers. Particularly negatively implicated in this conceptual scenario are African-American males. Several presuppositions have been integrated by the public toward the general conclusion that higher levels of teenage pregnancy and out-of-wedlock births among African-American females is reflective of low levels of African-American male responsibility. While little research and data are available on African-American teenage fathers, existing data on African-American males do not fully support the "irresponsibility" thesis. Several examples of myths concerning the African-American male can also be cited.

Myth #11: African-American males do not pay child support. While a smaller proportion of African-American than White females are awarded child support (36.3% and 70.6% respectively), 74.6 percent of White males and 72 percent of African-American males paid 77.4 percent of the full amount due. African-American males did nearly as well by paying 69.3 percent of the full amount due.[15]

Myth #12: African-American males do not pay alimony. In 1985, 24.4 percent of White females who were awarded alimony received payments. While a smaller proportion of African-American females were awarded alimony, 39.8 percent of those awarded alimony received payments.[16]

Myth #13: African-American fathers abandon their children. While the proportion of African-American males and females who marry after conception is lower than the proportion for Whites, both data and research indicate that there is African-American male involvement with their children. In American society, few family groups with children under 18 are maintained by the fathers alone. However, the proportion of such households headed by African-American males is actually greater than that of their White counterparts. In 1984, 3.3 percent of African-American households with children were tended by African-American males in comparison to 2.8 percent of White families. Of greater interest is the fact that in 1987, 33 percent of African-American men who raised their children alone were not married to the mother.[17]

This list of myths and misconceptions is not exhaustive. It is sufficient, however, to point out the need for a more careful analysis of existing data and research on teenage pregnancy. Equally compelling is the need for more extensive research on the African-American male's attitudes, beliefs, and values relative to family and familial responsibilities.

TEENAGE PREGNANCY INTERVENTION PROGRAMS: THE EMBODIMENT OF MYTHS

Over the last decade, numerous intervention programs have been designed for teenage mothers and their children.[18] Some intervention programs are based upon the assumption that early parenthood has certain adverse effects upon the life of the mother, such as interrupted education and birth complications. Thus, the focus of such programs ranges from efforts to maintain school attendance through the provision of child care to efforts to reduce child abuse by the teenage mother.[19] For example, the Children's Aid Society of Utah designed and implemented a program to teach teenage mothers how to care for their children.[20] Another group created a project that brought teenage mothers with infants and toddlers together in order to provide a support system for the mothers.[21]

In contrast to programs such as these, which seek to ameliorate only a few of the adverse effects of teenage parenting, the Continuing Education for Young Women (CEYW) program in Kalamazoo, Michigan is based upon a holistic strategy for addressing the needs of teenage mothers.[22] Such intervention programs seek to improve the life quality of the teenage mother as well as the quality of the parent-child interaction and are consistent with existing theory and data. They are based upon the premise that independently of the magnitude of the teenage pregnancy problem, positive socioeconomic outcomes may be negotiated through public and private efforts, Clearly, additional programs of this type are needed.

Beyond this point, actual and suggested intervention strategies have become as muddled as existing beliefs and misconceptions on the teenage pregnancy issue. Because both scholars as well as the media have transmitted the notion that teenage pregnancy is an increasing social and financial burden to the country, some extreme strategies have been suggested.[23] The actual enactment of measures to reduce the alleged teenage pregnancy-related increase in the welfare burden has led to programs to hold teenage fathers and their families financially responsible for the mother and child.[24] Of even greater concern is a renewed interest in the possible use of involuntary sterilization.[25] Such draconian solutions are proposed because the public has overestimated the magnitude of the problem.

The intellectual confusion over the nature of the problem has constrained the construction of effective strategies in other respects. For example, recent evidence has indicated that the most "at-risk" group for pregnancy-related physical problems may not be teenagers, but low income older mothers.[26] Yet, federal programs to service this population have been reduced and privately funded programs have been directed toward the teenage mother (middle income teenage mothers may be the group least in need of special obstetric care). Again, this commentary does not imply that teenage mothers *do not* need such programs. Rather, it points to the urgent need by other poor women for similar programs.

Similarly, the public and private sectors have adopted the "low incentive/weak values" paradigm and have proceeded to construct options for teenage and other AFDC recipients which emphasize the mother's entry into the labor force. Yet, there exists a basic contradiction in such strategy. Overwhelming support exists in the literature documenting that the major variable correlated with socialization problems in children is not *family* structure but parent-child interaction.[27] That is, nonerratic, thoughtful, and consistent use of parental discipline, ease and quality of communications, are key factors in the development of healthy children.

Given such data, the efficacy of a "pro-family" strategy designed to add the children of AFDC recipients to the growing pool of "latch-key" children must be questioned. Rather, the research suggests the need for parental skills training classes for teenage parents. Such programs would also need to include an interpersonal skills training component. (One such approach was successfully tried by Steven Schinke and Lewayne P. Gilchrist in Seattle, Washington.)[28]

Although a African-American AFDC recipient has only a 19 percent probability of remaining on AFDC for eight years or more, the belief that teenage pregnancy has led to the formation of an underclass of intergenerational welfare dependents has triggered a programmatic emphasis upon "self-sufficiency." Yet, the central problem transcends the issue of mere self-sufficiency. A nation that places great value on work has a *moral* responsibility to make work available for every potential worker. Thus, to speak of self-sufficiency, without full-employment is inherently contradictory.

Ralph Segalmon and Alfred Himelson in *The Futurist* also exemplify the faulty strategies that flow out of the defective existing analysis of the problem.[29] They postulate a need for divorce courts to order and enforce child support. Yet, evidence indicates that African-American males as well as White males are quite responsive to court-ordered child support. Further, they suggest that private rather than public funds provide relief to poor families. However, the proportion of private philanthropic funds allocated to social welfare was smaller in 1984 (22.4%) than in 1970 (31.1%).[30]

Teenage pregnancy is often seen as the result of a failure of values on the part of teenagers. Using this view, programs have been designed to promote "responsible" sexual behavior of teenagers through sex education and contraceptive counseling.[31] According to a recent study, most Americans approve of such strategies.[32] Few analysts, however, have pointed out that such strategies embody a basic contradiction in values— sex is "O.K." behavior, but pregnancy is "not O.K."[33] More importantly, research indicates that teenage pregnancy is often the consequence of the embracing of American values. Specifically, American youth are sometimes acting out a romantic love ritual which links sex, love, reproduction, and marriage. Joseph W. Scott, for example, found that high value attachment to "love" was most explanatory of teenage pregnancy in his sample of 123 teenage mothers.[34]

A RESEARCH AGENDA

The examples provided clearly demonstrate several informational areas of need. First, there exists a need for the reexamination and reinterpretation of existing census data. Empirical knowledge of the teenage pregnancy issue is clouded by several factors. Analysts often confuse universes when describing the data. For example, the proportion of the poor who are children has increased, but the proportion of children who are poor has decreased. Further, both the media and social scientists confuse levels, proportions, rates of change, and absolute versus relative changes. For example, while the level of out-of-wedlock births in the African-American community exceeds the level in the White community, Whites account for a higher proportion of total out-of-wedlock births than do African-Americans.

Similarly, the rate of increase in White out-of-wedlock births is nearly double the rate of increase in African-American out-of-wedlock births. The public is subjected to absolute numerical quantities when percentages would be more appropriate. When the public hears, for example, that $8 billion is now spent on teenage pregnancy, such data must be contexted by stating what percentage of total state and federal expenditures is represented by the $8 billion.

Second, effective programs to address teenage pregnancy must be based on new research paradigms which ask and answer different questions than those currently being addressed. For example, rather than using systemic and/or behavioristic models of the problem, models must be created which identify the direct linkages between individual decision-making behavior and systemic forces. Thus, researchers must ask "What are the psychosocial mechanisms by which unemployment, race- and class-based gender models, spatial segregations, among other things, insinuate themselves into the behaviors acted out by teenagers?"

Third, there exists a need for broad dissemination of accurate data about teenage pregnancy. Not only is the general public subjected to misinformation, but such distortions are also being perpetuated by the "experts." The increase in female-headed households among African-Americans is very much a African-American middle class problem rather than a teenage pregnancy-induced underclass problem. Contemporary African-American poverty is growing fastest among African-Americans with one or more years of college. These facts require different solutions than those which would be needed if prevailing myths were indeed true.

Fourth, intervention strategies must reintegrate the teenage father into the mother-child relationship. While there are few studies of the teenage father, there are even fewer programs targeted towards the father. Moreover, programmatic effectiveness is somewhat reduced because little is known about the fathers' attitudes, beliefs, values, and behavior. For example, do males encourage females to keep the baby? Do males also link sex, love, reproduction, and marriage, or do they see sex as recreational? Do males' own role model expectations shape their response to a pregnancy? While little is known about all teenage fathers, even less is known about African-American teenage fathers. Thus, these four areas are of critical importance if intervention strategies are to be directly linked to the nature and magnitude of the problem.

In view of these considerations, it would be difficult to mount effective educational and promotional campaigns without understanding the attitudes and motivations of the target groups, and the way demographics and personal factors affect them. Thus, some additional areas for further research are:

- The effects of age, gender, education, family background, and community context on knowledge and attitude of African-American adolescents;
- Assessing the knowledge of rights and responsibilities of fathers in general and unwed African-American fathers in particular;
- Assessing the beliefs and attitudes about legal paternity and child support requirements;
- Systematic examination of the effects of involving young African-American fathers in teenage pregnancy programs, stability of plans for the baby, rates of establishing paternity, child support payment or personal involvement with children.

NOTES

1. Charles Murray, *Losing Ground: American Social Policy, 1950-1980* (New York: Basic Books, 1986).
2. Unpublished data from the National Center for Health Statistics, Department of Health and Human Services, 1988.
3. Ibid.
4. Ibid.
5. See U.S. Department of Commerce, Bureau of the Census, *Marital Status and Living Arrangements: March 1987*, Table No. 9, pp. 42, 46, & 50.
6. U.S. Department of Commerce, Bureau of the Census, *Money Income and Poverty States in the United States: 1987*, Table No. 15, Number, Poverty Rate and Standard Error For Persons, Families, and Unrelated Individuals Below The Poverty Level in 1987 and 1986; p. 27.

7. Committee on Ways and Means, U.S. House of Representatives, *Background Material and Data on Programs Within the Jurisdiction of the Committee on Ways and Means: 1986 Edition*, March 3, 1986, p. 394.

8. U.S. Department of Commerce, Bureau of the Census, *Statistical Abstract of the United States, 1986*, "Aid to Families with Dependent Children (AFDC)—Percent Distribution of Recipient Families and Children, by Characteristics 1975 to 1982," No. 647, p. 382.

9. Spencer Rich, "Teenage Pregnancies Cost Welfare System $16 Billion 1985," *The Washington Post*, Wednesday, February 19, 1986.

10. Statistical Abstract, "Aid to Families with Dependent Children."

11. J.A. O'Neil, et al., *An Analysis of Time on Welfare*, June 1984, (HHS-100-83-0048); and Robert Hill, "The Black Middle Class: Past, Present, and Future," *The State of Black America: 1986* (New York: National Urban League, Inc., 1986).

12. Linda Held, "Self-esteem and Social Network of the Young Pregnant Teenager," *Adolesence* 16 (64) (Winter 1981): 905-912.

13. Sheppard Kellam, et al., "Family Structure and the Mental Health of Children," *Archives of General Psychology* 34 (1984): 1012-122.

14. Hill, "The Black Middle Class."

15. U.S. Department of Commerce, Bureau of the Census, *Statistical Abstract of the United States, 1986*, "Child Support and Alimony: 1985, Special Studies, Series p. 23, No. V. 52, August 1986, p. 11.

16. Ibid.

17. U.S. Department of Commerce, Bureau of the Census, Marital Status and Living Arrangements: March 1987, Table No. 9, pp. 42, 46, & 50.

18. Susan C. McDonough, "Intervention Programs for Adolescent Mothers and Their Offspring," *Journal of Children in Contemporary Society* (Fall 1984): 67-78.

19. Milling E. Kinard and Lorraine V. Klerman, "Teenage Parenting and Child Abuse: Are They Related?," *American Journal of Orthopsychiatry* (July 1980): 481-488.

20. Carolle A. Bell, "Ameliorating the Impact of Teenage Pregnancy on Parent and Child," *Child Welfare* 62 (2) (March-April 1983): 167-173.

21. Linda Kilburn, "An Educational Supportive Group Model for Intervention With School-age Parents for Their Children," *Social Work With Groups* (Spring 1983): 53-63.

22. Kyn-Taik Sung and Dorothy Rothrock, "An Alternative School For Pregnant Teenagers and Teenage Mothers," *Child Welfare* (July-August 1980): 427-436.

23. Maris A. Vinovskis, "An Epidemic of Adolescent Pregnancy? Some Historical Considerations," *Journal of Family History* (Summer 1981): 205-230; and Bell, "Ameliorating the Impact."

24. Cecilia Rivera-Casale, "The Relevance of Child Support Enforcement to School-Age Parents," *Child Welfare* (November-December 1984): 521-532.

25. Robert H. Blank, "Human Sterilization: Emerging Technologies and Re-emerging Social Issues," *Science, Technology, and Human Values* 9 (48) (1984): 8-20.

26. Mark W. Rocesa, "Maternal Age, Social Class, and the Obstetric Performance of Teenagers," *Journal of Youth and Adolescence* (August 1984): 363-374.

27. James Q. Wilson and Richard Herrnstein, *Crime and Human Nature* (New York: Simon and Schuster 1985).

28. Steven P. Schinke and Lawrence D. Gilchrist, "Adolescent Pregnancy: An Interpersonal Skill Training Approach to Prevention," *Social Work in Health Care* (Winter 1977): 159-167.

29. Ralph Segalmon and Alfred Himelson, *The Futurist*, October 1986, 18, 5, pp. 14-19.

30. U.S. Department of Commerce, Bureau of Census, *Statistical Abstract of the United States, 1986*, "Private Philanthropy Funds, by Source and Allocation: 1970 to 1984," No. 655, p. 388.

31. Melvin Zelnik and John F. Kantner, "Contraceptive Patterns and Premarital Pregnancy Among Women Aged 15-19 in 1976," *Family Planning Perspectives*, (May-June 1978): 135-142; and Rosalind J. Dorkin, "Pregnancy Among Low-Income Teenagers: A Social Structural Model of the Determinants of Abortion Seeking Behavior," *Youth and Society* (March 1980): 295-309.

32. Christine Rinck, et al., "A Survey of Attitudes Concerning Contraception and the Resolution of Teenage Pregnancy," *Adolescence* 18 (Winter 1983): 923-929.

33. Pearila Namerow, et al., "Attitudes Toward Sex Education Among Black, Hispanic and White Inner-City Residents," *International Quarterly of Community Health and Education*, 1982-83.

34. Joseph W. Scott, "The Sentiment of Love and Aspirations for Marriage and Their Association with Teenage Sexual Activity and Pregnancy," *Adolescence* (Winter 1983): 889-897.

13

Adolescent Fathers:
The Question of Paternity

Judith L. Rozie-Battle

This article analyzes pertinent legislation and court decisions as they affect adolescent fathers. It addresses paternity issues, child support concerns, and the legal rights and responsibilities of unwed and/or adolescent fathers, with a focus on their concerns. It concludes with the recommendation that communities develop improved programs to aid potential teenage fathers in understanding their rights and responsibilities.

The continuing concern over adolescent pregnancy rates generates concern for adolescent mothers and their offspring. The services developed focus on the female, who is perceived as the victim, and her child. Little effort has been geared toward the father of the child, who is perceived as the perpetrator.[1]

This attitude toward adolescent fathers is really not much different from the attitude of society toward fathers in general. Historically, the role of the father has been downplayed. The psychological and developmental needs of the child have been delegated as a responsibility and obligation of the mother. The father has not been viewed as a parent, he has only been perceived as a spouse/partner for the mother of the child. "To state the matter bluntly, except for his financial contribution, the father is a disposable parent."[2] In the case of adolescent fathers, the financial contribution is lacking or so minuscule that he indeed is a disposable parent in the eyes of society.

Only recently have a small number of agencies begun to include males in their programs for adolescent parents. The literature is just beginning to look at the importance of the adolescent father in the development and rearing of his offspring and as a support person to his partner. Researchers must look at the impact of adolescent fatherhood on the teenage male, the child, and the child's mother in order for service agencies to begin to develop and render appropriate services for these young men.

This article examines paternity issues, child support issues, and legal rights and responsibilities relevant to unwed and/or adolescent fathers. Pertinent court decisions and their impact on adolescent fathers are reviewed and analyzed. The focus is on the concerns for African-American adolescent fathers. This focus is important because of the high pregnancy rates in the African-American community, and the fact that the

African-American population is a very young population. Since the birth rate for younger adolescents has risen, a higher birth rate in the African-American community can be expected. In addition, the out-of-wedlock rate for African-American females ages 15 to 19 is six times greater than for their White counterparts.[3]

PATERNITY

Paternity, which is defined as "the state or condition of a father; the relationship of a father,"[4] is quite significant in all societies. In Western society, several factors make paternity important. Without an established legal father, a child is deprived not only of child support, but also of entitlements to other rights derived through parentage. These rights include Social Security, veteran's and worker's disability benefits. In addition, and of extreme importance, the child also loses family heritage, identity, and emotional support.[5]

There are essentially two ways to establish paternity. First, the natural father can, through his own volition, publicly acknowledge paternity. However, some states and the Uniform Parentage Act §§ 4, 6, require the mother's consent.[6] The father may acknowledge paternity in several ways: 1) by placing his name on the birth certificate; 2) through his conduct toward the child; or 3) by subsequent marriage to the mother of the child.

The second method of establishing paternity is through a judicial determination, known as a paternity suit or paternity adjudication. Historically, judicial means of ascertaining paternity have existed in all states. They assist welfare authorities who are otherwise left to support the child. Traditionally, the action was of limited scope and the primary objective was to charge the father with a duty to support his child.[7]

Paternity actions are generally viewed as civil, as opposed to criminal, proceedings. Thus, the required standard of proof is a *preponderance of the evidence*. This standard is defined as "evidence which is of greater weight or more convincing than the evidence which is offered in opposition to it; that is, evidence which as a whole shows that the fact sought to be proven is more probable than not."[8] There are a few courts that require the same evidentiary standard as in criminal proceedings—proof beyond a reasonable doubt. Still, a few others utilize the intermediate standard of proof referred to as "clear and convincing evidence," which is utilized in other civil proceedings such as termination of parental rights.

Until 1984, the statute of limitations on paternity actions varied from state to state. This is not unusual, since there is no uniform national family law. Traditionally, domestic relations have been left to the control of the state legislatures and courts, unless a state statute was in violation of the United States Constitution or federal legislation. Prior to 1984, the states' statutes of limitation on paternity actions varied from one year to eighteen years. In 1982, the U.S. Supreme Court made it clear that a one-year statute of limitation on support claims by illegitimate children violated the Equal Protection Clause by imposing a burden on these children not imposed on legitimate children.[9] The Court went further in 1983 when it struck down a statute of limitation with a two-year period.[10] Finally in 1984, federal child support legislation required that all states permit the establishment of paternity of any child at any time prior to such child's eighteenth birthday."[11]

Recent developments in the area of parentage include a Michigan decision where the appellate court found that the state's newly amended paternity statute of limitation (in accordance with federal requirements) could be applied retroactively to cases involving children born before its effective date.[12] In Texas, the appellate court found that a paternity suit may be filed after the death of the alleged biological father.[13]

A 1983 study conducted by Battle indicated that most African-American adolescent fathers were unaware of the linkages between legal paternity and benefits to the child. These same fathers were fairly well informed about how paternity was established, but there were exceptions. For example, 65.2 percent of the fathers knew paternity had to be established before the father could be required to provide child support.[14]

It is not clear that these young African-American men realize that fatherhood during adolescence makes them responsible for all the children they produce for at least the next eighteen years. This responsibility consists of more than financial support, although the monetary expectations may be the most frustrating. As indicated, state courts are interpreting the federal legislation very strictly and are holding young fathers responsible for these children at any point during the child's first eighteen years of life. So, even if a young man has not provided support for his child in the past, it does not mean that he will never be held responsible.

Information regarding paternity is important to African-American adolescent males in order to assist them in making responsible decisions regarding sexual activity and potential fatherhood. These young men must be made aware of the laws that protect the rights of their offspring born out of wedlock. Under the recent federal legislation and the general push from society to make fathers financially accountable to their children, these young men must realize there are long term consequences for their activities. The families, churches, schools, community, and social service agencies that have contact with these young men must provide them with knowledge that allows them to make informed and responsible decisions.

CHILD SUPPORT

Historically, child support was an obligation imposed primarily on fathers. As the traditional wage earners, they had an obligation to support their children. This obligation was particularly critical following divorce or in situations where the parents never married, because these families then became vulnerable and more likely to depend on public assistance for support.

Today, although in theory the child support obligation can be imposed on both parents equally, this is not the case in practice. This holds despite the trend of many states to modernize their statutes so as to hold both parents equally responsible and despite the court decisions that find the traditional support duty imposed on fathers discriminatory under equal protection laws. As a practical matter, as long as the tradition of favoring the mother in matters of custody proves resistant to change, "equality" in terms of support obligations continues to mean that the obligation of most fathers is fulfilled by making a financial contribution, while most mothers fulfill their obligation by personally caring for the children.[15] This is due, in part, to resistance to changing tradition and stereotyping of parental roles. This asymmetry in the legal obligation to provide child support is also due to the fact that in most cases fathers earn higher salaries than mothers.

A court order for child support is generally three-pronged. First, the court looks at each parent's earning ability. Second, it considers the needs of the child; and third, it takes into account the standard of living to which the child has been accustomed.

Under the Child Support Enforcement Amendments of 1984 (Pub. L. No. 98-378), states were mandated to establish child support guidelines no later than October 1987 to assist local officials and judges in making these determinations. Since that time, Congress has passed the Family Support Act of 1988 (Pub. L. No. 100-485), which requires that states establish guidelines for child support awards and review the established guidelines every four years to ensure that the application of the law results in appropriate child support awards.

The fact that most courts look at earning ability does not always take into consideration factors such as actual income, other support obligations, or remarriage by either spouse. Child support obligations are not etched in stone and can be modified by the court when either party can demonstrate a significant change in circumstances has occurred. There are no clear definitions for what constitutes a significant change in circumstances; therefore much discretion is left to the judge on a case by case determination. It is important to understand that the child support obligation runs from parent to child. This obligation does not run between parents. As a result, not only may a mother initiate proceedings against a father delinquent in his payments, on behalf of the child, but the child has the right to proceed if his/her mother fails to do so.

When looking to adolescent fathers for support, the income of these young men must be realistically considered. The Battle study found that approximately 39 percent of the African-American adolescent fathers interviewed were unemployed; only one-fifth were working in a full time capacity. In addition, only 15.2 percent of the fathers were making over $3000 per year.[16] In a study reported by Hendricks and Solomon, 34 percent of the African-American adolescent fathers interviewed felt that their problems were related to unemployment, lack of money, or not being able to complete school.[17] African-American males over twenty years of age are about 88.6 percent as likely to be employed as White males over twenty years of age, while African-American teenagers are only about 51.1 percent as likely to be employed as White teenagers.[18]

Keeping these statistics in mind, it is apparent that many African-American adolescent fathers will be unable to adequately provide support for their children. Yet, the Family Support Act of 1988 provides no exemptions for adolescents, the poor, or the disabled. This legislation is applied to all fathers. It does, however, require states to establish guidelines for child support awards and includes a section requiring states to establish procedures, within two years of enactment, to allow review of individual support orders at the request of either parent or a child support enforcement agency.

This section may provide an opportunity for fathers with little or no income to receive some realistic consideration under state established guidelines.

However, it is clear that states and courts are taking a firm stance in requiring fathers to provide support, as highlighted by the following cases. In a Massachusetts case decided prior to the implementation of the 1984 Amendments and the 1988 legislation, the Supreme Judicial Court upheld a lower court decision requiring a high school, adolescent father to pay child support for his out-of-wedlock child, although he was a recipient of AFDC benefits himself. The Court felt there was a strong public interest in immediately impressing a juvenile father with his obligations to his child and not waiting until he had reached majority to enforce his obligation.[19] In 1987, the U.S. Supreme Court held that a state had jurisdiction to find a totally disabled veteran, whose main source of income was federal veteran's benefits, in contempt for failing to pay child support.[20] These cases indicate the need for flexible guidelines that take into consideration the financial, physical, and mental condition of a father and his ability to pay child support orders.

In light of these efforts to hold fathers accountable for the support of their children, young fathers must be made aware that they are not an exception to the child support laws. The Family Support Act of 1988 will allow states to make wages of the absent parent subject to withholding whether or not the parent is in arrears. The only exceptions are where a parent can demonstrate there is no cause to withhold or where there is a written agreement between the parties providing an alternative arrangement. Close examination of these exceptions indicates that for the most part, only middle and upper income families would be in a position to come under the exceptions. This leaves the majority of African-American adolescent fathers unable to meet the requirements of the exceptions and therefore subject to mandatory withholding at the state's discretion.

A young father who acknowledges paternity or is judicially determined to be the father will have a heavy financial burden to bear for at least eighteen years, possibly longer if the child is disabled. Agencies that claim to provide services to young parents must not continue providing these services only to the mothers and their children. They must develop male components, preferably staffed with male role models, that provide specific services to young men and fathers.

Prior to fatherhood, the services should focus on prevention through education and information regarding consequences of behavior. If a young man becomes a father, he should be entitled to the same types of support services provided to mothers, such as health and mental health services, education, and employment training. The young father should be recognized and respected, not just for financial support, but for the psychological and emotional support he can provide to his child and in some cases, the child's mother.

LEGAL RIGHTS AND RESPONSIBILITIES

It is appropriate for an adolescent father to claim rights to and control over his out-of-wedlock offspring. The highest court of this nation has dramatically defined and shaped the rights of unwed fathers over the past sixteen years. However, the U.S. Supreme Court has indicated that with these rights go responsibility, both financial and emotional. This type of involvement is critical to trigger the rights of an unwed father. Rights may be limited or nonexistent unless the father has demonstrated his acceptance of his responsibility.

The most significant case granting rights to unwed fathers was decided in 1972 and took away from mothers the exclusive control of decisions regarding the adoption of their children born out of wedlock.[21] In *Stanley*, the Court found unconstitutional an Illinois statute that prevented an unwed father, who had lived with the mother and his three children as a family for many years, from participating in custody proceedings regarding his children following their mother's death. The Court found that Mr. Stanley was entitled to due process, notice and a hearing, prior to having his children removed from his custody. This decision put the adoption system in a turmoil while state legislators attempted to determine which procedures would comply with due process requirements and how far they were required to go in notifying absent fathers.

The Court, in a footnote to the decision, acknowledged that this due process requirement may increase costs but felt that the increase would be minimal. The Court stated that some fathers would not care and would not appear despite notice, therefore negating the need for a hearing in every case. The Court also pointed out that for those fathers who cared and claimed competence to care for their children, the burden of proving fatherhood fell on their shoulders.[22]

Following the confusion created by *Stanley*, the Court in 1978[23] denied an unmarried father strict veto power over the adoption of his child born out of wedlock. In that case, in an eleven-year period, the father had not legally acknowledged paternity, had only sporadically supported the child and had never lived as part of a family unit with the child. In another case, an unwed father, who had been living with the mother and his two children for five years, had contributed to their support and visited frequently following his separation from their mother, was allowed to prevent the adoption of his children by the mother's new spouse.[24]

Finally in 1983, the Court made clear its interpretation of unwed fathers' rights. In this case, the unwed father had rarely visited and had not supported his two-year-old child. Claiming his due process rights had been violated because he had not received notice or had an opportunity to be heard, he attempted to have the adoption of his child by the mother's husband invalidated.[25] The Court disagreed, saying:

> When an unwed father demonstrates a full commitment to the responsibilities of parenthood by 'com[ing] forward to participate in the rearing of his child,' *Caban*, his interest in personal contact with his child acquires substantial protection under the due process clause. At that point it may be said that he 'act[s] as a father toward his children.' But the mere existence of a biological link does not merit equivalent constitutional protection. The actions of judges neither create nor sever genetic bonds. The significance of the biological connection is that it offers the natural father an opportunity that no other male possesses to develop a rela-

tionship with his offspring. If he grasps that opportunity and accepts some measure of responsibility for the child's future, he may enjoy the blessings of the parent-child relationship and make uniquely valuable contributions to the child's development. If he fails to do so, the Federal Constitution will not automatically compel a state to listen to his opinion of where the child's best interests lie.[26]

Despite these clarifications by the Court, all of the questions have not been answered. The Court has not dealt with the case where the unwed father is not informed of pregnancy and is, therefore, unaware that a child has been born out of wedlock. In these situations, mothers may place the children for adoption immediately after birth, therefore denying the natural father the opportunity to acknowledge paternity or to have a relationship with his child. "Neither *Lehr* nor any of the earlier cases, articulates the interested and responsible unmarried father's rights immediately after the child's birth."[27]

However, in November, 1988, the U.S. Supreme Court heard arguments in a new case that again looked at the rights of unmarried fathers whose children are placed for adoption by their mothers. In *McNamara v. San Diego Department of Social Services*,[28] an unmarried father had not been in contact with the mother for eight months when their daughter was born in 1981. The father did not learn of the pregnancy and subsequent birth until the child was one month old, nor was he informed that the child had been placed in foster care to await adoption. The father immediately sought custody, which was denied when the child was four months old. The lower court determined that the child had bonded with the foster parents who wanted to proceed with her adoption. Therefore it held that the child's best interest was to stay with the foster parents. The lower court made this decision despite its finding that the father was "a good parent who can provide a good, loving home for this child."[29] In 1985, the father was stripped of his parental rights and his daughter was adopted. The father alleges that his rights were violated under the equal protection clause of the Constitution, "claiming that married fathers could not loose their parental rights unless they were found to have no interest or ability in parenting the child. And he noted that unwed mothers would not lose their parental rights under similar circumstances."[30] This case should be decided in 1989 and will clarify this very critical issue for unwed fathers.

Although these cases do not specifically state their application to adolescent fathers when referring to unwed fathers, it can be presumed that these decisions are equally applicable to all fathers, regardless of age. Historically, laws to protect children including adolescent fathers, have been based on assumptions that parents are responsible for their children and have primary control over them. Society is not willing to interfere with that control unless it is viewed as being in the best interest of the child. "[M]inors are assumed to exercise only limited judgment, they are accorded more protections and fewer liberties than adults."[31] However, the Court has held that "due process of laws is the primary and indispensable foundation of individual freedom."[32] Despite the fact that the Court limited its findings to this case, which involved the loss of liberty (incarceration), a strong argument can be made that the loss of rights to a biological child without due process is also a compelling liberty interest.

The direction of the cited cases demonstrates that an unmarried adolescent father will be required to make significant financial and emotional contributions to his child in order to have any right to visitation, custody, or an opportunity to be heard in potential adoption proceedings. This significant contribution may also provide the young father with some legitimate authority to determine health care, education, and day to day child rearing concerns pertinent to his child. A father will not automatically be entitled to involvement in and control over his child's life; he will have to earn this benefit by legitimizing his child's existence and taking responsibility for the financial and emotional needs of the child.

CONCLUSION

This article has attempted to provide information about pertinent legislation and court decisions regarding the rights of unwed adolescent fathers. It is hoped that young fathers and other young men, as potential fathers, will have a better understanding of the responsibilities they will owe to a child for whom they have acknowledged paternity or for whom paternity has been adjudicated.

The mere ability to conceive a child will not give these young men rights as fathers. They will need to demonstrate their competence and desire to contribute to the child emotionally and financially.

The information provided is particularly important to our young African-American men in understanding their role in the future of the African-American community. It is essential that the community develops improved preventative programs so that the choice to have children is associated with an awareness of the inherent responsibilities.

NOTES

1. Stanley F. Battle, Key Informant, "Adolescent Pregnancy: Problems and Prospects" (Massachusetts: Somerville Producers Group, Cable Access Television, 1987).

2. Jerry W. McCant, "The Cultural Contradiction of Fathers as Nonparents," *Family Law Quarterly* 21(3), (Fall 1987): 127-143.

3. *Blue Print For Action* (New York: National Urban League, July 1983).

4. Henry Campbell Black, *Black's Law Dictionary*, 5th Ed. (St. Paul, Minnesota: West Publishing Company, 1981), p. 1014.

5. Joyce E. Everett, "An Examination of Child Support Enforcement Issues," in Harriett McAdoo and T.M. Jim Parham (eds.), *Services to Young Families*, (Washington, D.C.: American Public Welfare Association, 1985), Chap. 3 .

6. Uniform Parentage Act, 1973 §4(a)(5),§6.

7. Harry D. Krause, *Family Law in A Nutshell*, 2nd ed. (St. Paul, Minnesota: West Publishing Company, 1986), p. 156.

8. Henry Campbell Black, *Black's Law Dictionary*, p. 1064.

9. *Mills v. Hableutzel*, 456 U.S. 91(1982).

10. *Pickett v. Brown*, 103 S.Ct. 2199(1983).

11. Consolidated Omnibus Budget Reconciliation Act(COBRA), Public Law No. 99-509, as codified in 42 U.S.C. §666(a)(9)(supp. III,1985).

12. *Smith v. Thompson*, 153 Mich. App. 441, 395 N.W. 2nd 700(1986).

13. *Manuel v. Spector*. 712 S.W.2nd (Tex. Ct. App. 1986).

14. Stanley F. Battle, Unpublished Supplemental Study, "Paternity Adjudication: Black Adolescent Fathers" (Minneapolis, Minnesota: The Ford Foundation, 1983), pp. 20-44.

15. Harry D. Krause, *Family Law in a Nutshell*, p. 209.

16. Stanley F. Battle, "Paternity Adjudication: Black Adolescent Fathers," p. 28.

17. Leo E. Hendricks and Annette M. Solomon, "Reaching Black Male Adolescent Parents Through Nontraditional Techniques," in Stanley F. Battle(ed.), *The Black Adolescent Parent* (New York: The Haworth Press, 1987), pp.111-124.

18. David H. Swinton, "Economic Status of Blacks 1987," *The State of Black America 1988* (New York: National Urban League, Inc., 1988), pp. 129-152.

19. *Commonwealth of Massachusetts v. a Juvenile*, 442 N.E. 2nd 1155, 1157 (1982).

20. *Rose v. Rose*, 107 S.Ct. 2029 (1987).

21. *Stanley v. Illinois*, 405 U.S. 645 (1972).

22. Ibid, footnote 9.

23. *Quilloin v. Wolcott*, 434 U.S. 246 (1978).

24. *Caban v. Mohammed*, 441 U.S. 380 (1979).

25. *Lehr v. Robertson*, 463 U.S. 248 (1983).

26. Ibid.

27. Harry D. Krause, *Family Law in a Nutshell*, p. 174.

28. Andrea Neal, "Supreme Court Preview," *American Bar Association Journal* 74 (December 1988):36.

29. Ibid.

30. Associated Press, "High Court Will Look At Unwed Father's Rights," *The Hartford Courant*, April 19, 1988, p. A3.

31. *In re Gault*, 387 U.S. 1 (1987).

32. Ibid.

14

An Epidemiological Perspective of Minority Teenage Males: A Preliminary Report

Neela P. Joshi

The demographics, sexual behavior, use of contraceptives, and fatherhood status of 150 minority males under the age of 19 years are described in this preliminary report of a two-year prospective longitudinal study. Nearly all of the subjects were from families of low socioeconomic status. More than half the subjects were living in a single parent household headed by the mother. Three groups of males were identified: Not sexually active (21 or 14 percent), sexually active nonfathers (107 or 71.3 percent) and fathers (22 or 14.6 percent). The majority of the subjects (86 percent) reported having had sexual experiences before the age of 15. Thirty-five of these youth were aware that the activity had resulted in at least one pregnancy.

Teenage pregnancy and parenting are major public health problems in the United States. In 1985, there were approximately 3.7 million births.[1] Of these, 12.7 percent or 477,705 were to women 19 years of age and under. This percentage has changed very little since 1976. In order to deal with this problem, many special programs to provide services to pregnant and parenting teenagers have been developed in the last twenty years. Many papers which examined factors responsible for and the consequences of teenage pregnancy and parenting have been published.[2]

What about the teenage father? Prevalence of teenage fatherhood is high even though accurate rates cannot be calculated due to reporting difficulties. For example, of the approximately 3.7 million births in 1985, 500,100 birth certificates had no information on the father.[3] This is largely due to the fact that mothers are unmarried and do not provide information regarding the father on the infant's birth certificate. In spite of this probable underreporting in 1985, 107,650 births (22 percent of all births to teenage mothers) involved fathers 19 years of age and under.[4]

The risk of becoming a father in adolescence is high for African-American and Hispanic males due to a high prevalence of sexual activity and a low use of contraceptives among these groups.[5] The number of births per 1,000 unmarried teenagers is more than six times greater among non-Whites than Whites. It has been suggested that successful pregnancy prevention programs for adolescents need to include males.[6]

However, despite the high prevalence of teenage fatherhood and the need, service providers have failed to include male partners in prevention programs.[7]

In a 1980 review, Earls and Siegel have noted that there is a paucity of research on teenage fatherhood.[8] It is believed that this is due to difficulties in capturing this population for observation which in turn leads to inadequacy of information for designing appropriate services. Since the Earls and Siegel review, considerable gains have been achieved in research regarding teenage fathers.[9]

The existing literature contains demographic information, data on attitudes toward sexuality and contraceptive behavior, and on educational/vocational and marital outcomes of teenage fathers.[10] In addition, emotional stress and difficulty surrounding adjustment to the pregnancy, and the degree to which the adolescent father fulfills the husband/father role in the first year or two of a child's life have been studied to some extent.[11]

Most of these studies are cross-sectional or retrospective. They identify the father through the pregnant teenager and information is obtained from him while he is in a crisis situation; that is, becoming a father. Very little information is available on the psychological, behavioral, and situational characteristics of minority adolescent males who are expectant fathers. There are also no observations regarding how changes in these characteristics over time affect sexual behavior and fatherhood status. It was, therefore, decided to observe a sample of inner city minority adolescent males over a period of time. The major objectives of this study were:

1. To identify three groups of males at the baseline interview: not sexually active, sexually active non-fathers, and fathers;
2. To obtain information on these three groups regarding situational, behavioral and psychological characteristics at the initial and follow-up interview;
3. To compare these three groups on situational, behavioral and psychological characteristics initially and at follow-up;
4. To observe change in fatherhood status over time; and
5. To ascertain whether there are many predictive associations between situational, behavioral and psychological characteristics and becoming a father during adolescence.

The design is a prospective, longitudinal study. Initial and follow-up observations were made on situational, behavioral, and psychological characteristics of 150 minority males age 19 years or under. The project site was an adolescent clinic in an urban municipal hospital which serves predominantly poor youth from surrounding neighborhoods. (The hospital's pay mix is: 40 percent Medicaid, 41 percent self-pay, 13 percent third party and 6 percent other.)

In this article, we report preliminary descriptive data on the demographics, sexual behavior, and use of contraceptives in the sample population at the time of initial interview.

MATERIALS AND METHODS

Subjects

Information regarding the project was widely disseminated to community agencies as well as the hospital personnel via group presentations and flyers. Posters displayed in well traveled areas provided salient project information with a telephone number for contact. In addition, a list of adolescent males attending the hospital-based Adolescent Center was prepared from the appointment log. A brief letter of project information was mailed to every adolescent male on this list. Flyers were also distributed in area schools. A youth volunteer assisted in distributing the flyers to adolescents at various youth meeting sites. Thus, a total of 600 adolescent males received brief project information—400 through letters, 150 through flyers and outreach, and 50 through direct contact when the adolescents had completed their clinic visit in the Adolescent Center.

As a result of these efforts, 150 English-speaking males were enrolled in the project over a three and a half month period. Informed consent was obtained from each participant and the parents of minors in accordance with Institutional Review Board Protocol. The initial interview with each participant was completed at the time of enrollment. Each participant was paid $10 for participation in the project.

Interviews

The participants were interviewed in an office at the Adolescent Center. Answers to all questions in the interview-protocol were recorded by a trained interviewer who read each question slowly to the participant. The completion time for each interview was approximately 45 minutes.

The interview provided information on demographic factors, educational status, sexual behavior, and use of contraceptives. Fatherhood was ascertained during the interview. For participants who were fathers, additional questions were asked regarding the current relationship with the mother and child, the nature of child support, and the nature of family support received by the subject.

The results reported here are based on frequency analysis of the data on demographic factors, sexual behavior and contraceptive use.

RESULTS

Demographic Characteristics

Age: The majority of participants (84 percent) were 15 years of age or older. A breakdown for age by years and as a percentage of the total sample is shown in Table 1.

Ethnicity: Of the 150 respondents, 105 (70.4 percent) were African-American, 14 (9.3 percent) were Hispanic and 29 (19.3 percent) were racially mixed although they consid-

TABLE 1
Number of Participants in Each Age Group With
Percentage Distribution of the Total Sample

Age (years)	Number (participants)	Percent (total Sample)
10	1	0.7
12	1	0.7
13	11	7.3
14	11	7.3
15	22	14.7
16	41	27.3
17	28	18.7
18	22	14.7
19	13	8.7
Total	150	100

ered themselves African-American. Information regarding ethnicity was missing from two participants.

Marital Status: Only 8 (5.3 percent) of the respondents were married at the time of the initial interview.

Household Composition: Just over one quarter of the sample—40 (26.7 percent)—reported the presence of both a father and a mother in the household. Seventy seven (51.3 percent) respondents stated that they were living with their mother who was a single parent and head of the household. In response to the question "When you were growing up, did you live with both your father and mother?" 105 (70 percent) of the subjects responded affirmatively. However, even when the father was present in the household while they were growing up, the majority of the respondents 94 (63.1 percent)—reported that they had a closer relationship with their mother than with other members of the household. Only 21 (14 percent) reported being closer to their father, whereas 26 (17.3 percent) reported being close to neither parent.

Religiosity: In this report, religiosity is defined as having an active membership in a church. Most of the respondents (78.7 percent) reported that they were not active members of any church. Well over one-third (40 percent) indicated no religious preference; 18 percent were Baptist; 18.7 percent were Roman Catholic; and the remainder were spread among other denominations.

Sexual Behaviors and Use of Contraception

Respondents were asked whether they ever had sexual intercourse. The majority (86 percent) responded in the affirmative. These 129 respondents were then asked a series of questions regarding their age at first intercourse, current sexual activity, number of partners, and experience with sexually transmitted diseases (STD). As can be seen from Table 2, 90.6 percent of these sexually experienced participants had their first sexual encounter before the age of 15. Almost one-fourth of those who reported being sexually active stated that they had more than one partner. Sixteen percent (16 percent) reported having had a sexually transmitted disease.

TABLE 2
Age at First Intercourse, Current Sexual Activity,
Number of Partners and History of Sexually Transmitted
Disease (STD) in 129 Respondents

	Number of Respondents	Percent
I. Age at first intercourse		
under 15 years	116	89.9
15 years or more	12	9.3
Do not remember	1	0.8
Total	129	100
II. Current sexual activity		
Yes	82	63.7
No	47	36.3
Total	129	100
III. Number of sexual partners		
One	62	75.6
More than one	19	23.1
No response	1	1.3
Total	82	100
IV. Ever had STD		
Yes	20	16.1
No	109	83.9
Total	129	100

Participants were also asked a series of questions regarding the use of contraception. Most (85 percent) reported having used a method of birth-control at some time. This percentage dropped drastically to 33.9 percent when the respondents were asked whether they used contraceptives all the time. Condoms and use of oral contraceptive pills by the partner were the most frequently used methods in this sample. It is interesting to note that almost a third declined to state their reason for not using a contraceptive. Almost 25 percent thought that contraceptives were not readily available, and only a small percentage (3 percent) stated that they wanted their partner to become pregnant (see Table 3.)

Pregnancy and Fatherhood Status

Those 120 respondents who reported having had sexual experience were asked whether the activity had resulted in a pregnancy. There were a total of 45 pregnancies reported by the sample, with thirty-nine subjects (30.2 percent) reporting at least one. Of the total pregnancies, 23 (51.1 percent) resulted in a live-birth and 22 (48.9 percent) in abortions or miscarriages. The number of respondents reporting a pregnancy and the outcome are shown in Table 4.

SUMMARY AND DISCUSSION

This is a preliminary report regarding some demographic characteristics, sexual behavior and fatherhood status of 150 minority males under the age of 19 years from

TABLE 3
Use of Contraceptives and Pattern of Use in 129 Respondents

	Number of Respondents	Percent
1. Ever used Birth-Control		
Yes	110	85.3
No	19	14.7
	129	100
2. Always used		
Yes	40	33.9
No	70	66.1
	110	100
3. Used first time		
Yes	40	33.9
No	70	66.1
	110	100
4. Used last time		
Yes	77	70.0
No	33	30.0
	110	100
5. Commonly used methods		
Condom:		
Yes	102	92.7
No	8	7.3
	110	100
Oral Contraceptive Pill:		
Yes	65	59.1
No	45	40.9
	110	100

TABLE 4
Fatherhood Status of Respondents Reporting Pregnancy
and Live Births
(Analysis of 129 respondents who reported ever having had
sexual experience)

	Number	Percent
I. Ever gotten anyone pregnant?		
Yes	39	30.2
No	90	69.8
	129	100
II. Total Number of Pregnancies reported	39	45
III. Outcome or 45 pregnancies		
Live birth	23	51.1*
Abortion and Miscarriage	22	48.9
Total	45	100

* Of 129 sexually experienced males, 17% reported being a father (having a live birth).

urban, low-income neighborhoods. The study population suffers from inherent selection bias, in addition to an overrepresentation from urban, minority, and low-income groups. As such, it is generalizable only to urban, minority, low-income populations. This is because the study reflects only those minority teenagers who agreed to be interviewed. Of the 600 adolescent males who received brief project information, the first 150 (25 percent) who chose to get detailed information regarding the project and agreed to be interviewed were recruited in the project. Even though the remainder were similar in age, ethnicity and socioeconomic status, there is no further information on them.

The preliminary findings support the existing evidence that more than half (51.3 percent) of the teenagers from poor urban neighborhoods live in a single parent household headed by a female. Most reported being close to their mothers while growing up. Many (78.7 percent) were not active members of any church. The majority of these males (90.6 percent) reported engaging in sexual activity before they were 15 years of age. Of those who were sexually active, a substantial number (25 percent) have more than one sexual partner and only a third (33.9 percent) reported using contraceptives all the time. Further, 30.2 percent reported being aware of their partner becoming pregnant. Approximately half (51 percent) of these pregnancies resulted in live births. This means that 17 percent of the sexually experienced teenage males became fathers.

Further analysis will include self-esteem, ego development, school/job status, and the future outlook of the three groups of respondents. Comparisons will be made among the three groups at the initial and follow-up interviews to assess changes in fatherhood status as well as on these characteristics.

NOTES

1. National Center for Health Statistics, *Monthly Vital Statistics Report* 36 (4), Supplement (July 17, 1987).

2. B.S. Zuckerman, K.D. Walker, and D.A. Frank et al:, "Adolescent Pregnancy: Biobehavioral Determinants of Outcome," *Journal of Pediatrics* 105 (1984): 857-863; and K.A. Moore and R.F. Wertheimer, Teenage Childbearing and Welfare: Preventive and Ameliorative Strategies," *Family Planning Perspectives* 16 (1984): 285-289.

3. National Center for Health Statistics, *Monthly Vital Statistics Report*.

4. Ibid.

5. L.B. Johnson and R.E. Staples, "Family Planning and the Young Minority Male: A Pilot Project," *The Family Coordinator* (October 1979): 535-543; M.L. Finkel and D.J. Finkel, "Sexual and Contraceptive Knowledge, Attitudes and Behavior of Male Adolescents," *Family Planning Perspectives* 7(6) (1975): 256-260; and W. Baldwin, "Trends in Adolescent Contraception, Pregnancy and Childbearing," in *Premature Adolescent Pregnancy and Parenthood*, ed. E.R. McAnarney (New York: Grune and Stratton, 1983), 3-9.

6. L.E. Edwards, M.E. Steinman and K.A. Arnold et al. "Adolescent Pregnancy Prevention Services in a High School Clinic," *Family Planning Perspectives* 12 (1980): 6-14.

7. M.H. Wallace, J. Weeks and A. Medina, "Services for Pregnant Teenagers in the Large Cities of the United States: 1970-1980," *Journal of American Medical Association* 248(8) (1982): 2270-2273.

8. F.L. Earls and B. Siegel, "Precocious Fathers," *American Journal of Orthopsychiatry* 50(3) (1980): 469-480.

9. See L.E. Hendricks, C.S. Howard, P.P. Caesar, "Help Seeking Behavior Among Select Populations of Black Unmarried Adolescent Fathers: Implications for Human Services Agencies," *American Journal of Public Health* 71 (1981): 733-735; and R.L. Barret, and B.E. Robinson, "A Descriptive Study of Teenage Expectant Fathers," *Family Relations* 31 (1982): 349-352; A.B. Elster and S. Panzarine, "Teenage Fathers: Stresses During Gestation and Early Parenthood," *Clinical Pediatrics* (October 1983): 700-703.

10. F.P. Rivara, P.J. Sweeney and B.F. Henderson, "Black Teenage Fathers: What Happens When the Child is Born?" *Pediatrics* 78(1) (July 1986): 151-158.

11. M.M. Brown-Robbins and D.B. Lynn, "The Unwed Fathers: Generation Recidivism and Attitudes About Intercourse in California Youth Authority Wards," *Journal of Sex Research* 9(4) (1973): 334-341; and F.F. Furstenberg and K. Talvitie, "Children's Names and Paternal Claims," Journal of Family Issues 1(1) (1980): 31-57.

15

Reaching African-American Male Adolescent Parents through Nontraditional Techniques

Leo E. Hendricks and Annette M. Solomon

Despite considerable attention in the literature given to African-American adolescent fathers by human service professionals, efforts to document how workers might reach out to them more have been few. Even less is available on how to reach African-American adolescent fathers through nontraditional techniques, for new approaches are needed. As a step toward alleviating this nagging gap in the literature, this article utilizes data from studies conducted in Tulsa, Chicago, Columbus, Ohio, and Washington, DC to provide suggestions for reaching out to African-American male adolescent parents through nontraditional means. Major issues include but are not limited to the following: (1) needs of African-American male adolescent parents; (2) nontraditional techniques for reaching this group of parents; (3) planning the initial assessment meeting, including possible barriers to the process and factors that contribute to its success; (4) do's and don'ts for helping African-American adolescent fathers stay in treatment or in a counseling relationship; and (5) ways young African-American fathers may be helpful not only to themselves but also to mothers and their children.

Some researchers have given persistent attention to the study of African-American teen males as fathers.[1] Efforts, however, to document how human service workers might reach out to them have been few[2] while much less information is available on how to reach African-American adolescent fathers through the use of newer nontraditional techniques. It is a small wonder then that human service workers express feeling quite uncomfortable about their endeavor to obtain knowledge on how they may reach out effectively to young African-American male parents. Too many questions remain unanswered: What are the needs of African-American male adolescent parents? What strategies and approaches are successful in reaching out to young African-American fathers versus those that are not? In what ways may a young African-American father be helpful not only to himself but also to the mother and his child?

As a step toward trying to put an end to this irksome gap in the literature, this article uses data from studies carried out in Tulsa, Oklahoma, Chicago, Illinois, Columbus,

Originally published in *Child and Youth Services*, Vol. 9, No. 1, 1987. Reprinted with permission of the Haworth Press, Inc.

Ohio, and Washington, DC, as well as interviews with selected practitioners working with teen parents.

This research presumes that unmarried African-American adolescent fatherhood is a stressful situation. For purposes of the study, stress was conceived as characterizing a discrepancy between demands impinging on a person—whether these demands be external or internal, challenges or goals—and the individual's (potential) responses to these demands.[3] In short, any or all forces to which a human being is subject may contribute to stress. Pertinent factors for discerning stress in unmarried teen fathers relate to the nature and outcome of each father's struggle with similar problems, notably the dilemmas of adolescence; his relationship with the unmarried mother; and family, social, and economic pressures.[4]

METHODS

The data are drawn from a cross-sectional study of 133 recent, first-time, unmarried African-American adolescent fathers residing in Tulsa, Oklahoma (N = 20); Chicago, Illinois (N = 27); Columbus, Ohio (N = 48); and Washington, DC (N = 38). Prior to the selection of the study population, an unmarried adolescent father was defined as an unwed male who was a father, or an acknowledged father-to-be, and under the age of 21 years. In addition to these criteria, subjects were required to be residents of either Tulsa, Chicago, Columbus, or Washington, DC.

Respondents were chosen with the help of social service staff from selected teen parenting agencies located in the specified cities. By and large, these agencies offered educational, helath, and social services to young women and their families. Investigators were assisted in the identification and selection of the young fathers by the unwed teen mothers registered with these agencies when the studies took place.

All subjects, with the exception of the Washington, DC sample, were paid for their participation in this investigation. Subjects in Chicago were paid $5.00, those in both Columbus and Tulsa, $10.00.

Data were collected by four adult males and two adult females in face-to-face, private interviews. Questions pertained to the social and demographic traits of the population; their sexual knowledge, attitudes, and practices; problems they faced and how they coped; their relationships with the mothers of their children; and their interest in their children. Each subject was informed that all information would be kept confidential and anonymous, and that he could refuse to answer a question or discontinue the interview at any time.

RESULTS

Table 1 provides some insight about who these young fathers are, according to the major scoiodemographic variables chosen for this study. When comparisons were made among the four samples of fathers, important differences were found to exist among them. Young fathers in Tulsa and in Washington were more likely to be older at the

TABLE 1
Distribution of Socio-Demographic Traits of Unmarried Adolescent Fathers by City

Traits	Tulsa N	Tulsa %	Chicago N	Chicago %	Columbus N	Columbus %	Washington D.C. N[a]	Washington D.C. %	p-value[b]
Age at birth or conception of child									
≤ 17	7	35	17	63	38	79	11	30	.01
≥ 18	13	65	10	37	10	21	26	70	
Age of first coital experience									
≤ 12	7	35	13	48	27	56	23	61	NS[c]
13–14	6	30	6	22	14	29	11	29	
15–17	7	35	8	30	7	15	4	10	
Family size									
≤ 3	4	20	4	15	9	19	5	13	NS
4	4	20	7	26	5	10	9	24	
≥ 5	12	60	16	59	34	71	24	63	
Father at home									
Present	13	65	15	56	29	60	13	34	.05
Not present	7	35	12	44	19	40	25	66	
Sisters who are unwed mothers									
Yes	8	40	12	44	25	52	20	53	NS
No	12	60	15	66	23	48	18	47	
Brothers who are unwed fathers									
Yes	7	35	8	30	17	35	18	47	NS
No	13	65	19	70	31	65	20	53	
Grade completed									
≤ 12	5	25	14	52	31	65	29	76	.01
> 12	15	75	13	48	17	35	9	24	
Employment status									
Employed	12	60	7	26	27	56	18	47	.05
Not employed	8	40	20	74	21	44	20	53	
Active church member									
Yes	8	40	11	41	11	23	6	16	.08
No	12	60	16	59	37	77	31	84	

[a]Missing value not included.
[b]p-value calculated by Chi-square statistics.
[c]Not statistically significant.

birth or conception of their children than fathers in Chicago and Columbus (p < .01). Further, young fathers in Tulsa were more likely to have completed 12 or more years of school than were fathers in Chicago, Columbus, or Washington, DC (p < .01). In both Tulsa and Columbus, young fathers were more likely to be employed than those in Chicago and Washington (p = .05). In Washington, DC, subjects were more likely not to be active church goers (p = .08) and to have grown up in a house with one parent (p = .05). More generally, the fathers were likely to have had their first coital experience with a girl when they were 12 years old or less. Further, these young men usually came from families with at least five children. In fact, 65 percent of all fathers sampled were members of families with five or more children. No statistically significant differences were found among the fathers in regard to having siblings who were unwed parents; it was interesting to note that, with the exception of those in Washington, DC, these adolescent fathers were more likely to have sisters than brothers who were unwed parents.

Needs of African-American Adolescent Fathers

The primary, essential characteristic of effective outreach to African-American adolescent fathers is knowledge and understanding of their needs. Toward that end, fathers in this study were asked the question: "In your opinion, and from what you have seen yourself, what are some of the problems you have faced as a young father?" When taken together, problems encountered by these African-American fathers suggest they need counseling about relationships as well as assistance with employment, job training, and education. For example, 46 percent indicated they had problems in a relationship or the problem was in the "other person." The nature of emotional and/or social difficulties for a father could be with his family of origin; restriction of his freedom imposed by responsibility for the child; the duty of providing for the child, or not being able to see his child as often as he would desire; problems with his girlfriend or unwed mother; problems with various members of the unwed mother's family; and not wanting the young woman to have the baby.

With regard to more external factors in the young men's lives, 34 percent of the fathers indicated problems related either to unemployment, lack of money, or not being able to finish school. Few of the African-American fathers perceived their difficulties as the result of some personal failing. Those that did, indicated they were having a problem coping with being a father and setting a "good example" in the child's presence.

To obtain a clearer picture of what kinds of problems young African-American fathers were likely to seek help with, they were asked: "When you ask someone for help with a personal problem, what types of problems do you discuss with them?" Chicago and Tulsa fathers were likely to bring up issues about themselves or about external causes, especially employment. In contrast, a father in Columbus discussed with others problems that concerned another person more than discussing himself; while the Washington, DC fathers probably discussed problems relating to relationships, financial responsibilities, or life goals.

TABLE 2
Distribution of Responses by City to Question: "Who Would You Go To First With a Problem?"

Source of Help With Problem

City	Family		Friend		Social Service Agency		Total	
	N	%	N	%	N	%	N	%
Tulsa	19	95	1	5	—0—	—0—	20	15
Chicago	23	85	4	15	—0—	—0—	27	21
Columbus	42	88	5	10	1	2	48	36
Washington, D.C.	31	84	5	13	1	3	37	28
Total	115	87	15	11	2	2	132	100

"Who would you go to first with a problem?" Answers revealed a majority of the young fathers—regardless of city of residence—most likely went to their family first for help with a problem (Table 2). Subjects were next asked: "If you had a personal problem, who or where would you go to for advice or help?" Responses indicated a majority of the young fathers in each city would go to their mother or father for advice or help, mostly to their mothers. This finding was not too surprising since it was also found that when these young African-American fathers were growing up, a majority of them, in each city, reported they were closer to their mothers than to other persons in their family.

Clergy, friends, and school teachers were used rarely as a source of help. Only one father from the entire study population said that he would go to a minister. This was also not unexpected, as in each of the four cities, a majority of the fathers were not active church members. Only two of the fathers from the combined study population said they would seek help from a social service agency; however, data obtained from the Washington, DC sample revealed that while young African-American fathers were not prone to seek a social service agency for help, 51 percent indiated they would seek out a human service agency if they wanted to know about their rights as a father and the rights of their children.

Feelings for the Mother and the Child

Human service workers must understand how a young father feels about the young mother and his child.[5] When asked to describe the relationship between themselves and the young mothers both before and after the pregnancy, fathers were more likely to report that it was one of love, and 94-100 percent expressed an interest in their children's future.

OUTREACH TO YOUNG AFRICAN-AMERICAN FATHERS:
SUGGESTED STRATEGIES

In light of findings reported here, reaching out to African-American adolescent fathers may be a difficult task because of the variation in their spiritual, physical, and concrete needs. Nevertheless, one may succeed in reaching out to the young African-American male parent by employing a combination of traditional and nontraditional techniques. Workers need to accept the young African-American father as he is and start out building a relationship with him in small ways. One way is to offer practical help, such as providing information to young African-American fathers concerning their legal rights and responsibilities. This may include information about paternity suits, the legal significance of having the child bear his name if he does not marry the mother, the possible effect of fatherhood on his status as a student, and so on. In relation to schooling, practical assistance could be helping with arrangements for tutoring to return to school or to achieve a high school equivalency diploma (GED). Because a number of the fathers were observed to be unemployed, vocational counseling, training, and placement could help attract them to an established agency. Unless a human service worker can help resolve the young father's practical problems, it is difficult to focus on other less visible but important problems.[6]

Meeting practical needs of young fathers, however, requires a special approach by an agency. Given that these fathers tended to receive sex education first from a friend, and tended to spend two to four days a week with their peers after school, work, or in the evenings, the use of peer counselors may be advisable. Through contacts at pool halls, basketball courts, and recreational centers, these counselors could be helpful to other human service workers in opening up communication with young fathers. Information concerning fathers' rights, sex education, the role of a father, and consumer education could be discussed freely. Some investigators[7] caution, however, that these counselors must not act as "just a pal." If these counselors meet the young fathers in their own environment, the fathers want to feel the counselors have something special to offer.

In meeting the practical needs of young African-American fathers, human service workers can also be aided by the young men's mothers, whom the majority of the respondents said they were closer to when growing up. Gottlieb has pointed out that mothers combined expert knowledge along with being the person who makes the greatest investment in the young man's well-being.[8] Involving mothers or both parents of young fathers may make reaching young fathers easier.

This investigation, as noted, indicated that a majority of the fathers perceived their relationship with the mothers of their children to be one of love; they also expressed a marked interest in their children's future. If outreach efforts are predicated on the interest young fathers have for the mothers and their children, human service agencies will appear more accepting, and perhaps access will increasse for all adolescents, including young fathers. Regardless of their motivation, young fathers are more likely to become involved if they are not threatened by an agency's sponsorship, its setting, or fear of legal action. Furthermore, once young fathers are involved in an agency program, it is critical to serve them after the birth of their child as well as before.[9]

TREATMENT WITH ADOLESCENT AFRICAN-AMERICAN FATHERS

While the knowledge base is far from complete or harmonious, some strategies and techniques have proved effective in outreach efforts to and in establishing positive relationships with African-American adolescent fathers.

Adolescent mothers may bring a young father into a worker's office for a meeting. However, a joint counseling session is not recommended for the teen father's first visit. The relationship of the young woman and man may not be stable enough for such a meeting to be productive. Telephoning young fathers and offering to help with a personal problem especially around employment, job training, or employment couseling might constitute successful outreach. In fact, many workers find that meeting the employment needs of a teen father is a major step to having a first meeting with him. Unless there is some tangible incentive for him, it is difficult to get the young father to come in for a counseling session.

Some practitioners have utilized the media (i.e., radio, television, and newspapers) to reach out to adolescent fathers. For example, one enterprising clinician reported attracting young males to a family planning clinic by placing advertisements in the Monday sports section of the local newspaper during the football season. Through these advertisements, young males were offered the following services that could be perceived as tangible rewards:

—physical examinations;
—diagnosis and treatment of sexually-transmitted diseases;
—sex education; and
—counseling.

The young men were told they could receive these services free of charge and on a walk-in basis. The results of these advertisements revealed that the younger teen males (17 and under) were likely to come into the clinic for physical examinations; older adolescent males (18 years or older) sought services for sexually-transmitted diseases.

Some workers report success in reaching young fathers through public service announcements over radio and television. Others place posters in pool halls, video arcades, around basketball courts, or wherever teen males are known to frequent. Another approach is to direct messages to mothers through posters placed in grocery stores.

Among the negatives is setting a specified time for the young father to come in for an interview. It is better to ask the young man something like the following to encourage him to come into the office: "Can you come in the morning, between the hours of thus and so? Or is the afternoon better for you, between the hours of thus and so?" To the extent it is possible, arrange a meeting with the young African-American father at a time convenient for him. Also, perhaps the meeting can be held at his home or some other mutually-agreed upon site.

The initial interview with a young African-American father is crucial to a productive client-worker relationship. Failure to understand the young father's life circumstances may precipitate a mishandling of the first interview and prevent the possibility of even addressing the young father's presenting problem. A worker needs to be abreast of the state of African America in general, and the local community, in particular. Does the young African-American father come from a family living below the poverty level? From an intact or female-headed household? Are these clients sometimes school dropouts? Unemployed? Has the young father grown up in a neighborhood where most of the recreational facilities were so stressed and overcrowded they became a source of frustration and discontent? Answers to questions on this order may be obtained from several sources, including non-profit organizations such as the Children's Defense Fund[10] and the National Urban League.[11] Or information may be sought from local, state, or federal agencies dealing in these statistics.

THE FIRST INTERVIEW

Often, the life circumstances that help prompt an interview manifest themselves in nonverbal communication during the interview. For example, nods, fingernail picking, slouched posture, lack of eye contact, and wearing either a hat, coat or jacket must not be overlooked, nor misinterpreted as hostile, uncooperative, or being closed or inarticulate. Not infrequently, practitioners report that seeing a human service worker for any reason prompts a young African-American male to make the statement: "I'm not crazy."

In addition to being abreast of the young father's life circumstances, it is important to be aware of complaints a young African-American male parent may have toward human service workers. To that end, we learned in an interview with four African-American adolescent males that these complaints may be of the following nature:

> . . . Don't like the fact the conversations are taped. . . . Nobody likes to be on tape. . . .
>
> They (i.e., human service workers) tells you he doesn't think your problem is unique. You want to think it is or else you wouldn't go to see them. . . .
> . . . They ask you a lot of questions that don't even pertain to the problem. Or are they just being nosy. . . .
> . . . They "dig" into your past, your fears. People don't want to remember the past. . . . Rather leave those things in the past . . . leave the office worse off than when you came in. . . .

Further comments were made by these young African-American males about what they disliked about their human service workers and their offices:

> . . . Can't keep my hat on. It's (the hat) like a security blanket. . . .
> . . . They (i.e., human service workers) don't seem to make . . . you feel comfortable. . . .
> . . . They use big words I don't understand. . . .
> . . . They sometimes try to use teenage slang and they sound stupid. . . .
> . . . They are always writing while I talk. . . .
> . . . They (i.e., the offices of human service workers) should have something that appeals to everyone—magazines, music.
> . . . Everyone doesn't drink coffee. . . .

. . . The offices are too clean. . . They should look lived in. . . .

Young African-American male parents tend to have several needs they define themselves as their priorities. Very often their priorities include the following:

—employment
—job skills training
—emergency financial assistance
—housing
—GED preparation, entry back into public schools, or entry into an alternative educational setting.

Other needs may be less clearly stated and will need more definition. Wisdom dictates that a worker not attempt to assess all of a young father's needs in the initial interview, especially since this may engender misunderstanding or hostility between him and the worker. It is far better to have a second visit with the young father to complete the intake process. The initial assessment should focus on the young father, not on the worker's successful completion of required agency forms.

Moreover, it is not advisable or considerate during the young African-American father's initial visit to ask him a lot of questions or to discuss goals, child support, and what he plans to do about the baby. Young fathers often associate coming to a worker's office as reflective of their being in some sort of trouble. Instead of talking a lot, listen generously to the young father and let the interview center around him, so he may express his concerns about the pregnancy if he wishes. Put in another way, a worker might ask how becoming an adolescent father has affected his life and what may be done to help him with his immediate needs. Only after pressing concrete needs are met does an adolescent father tend to entertain much discussion concerning the young mother and his child. When these observations are taken in concert, they suggest strongly that the pregnancy may be secondary to the young father's concrete needs.

Creating a comfortable therapeutic environment initially will encourage young African-American fathers to return; more challenging material should be saved for later sessions. Nonthreatening questions are more appropriate for an African-American adolescent father in the intake interview: his name, address, social security number, the name of a person who may be contacted when the client can't be reached directly. What has his work experience been? Do not suggest contacting or probing too deeply about his employer because his experience with his employer may be unfavorable. Trust, rapport, and productive communication are likely to be established more readily during an initial interview with the adolescent father, when he and the worker sit side by side rather than being seated opposite one another. This seating arrangement tends to promote honesty and trust between the young father and the worker.

THE COURSE OF TREATMENT

Other factors may contribute to encouraging an adolescent father to consider remaining in treatment:

1. During sessions, telephone conversations, and so on, address the young father as "Mr." until you gain his permission to call him by his first name.
2. Relax the young father by offering him a soft drink prior to the start of the session.
3. Have all calls held during sessions to contribute to his awareness that the counseling process and the young father's participation are important.
4. Have magazines displayed that the young father may identify with, especially those having to do with sports.
5. Be apprised of the language the adolescent father may use since he may not have a good command of standard English.
6. Be prepared to discuss current events in the local community.
7. Keep interview sessions brief, no more than 45 minutes at a time.

Once a helping relationship with a young African-American father stabilizes and concomitantly, some of his immediate needs have been addressed, the following areas are suggested for an African-American teen father to work on, and it is hoped, achieve if they have bearing on that young father's life:

1. Standing by the unmarried mother, which lends some dignity to their relationship and is of extreme importance to her;
2. Participating in planning for the birth of their child;
3. Meeting financial responsibilities, if possible;
4. Examining thoughts and feelings revealed by the out-of-wedlock pregnancy;
5. Recognizing the meaning and responsibilities of marriage and parenthood, if appropriate;
6. Developing a positive attitude toward getting help from the agency;
7. Understanding his attitudes and feelings toward the mother of his child;
8. Understanding his attitude toward sex and the meaning and consequences of sexual relations; and
9. Recognizing his attitude toward fatherhood, which may include his seeing the child, and participating in parenting.

These areas, as well as an agency's role in providing assistance through its services, are proposed to the young African-American father in the first few sessions with him and taken up again at appropriate times during ongoing counseling sessions.[12]

NOTES

The authors are grateful for research assistance and conducting interviews to Tony Hawkins, Michael McCoy, Teresa Montgomery, Janice Williams, and David Hooper; to Cleopatra S. Howard for supervising the field operations; to Dorothy J. Vance for typing the manuscript; and to Dr. Lawrence E. Gary, Director of the Institute for Urban Affairs and Research, for his support of this research. This article was made possible in part through award IROI-MH25551-01 from the Center for Minority Group Mental Health Programs (NIMH), and award 90CW637-01 from the Children's Bureau of Administration for Children, Youth and Families.

1. L.E. Hendricks, *Unmarried Adolescent Fathers and Their Controls: The Washington, DC sample.* Final report (Washington, DC: Howard University, Institute for Urban Affairs and Research, 1983); L.E. Hendricks, *A Comparative Analysis of Three Select Populations of Black Unmarried Adolescent Fathers.* Final Report, Vol. 2 (Washington, DC: Howard Unviersity, Institute for Urban Affairs and Research, 1982); L.E. Hendricks, *Unmarried Adolescent Fathers: Problems They Face and The Ways They Cope With Them, The Tulsa, Oklahoma sample.* Final Report (Washington, DC: Howard University, Institue for Urban Affairs and Research, 1979).

2. L.E. Hendricks, "Suggestions for Reaching Unmarried Black Adolescent Fathers." *Child Welfare,* LXII, (1983): 141-146; and J. Kahn, *Fathers Outreach Report: Objectives and Interventions.* (Salt Lake City: University of Utah Medical Center, September 1982—January 1983).

3. D. Mechanic, *Medical Sociology: A Selective View* (New York: The Press, 1968).

4. J. Caughlan, "Psychic Hazards of Unwed Paternity," *Social Work* 5 (1960): 29-35.

5. F.F. Furstenberg, Jr. "The Social Consequences of Teenage Parenthood," *Family Planning Perspective* 8 (1976): 148-164; R. Pannor, "The Forgotten Man," *Nursing Outlook* 18 (1970): 36-37.

6. M. Howard, "Improving Services for Young Fathers," *Sharing,* (Spring, 1975): 10-22.

7. L.B. Johnson and R.E. Staples, "Family Planning and the Young Minority Male: A Pilot Study," *The Family Coordinator* 28 (1979): 535-543; Howard, Improving Services for Young Fathers.

8. B.H. Gottlieb, "The Contribution of Natural Support Systems to Primary Prevention Among Four Social Subgroups of Adolescent Males," *Adolescence* 10 (1975): 207-220.

9. Howard, "Improving Services."

10. Children's Defense Fund, *American Children in Poverty* (Washington, DC: Author, 1984).

11. National Urban League, *The State of Black America 1984* (New York: National Urban League, Inc.: 1984).

12. R. Pannor, "Casework Services for Unmarried Parents," *Children* 10 (1963): 65; and M. Rowan and R. Pannor, *Casework with the Unmarried Father* (New York: Child Welfare League of America, 1964).

16

Family Planning and the Young Minority Male: A Pilot Project

Leanor Boulin Johnson and Robert E. Staples

This article is a report of the first coordinated program of its kind aimed at young African-American, Spanish speaking, Asian and American Indian males in relation to family life education, family planning and parental concerns. The project sought to develop an approach to the promotion of sexual responsibility and the reduction of repetition of unwanted, out-of-wedlock pregnancy through goal-directed support and assistance to unwed fathers and potential unwed fathers, 14 to 24 years of age.

Because family support systems of minorities are severely handicapped by the effects of poverty and discrimination, the consequences of combining parenthood with adolescence are compounded for the minority parent. Yet, little is known about the psychosocial development of minority youth with respect to their sexuality, the resulting problems that emerge when out-of-wedlock pregnancy occurs, and minority youth's relationships to family planning agencies. This knowledge is virtually nonexistent for minority males. While many agencies operating in minority communities deliver counseling and family planning services to the unwed mother,[1] the father is usually involved only superficially or punitively—when efforts are made to establish legal paternity as a means for assessing financial responsibility.[2]

This omission, however, is not unique for minority males. The present sexist value system robs the term "fatherhood" of the richness of connotative meaning elicited by that ascribed to "motherhood." A father is a person who provides financial security. This narrow definition obscures his potential contribution to the psychological well-being of the mother and child and has led social agencies to generally ignore the adolescent father, who is frequently without financial resources.[3] It is, perhaps, this single fact of inadequate economic provision which has resulted in the social agency's premature conclusion that unwed fathers are unwilling to contribute to the future of their child and the support of the mother.

Originally published in *The Family Coordinator*, October 1979 (now *Family Relations*). Reprinted with permission of the National Council on Family Relations.

This sexist assumption is extended further by the traditional double standard which holds that, although it was the boy's fault for getting the girl pregnant, she failed to exercise the negative control expected of females. Hence, he is not really responsible. Frequently, the girl's parents forbid the boy to see their pregnant daughter. His absence is interpreted as an uncaring attitude and, again, he is ignored or treated punitively.[4] This situation is further compounded when minority males, particularly African-Americans, are involved. Sociological theory purports that slavery broke the African-American man's sense of family responsibility.[5] Thus, it is assumed that African-American women do not expect or demand that their African-American men support them.

Recent evidence suggests that the matrifocality of present theory and social services is myopic. Although a popular belief is that informal adoptions result primarily from irresponsible males, there are numerous case studies which describe situations where children born out-of-wedlock are informally adopted by the father or his relatives.[6] A study conducted at Los Angeles Vista Del Mar Child-Care Service, and another at the juvenile division of the Philadelphia County Court, demonstrated that most unwed fathers are willing to face their feelings and responsibilities.[7] Although Misra's study of lower income African-American males focused upon those who were married, his findings suggest that unmarried males do not consider family planning a domain of the female, but rather a joint responsibility to be shared by both partners.[8] In Johnson's 1978 survey of 313 southern African-American college students, a large majority of both males and females disagreed that contraception was entirely the sexually active unmarried female's responsibility.[9] Furthermore, the frequency of disagreement was higher for males than for females (71.5% and 65.4%, respectively). A survey of 421 male high school African-Americans, White and Hispanic students revealed that despite the fact that a slight majority responded that birth control was the female's responsibility, the same percentage believed that a male respects his partner when he uses a condom.[10] When it is realized that the fertility decline in the Western world has largely resulted from male methods of family planning, and that the leading form of contraceptives, especially among teenagers, are methods which involve male initiative, the need to focus attention upon males is evident and urgent.[11] However, when minority males are the target, the task is more difficult.

A CULTURALLY RELEVANT APPROACH

Race and cultural practices are two significant factors which influence the perception of sex roles and sexuality. Any family planning program which ignores either the history of majority-minority relations or cultural norms is headed for difficulty.

Most Anglo-oriented social agencies are uneasy and unfamiliar with the appropriate ways of approaching the inner-city male. The chasm in cultural understanding between poor minorities and Anglo health practitioners has resulted in what social workers and ethnic spokespersons define as the "failure to reach" minority clientele. Past discrimination and the trend toward militancy and racial polarization further intensify this discomfort.[12]

Government agencies' violation of cultural beliefs and norms, as well as public actions which threaten the minorities' right to exist, only serve to make public family clinics suspect.[13] For instance, there is sufficient evidence supporting a relationship between fears of racial genocide and family planning practices. The fear of genocide among Indians is understandable given their particular history and present population size. This same attitude is present among African-Americans and Asian-Americans. One study indicates that among African-Americans, those most expressive of genocide fear were males, subjects under age twenty-eight, and those who were not high school graduates. Over half of these young African-American males agreed that birth control programs are a plot to eliminate African-Americans, and 39 percent of the entire sample were in agreement with them. However, these same data indicated that, regardless of gender, age, education, or region, the majority wanted family planning clinics if they were controlled by African-Americans.[14]

Genocide fear is also evident in the Chinese community. The San Francisco Chinatown Planned Parenthood Clinic is the biggest and one of the most successful minority programs operating today. Yet, because a significant number of people felt that it was a government plot to control them and/or felt its services had strings attached, the initial attempt completely failed. It was only after involving the people through a series of seminars, educational classes, etc., that the clinic reopened with great success.[15]

It is important to note that the notion of birth control as genocide does not capture the full complexity of needed cultural considerations. While the European-based family systems focus upon contrarity, polarity and primacy of individualism, minority families tend to be communistic, expressive, spiritual, and particularistic.[16] A number of examples elucidate this point.

The Chinatown population is characterized by an unusually persistent social isolation. Thus, language is not the only major concern.[17] It is essential that a family planning program recognize the influence of old world norms and institutions, particularly the close affinity between Confucian philosophy and family formation. The status of men and women is distinct, and the indelible line of family authority remains intact throughout life. Parents expect unquestionable obedience regardless of their child's age.[18] Thus, in order to both serve the Chinese male and preserve the family as the citadel of the Chinese community, family planning programs must open up communication among family members and work with their conservative sexual attitudes (e.g., privacy of sex and propagation as the sole function of coitus).

In both the African-American and Latino (particularly Latino, the most recent immigrants) communities, it is important to recognize the impact of significant others. These two groups are known to have strong consanguine and fictive kinship ties which serve as emotional, psychological, and financial support systems. The rights and obligations of nonconsanguine *compadrazgo* (godparents) are similar to those of any blood relative and are highly valued in the Mexican-American community.[19] Similarly, within the African-American population, the "play" aunt or uncle is often the source of unlimited support. When such fictive relationships exist, a relevant delivery service will seek to effectively utilize them.[20]

Similarly, delivery services to Indian males will not be effectively met unless recognition is given to their pattern of etiquette (e.g., the value of non-interference in the affairs of others), their adherence to the ethic of mutual aid to kin, and their religious orientation (e.g., oneness with nature, and community identity and participation).[21]

The role of the male virility cult and family planning in the Chicano and African-American community is still another illustration. Within these cultures there is evidence that a link exists between the ability to have sexual relations with women, the subsequent birth of children, and the self-image of the male. The Spanish-speaking groups have coined the word *machismo* (which literally means that the ability to have children defines the status of a man in his society) to refer to this concept of masculinity. For the Chicano this notion is often intertwined with the anticontraceptive teachings of Catholicism as well as with the traditional patriarchy. If these males are convinced that contraceptives will detract from their masculinity, they may be reluctant to use them.

THE YOUNG INNER-CITY MALES PROJECT

Recognizing the immediate need and the complex nature of determining a delivery system for inner-city minority males, the Los Angeles Young Inner-City Males Project has begun to develop the first coordinated program designed to provide culturally oriented family life planning and educational services to African-Americans, Chicanos, Asians, and Indians living in urban poverty pockets.

Funded by a DHEW contract, the Young Males Pilot Project was implemented in 1974 by Naomi Gray Associates (NGA), a minority owned and directed family planning, social welfare, and health consultant firm. In order to enlist the cooperation of agencies in the 4,000 square miles of geographic area to be served, the NGA worked in cooperation with the Los Angeles Regional Family Planning Council (LARFPC).[22] This council is unique in that it coordinates the programs of all family agencies, including those serving ethnic populations. Its grantsmanship and vision have provided money to establish new clinics and "grass-roots" participation in its program planning.[23]

The organization of the Young Males Project is presented in Figure 1. The project staff consists of Naomi Gray as project director, a project coordinator who is a former statistical analyst of LARFPC, a part-time, Spanish-speaking consultant who works three days a week, four outreach counselors who are paid for only ten hours a week (all work overtime because of enthusiasm and commitment), and six peer group counselors. The outreach and peer group counselors represent each of the four target ethnic populations—African-American, Chicano, Asian, and Indian. The outreach counselors were selected from a large pool of applicants and have proven to reflect the cultural concerns of their respective communities. The peer group workers were hired to aid young fathers in working out their own solutions to emotional problems, attitudinal relationships with the mother of their child, their identification as fathers, vocational and educational goals, and legal problems and responsibilities.

With the exception of the Asian-American community (Chinatown), each ethnic community has a peer outreach counselor who works within the community and with

FIGURE 1

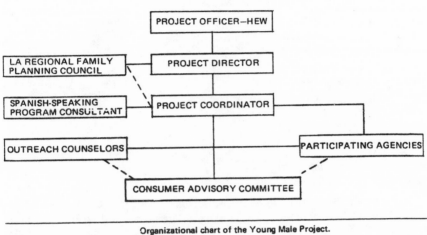

Organizational chart of the Young Male Project.

the participating delegate agency. The LARFPC provides the counselors with office space and telephones. For each agency there is a liaison person who is assigned to work with the counselor and the Young Males Project.

A 21-member (ages from 13-21) Consumer Advisory Committee consisting of members from each of the ethnic areas was organized and successfully worked with the staff in: (a) evaluating the relevance of educational and promotional materials for teenage populations (e.g., sex education films were evaluated and rated, and groundwork was established for rewriting existing material at the reading level of the target group); (b) giving feedback information on program effectiveness; (c) suggesting exploratory areas for the project; and (d) serving as a sounding board on issues affecting the program.

A one-day training session entitled "The Role of the Minority Male in Traditional and Contemporary Family Life" was designed to outline program goals for the personnel of cooperating agencies and the project staff. This session was held in late September of 1974 in the LARFPC office; approximately 25 persons attended. The project staff met monthly to address new training needs and to insure the project's optimal responsiveness to the needs of the target populations.[24] In addition, a resident physician and a lawyer were invited to instruct the youth counselors in the medical and legal issues of teenage parenting.[25]

In order to sensitize the young males to their sexual and parental responsibilities and to meet their needs in coping with their environment, it was realized that efforts were needed to allay community suspicion about the nature and purpose of the project. Thus, the cornerstones of the program were the peer group and outreach counselors.

TABLE 1
The Number of Contacts Interviewed
by Age, Ethnic Group and Marital Status

	Total	Group 1 Age 12–14	Group 2 Age 15–17	Group 3 Age 18–20
Total Number of Respondents	118	21	53	44
African-Americans	39	6	20	13
Chicanos	35	3	19	13
Asians	44	12	14	18
Total Number Married	14	0	5	9
African-Americans	3	0	0	3
Chicanos	3	0	1	2
Asians	8	0	4	4

Outreach Counselors and Their Activities (Implementation Phase)

The counselors began their 10-hour-a-week contact with the community after 16 hours of formal basic training.[26] Their primary duties were to determine the most practical and innovative means of attracting males to established clinics and to make suggestions to the staff for noninstitutional delivery services. Through contacts in the street, pool halls, basketball games, recreational centers, parties, and homes for boys, the counselors have been able to gain the confidence of their respective target groups. In addition, an enthusiastic working relationship was established with several of the local high schools, youth groups, and organizations.

Within three months the staff made contacts with 437 young individuals, 83 adults/parents, and 73 agencies; conducted sessions with 47 groups (total attendance of 401); and made 6 referrals. Within 12 months approximately 1,000 sexually active young males were reached through face-to-face contacts, with at least 40-50 percent being involved in the ongoing program and 200 receiving intensive consultation and other services.

The counselors' most significant contribution rested with their success in opening up communication among males so that information and feelings concerning family planning, sexual activities, father's rights, relationships with females, and attitudes about condom use were freely discussed. The counselors learned that these males expressed annoyance with the prying and intrusiveness of existing family planning agencies.[27] As a result of this irritation, they used agencies only in a crisis situation. Systematic information on the males' general sexual knowledge, attitudes, and practices was gathered by a preliminary (i.e., utilized for a 60-day trial period) one-page reporting form. With the exception of the Indian counselor, who joined the staff much later, the counselors returned 118 completed forms (see Table 1). In general, most of the males were misinformed, ignorant about venereal disease detection and treatment, and unfamiliar with the wide variety of contraceptive methods (some had never seen a condom). While there were no significant statistical differences between the responses of the three ethnic groups, differential responses were evident by age group.

TABLE 2
Knowledge and Attitudes
Toward Birth Control by Age Groups

	Age Group					
	12–14		15–17		18–20	
	%	(N)	%	(N)	%	(N)
Has Knowledge About Birth Control						
Yes	5	(1)	21	(11)	60 '	(26)
A Little	5	(1)	35	(18)	20	(9)
No	19	(90)	44	(23)	20	(9)
Attitudes Toward Birth Control						
Positive	35	(7)	45	(23)	39	(39)
Negative	0	(0)	4	(2)	0	(0)
No Thoughts	65	(13)	39	(20)	37	(16)
Not His Problem	0	(0)	12	(6)	23	(10)
Uses Condoms						
Yes	0	(0)	24	(12)	36	(15)
No	100	(16)	76	(38)	64	(27)
Would Like to Know More About Birth Control						
Yes	85	(18)	73.5	(39)	41.6	(18)
No	5	(1)	16.9	(9)	52.4	(23)
No Opinion	10	(2)	7.5	(4)	5.5	(2)
Knows Enough	0	(0)	1.8	(1)	2.4	(1)

Of those who confined their sexual partners to one woman, 76 percent were 12-14 year olds, 26 percent were age 15-17, and 30 percent were 18-20 year olds. The data suggest that education about venereal disease was most relevant to the older teenager who had two or more sexual partners. Data about the males' knowledge and attitudes toward contraceptives are presented in Table 2. Twenty-four percent of the males under fifteen years of age were uninformed and none had ever used a condom. Seventy-nine percent of those aged 15-17 and 40 percent of those aged 18-20 had little or no birth control knowledge, and 76 percent and 64 percent respectively reported not using the condom. Those respondents who used the withdrawal or rhythm method or douching were coded as having little or no knowledge.

It is evident that, while the majority of those under 18 years of age held neutral or positive attitudes toward family planning and expressed a desire to learn more about birth control, only a minority of older males expressed interest in further knowledge. In fact, the older the age group, the more likely they were to feel that birth control was their partner's problem.

Not a single male in the 12-14 age group felt his partner knew about birth control methods. Thus, the partner's awareness appears to be equivalent to the males' own inadequate knowledge. Since a higher percentage of the older age groups was married, it is not surprising that a greater number of them were aware of their partner's birth control knowledge and method.

Table 3 shows that few in any age group were aware of the increased risk of teenage pregnancy. Yet, there was an almost unanimous wish not to impregnate their partner.

TABLE 3
Attitudes Toward Teenage Pregnancy

	Age Group					
	12–14		15–17		18–20	
	%	(N)	%	(N)	%	(N)
Attitudes Toward Getting Girl Pregnant						
In Favor	0	(0)	0	(0)	2	(1)
Against	100	(100)	98	(51)	89	(40)
Don't Care	0	(0)	2	(1)	7	(3)
In Favor of Child Later	0	(0)	0	(0)	2	(1)
Knowledge of Increased Risk of Teenage Pregnancy						
Is Aware	10	(2)	14	(7)	17	(7)
Is Not Aware	90	(19)	86	(45)	83	(36)

Perhaps that wish results from their belief that they and others their age are too young for parenthood. However, wishes and existing realities are in conflict. The males' lack of knowledge is compounded by the slow and often negative response of existing agencies and health care providers. In fear of community reaction, many pharmacists will not even put up condom displays.[28] In view of low reading levels, instructions on boxes of condoms are of little use. Thus, in an effort to improve the rapport between health care delivery units and males, the counselors encouraged drug store clerks to explain the proper use of condoms. In addition, LARFPC supplied contraceptive kits for demonstration and a supply of condoms for distribution.

In sum, these counselors' practical training and intimate knowledge of the culture made them valuable resource persons not only for the young client, but also for his significant others who are more entrenched in traditional institutions.[29] After the project was re-funded for another two years, a smaller scale Teens Incentive Project (TIPS) was established in the Watts area of Los Angeles. However, the limited funding resulted in services being scaled down considerably. Due to the lack of follow-through by the federal government and local schools, many of the project's suggestions and plans have not been implemented. This project did stimulate more interest in the unmarried young male's responsibility in contraceptive use and his role as a father; in addition, the San Jose Health Department received funds for a male's outreach program in family planning, and the Chinatown Clinic in Los Angeles was established. Other projects sprang up in various cities in the United States (e.g., the Chicano project in Denver, Colorado), although few focused on the minority male population. Thus, the situation still exists where unmarried parenthood continues to be the responsibility of women and the special needs of minorities are not being served.

RECOMMENDATIONS

This pilot project has demostrated that, until the young minority male is more directly involved in decisions about sex and parenthood, we will continue to experience an increasing number of out-of-wedlock pregnancies. While most of the attention has been focused on teenage girls, it is often the young male who determines whether he or his sexual partner will use a birth control method.[30] Hence, it is incumbent upon us to provide information and services to both male and female adolescents. Although the logical source of sex education should be the parents, there is little indication that many parents are willing or able to fulfill that role.

Hence, other institutions will have to carry out this function. Public schools, in particular, should provide sound sexual education as early as age 12 to young, minority males. A teaching and training curriculum for family life, family planning, and sex education materials (both written and visual) should be introduced into the junior high and high school curriculum. Such a curriculum should include instruction on the meanings of parenthood and value clarification in relation to the minority male's culture, as well as the technicalities of contraceptive use. The curriculum should not be just a narrow "pelvic-centered" one but provide the positive concepts of the minority male's image, history, and cultural variations.

The same range of services provided the young female population should be made available to young minority males. Since they will have unique needs, we suggest that clinics be based in the minority communities and under community control. We would like to see these clinics specifically designed to serve the young minority male population and manned by properly trained teens who would act as counselors, interviewers, etc. In this way they would achieve greater success in meeting their objectives. A health department, hospital, or family planning center could set aside one morning during nonschool hours for teens who would feel more comfortable accepting services under these circumstances. Given the existence of special clinics for young minority males, their special concerns, fears, and needs should be addressed. Sensitivity to their need for anonymity and privacy should have primacy. Thus, confidentiality and privacy can help assure their continued use of the clinic services.

On the legislative front, young people under eighteen still encounter considerable difficulty in obtaining contraceptive services without parental consent in some states— it is particularly difficult for minorities to obtain this service. Given the high rate of teenage pregnancy, condoms should be as readily available as other merchandise in a drug store. Too often the young male is embarassed to go through the procedure of requesting condoms from a pharmacist. A counter display of condoms could obviate this awkward process for many young men. For young males who have fathered an out-of-wedlock child, discriminatory laws related to custody, visitation rights and adoption should be mitigated. Basically, American laws do not recognize the parental rights of the unwed father except for financial support. In most states the unwed father's parental rights can be terminated without his consent. If we want to encourage greater participation in child rearing by the young unwed father, it is essential that he be permitted more parental rights than are now allowed by law.

We cannot overlook the link between economic opportunities and the young minority male's attitudes toward and enactment of the father role. At this point in time there is little realistic basis for hope of young minority males taking a more active and responsible role in child bearing and rearing until their employment prospects improve.

Due to an unemployment rate that remains around 40 percent, limited education, and continued racial discrimination in employment practices, the chances of a young minority male obtaining a steady job to support the mother and their child are restricted. Moreover, young minority males who do not have access to conventional expressions of masculinity, such as the ability to sustain themselves and their families through meaningful employment, will often express it through sexual activity, the result of which may be a child they cannot support.[31]

NOTES

This project was supported by Health Services Administration, Bureau of Community Health Services, Dept. of H.E.W. Contract HSA 105-74-201.

1. Although the existing agencies are female oriented, only half of sexually experienced teenage females are believed to have access to a clinic or physician. Cited in R. Slovenko, "Financing Abortion: Ploys Revisited." *SIECUS Report* 6 (1978): 4.

2. Naomi Gray Associates. *To Conduct a Program on Sexual and Parental Responsibilities in Family Life and Family Planning: A Multi-Service Project for Young Inner-City Males*, Progress Report. (Los Angeles: Naomi Gray Associates, 1974).

3. R.D. Parke and D.B. Sawin, "Fathering: It's a Major Role," *Psychology Today* 10 (1977): 108-109, 111-112.

4. L. Connolly, "Boy Fathers,"*Human Behavior* 7 (1978): 40-43, 45.

5. D.P. Moynihan, *The Negro Family: The Case for National Action*. Office of Policy Planning and Research, United States Department of Labor, 1965.

6. R. Hill, and L. Shackleford. "The Black Extended Family Revisted," *The Urban League Review* 1 (2) (1975): 18-24; and C. Stack, *All Our Kin: Strategies for Survival in a Black Community* (New York: Harper, 1974).

7. Connolly, "Boy Fathers."

8. B.D. Misra, "Correlates of Males' Attitudes Toward Family Planning." In D. J. Bogue (Ed.), *Sociological Contributions to Family Planning Research* (Chicago: University of Chicago Press, 1967), 161-167

9. L. B. Johnson, Unpublished research at Florida State University, 1978.

10. M. Finkel, and D. Finkel, "Sexual and Contraceptive Knowledge, Attitudes and Behavior of Male Adolescents," *Family Planning Perspectives* 7 (1974): 256-260.

11. J. E. Lieberman, "Specialist Tells Experts Educate Boys Sexually," *Tallahassee Democrat*, November 6, 1977; and D.J. Bogue, *Sociological Contributions to Family Planning Research*.

12. Naomi Gray Associates, *To Conduct a Program*.

13. L. B. Johnson, The Sexual Oppression of Blacks. In H. Gochross and J. Gochross (Eds.), *The Sexually Oppressed*. (New York: Association Press, 1977); and L. C. Landman, "Los Angeles Experiment with Functional Coordination: A Progress Report." *Family Planning Perspectives* 3, (1971): 5-14.

14. W. Darity, and C. Turner, "Family Planning, Race Consciousness and the Fear of Race Genocide," *American Journal of Public Health* 62 (1972): 1454-1459; and C. Turner, & W. Darity, "Fears of Genocide Among Black Americans as Related to Age, Sex and Religion," *American Journal of Public Health* 63 (1973): 1029-1034.

15. Naomi Gray Associates, *To Conduct a Program*.

16. W. Nobles, "Africanity: Its Role in Black Families," *The Black Scholar* 9 (1974): 10-17; and C.A. Hernandez, M.J. Haug, & N.W. Wagner, *Chicanos: Social and Psychological Perspectives* (St. Louis: Mosby, 1976).

17. S.M. Lyman, "Contrasts in the Community Organization of Chinese and Japanese in North America." In N.R. Yetman and C. H. Steele (Eds.) *Majority and Minority* (2nd ed.). (Boston: Allyn, Bacon, 1975).

18. S. Sue, and N.N. Wagner, *Asian-Americans: Psychological Perspectives* (Berkeley, CA: Science and Behavior Books, 1973).

19. Recent data show that *compadrazgo* is viable, but the frequent casual use of the term "compadre" among Mexican-Americans perhaps makes the relationship more conspicuous than is warranted (see below, Grebler, Moore, and Guzman).

20. L. Grebler, J.W. Moore, and R.C. Guzman, *The Mexican-American People*. (New York: Free Press, 1970); Hernandez, et al. *Chicanos*; and W. Nobles, "Africanity: Its Role in Black Families."

21. C.H. Steele, "The Acculturation/Assimilation Model in Urban Indian Studies: A Critique." In N.R. Yetman and C.H. Steele (Eds.), *Majority and Minority*, 2nd ed. (Boston: Allyn, Bacon, 1975); and M. Wax, and R. Wax, "Federal Programs and Indian Target Populations." In N.R. Yetman and C.H. Steele (Eds.), *Majority and Minority*. (Boston: Allyn, Bacon, 1971).

22. In 1968 the LARFPC, a nonprofit corporation of eleven public and private health agencies, hospitals and social agencies, received $448,000 (the largest grant to a family planning project) from the Office of Economic Opportunity

to establish a coordinating agency for the delivery of family planning services to poor people within Los Angeles County. Since then the delegate agencies have doubled, clients have steadily increased, and the funding has increased tenfold (for further background on LARFPC see Landman, 1971). Participating agencies of LARFPC included the Allso-Pico Family Planning Clinic; American Indian Free Clinic, Inc., Compton; Elias Chico Family Health Center, La Clinica Familia del Barrio; Martin Luther King, Jr. General Hospital Family Planning Program; Westland Health Services, Inc.; and White Memorial Center, Family Planning Program. Also cooperating was ANC Mothers Anonymous, Watts.

23. The LARFPC contains a 50-member council of family planning consumers who represent various ethnic, geographic, and educational backgrounds, have received subsidized family clinic services and show continued interest in the council.

24. On February 26-28, 1975, the Indian group found it necessary to conduct a National Family Planning Forum for Indians in Phoenix, Arizona. The central aim of the conference was family planning enrichment and the exchange of the unique concepts and purposes of each of three tribes—Sioux, Navajo, and Chippewa.

25. Naomi Gray Associates, *To Conduct a Program.*

26. Carol Smith, a sex educator and nurse/midwife and a member of the obstetrics and gynecology department of the Martin Luther King, Jr. Hospital, assumed primary responsibility for training the staff in human sexuality, counseling, rap sessions, human reproduction, and birth control methods. Limited time and money resulted in a no-frill training program.

27. These feelings have support elsewhere. In a study of forty clinics in eight major U.S. cities it was found that violation of confidentiality or "fear of parents finding out" was the primary reason teenagers cited for not using clinics (Slovenko, 1978).

28. "Open Display of Condoms Results in Increased Sales," *Family Planning Perspectives* 8 (1976): 134.

29. Naomi Gray Associates, *To Conduct a Program.*

30. Bogue, *Sociological Contributions to Family Planning,*: and Lieberman, "Specialist Tells Experts."

31. There is a need for basic research studies on the young minority male's sexuality. While a few studies and articles exist about the sexual attitudes and practices of young black males, there is very little information on Latino, Asian and Indian males. We need to know what cultural values, if any, are connected to their sexual practices and how effective family planning programs can be constructed which will be compatible with their cultural values. Research might provide the answer as to whether their sexuality is linked to cultural values or is a function of poverty and poor education. No matter what our efforts may produce, we should continue to stress that fatherhood is a role that embraces a variety of support functions that exist beyond the act of conception.

ABOUT THE AUTHORS

ALVA P. BARNETT, Ph.D., is Assistant Professor, School of Social Work, University of Nebraska, Omaha, NE 68182-0293.

STANLEY F. BATTLE, Ph.D., is Associate Professor, School of Social Work, University of Connecticut, 1798 Asylum Avenue, West Hartford, CT 06117-2698.

HELEN L. EVANS, Ph.D., is Core Faculty, Illinois School of Professional Psychology, 220 S. State Street, Chicago, IL 60604.

ROBERT C. EVANS, Ph.D., is Associate Professor, School of Social Work, Aurora University, 347 Gladstone, Aurora, IL 60506.

BRUCE R. HARE, Ph.D., is Associate Professor of Sociology, the State University of New York at Stony Brook, Long Island, NY 11790.

LEO E. HENDRICKS, Ph.D., is a private consultant, 3055 Harrison Street, N.W., Washington, D.C. 20015.

LEANOR BOULIN JOHNSON, Ph.D., is Associate Professor, Department of Family Resources and Human Development, Arizona State University, Tempe, AZ 85287-2502.

DIONNE J. JONES, Ph.D., is Senior Research Associate, National Urban League Research Department, and Editor of *The Urban League Review*, 1111 14th Street, NW, Washington, DC 20005.

NEELA P. JOSHI, M.D., is Assistant Professor of Pediatrics, Boston University School of Medicine, and Director, Adolescent Center, Boston City Hospital, 818 Harrison Avenue, Boston, MA 02118.

KAREN J. PITTMAN, M.A., is Director, Adolescent Pregnancy Prevention Policy Division, Children's Defense Fund, 122 "C" Street, NW, Washington, DC 20001.

CYPRIAN L. ROWE, Ph.D., is Assistant Professor, School of Social Work, University of Maryland, 525 West Redwood Street, Baltimore, MD 21201, and he is a Marist Brother.

JUDITH L. ROZIE-BATTLE, J.D., is a consultant, Department of Health Services, 117 Washington Street, Hartford, CT 06106.

ALTHEA SMITH, Ph.D., is Asssociate Professor, Boston University, Graduate School of Social Work, 264 Bay State Rd, Boston, MA 02215.

ANNETTE M. SOLOMON, M.S.W., A.C.S.W., is Director of the Interagency Center for PINS (Persons in Need of Supervision), Washington Urban League, Washington, DC 20001.

ROBERT E. STAPLES, Ph.D., is Professor, Department of Social and Behavioral Sciences, University of California, San Francisco, CA 98143.

JOHN M. TABORN, Ph.D., is Associate Professor, Department of Afro-American Studies, Psycho-Educational Studies and the Center for Youth Development and Research, University of Minnesota, Social Sciences Building, 267 19th Avenue South, Minneapolis, MN 55455.

RONALD L. TAYLOR, Ph.D., is Professor, College of Liberal Arts and Sciences, Department of Sociology, University of Connecticut, Box U-68, Room 121, 344 Mansfield Road, Storrs, CT 06268.

ROBERT O. WASHINGTON, Ph.D., is Vice Chancellor for Research and Graduate Studies and Dean of the Graduate School, University of New Orleans, New Orleans, LA 70148.

BETTY J. WATSON, Ph.D., is Senior Research Economist, National Urban League, Inc., 1111 14th Street, N.W., Washington, DC 20005, and Assistant Professor of Marketing, Howard University, Washington, DC 20059.